William Lindsay Alexander

Zechariah

His Visions and Warnings

William Lindsay Alexander

Zechariah
His Visions and Warnings

ISBN/EAN: 9783744662680

Printed in Europe, USA, Canada, Australia, Japan

Cover: Foto ©Lupo / pixelio.de

More available books at **www.hansebooks.com**

LONDON:
& CO., 21 BERNERS STREET.
MDCCCLXXXV.

PREFACE.

THE following papers on Zechariah were issued, first, in the *Homiletic Magazine* (late *Quarterly*), and were scattered through seven volumes of that periodical. On the decease of Dr. Lindsay Alexander they were collected, and under arrangement with the Author's family are now sent forth in a handy form, such as will be welcomed by the many former students, hearers, and admirers of the venerated author. As the various papers came fresh to my hand I was delighted with them, and a careful revision only impresses one with their scholarly and suggestive character. They will make the study of one of the minor prophets an increasing joy to many a minister.

It was intended to prefix to this volume a brief biographical sketch of Dr. Alexander, but the intention

CONTENTS.

	PAGE
I. THE RIDER IN THE MYRTLE GROVE	1
II. THE HORNS AND THE WORKMEN	17
III. THE MAN WITH THE MEASURING LINE	23
IV. THE HIGH PRIEST AND THE ADVERSARY	37
V. THE CANDELABRUM AND OLIVE-TREES	59
VI. THE DRIVEN PARCHMENT	78
VII. THE WOMAN AND THE MEASURE	87
VIII. THE FOUR WAR-CHARIOTS	94
IX. EVIL DENOUNCED	111
X. ISRAEL CHEERED	126
XI. ENEMIES REBUKED	146
XII. APPROACHING DELIVERANCE	162
XIII. PRIVILEGES OFFERED	175
XIV. ISRAEL'S FULL SALVATION	189
XV. THE FALLEN CEDAR	206
XVI. THE UNFAITHFUL SHEPHERD	213

		PAGE
XVII.	THE GOOD SHEPHERD REJECTED	224
XVIII.	THE EVIL SHEPHERD'S DOOM	241
XIX.	ISRAEL'S CONFLICT AND VICTORY	246
XX.	PENITENCE AND GRACE	258
XXI.	PURIFICATION AND ENLIGHTENMENT	271
XXII.	THE FLOCK SCATTERED	286
XXIII.	JERUSALEM ELEVATED	300
XXIV.	THE PERFECT AND SPIRITUAL KINGDOM	320

ZECHARIAH'S VISIONS AND WARNINGS.

I.

THE RIDER IN THE MYRTLE GROVE.

"Upon the four and twentieth day of the eleventh month, which is the month Sebat, in the second year of Darius, came the word of the Lord unto Zechariah, the son of Berechiah, the son of Iddo the prophet, saying, I saw by night, and behold a man riding upon a red horse, and he stood among the myrtle trees that were in the bottom; and behind him were there red horses, speckled, and white. Then said I, O my Lord, what are these? And the angel that talked with me said unto me, I will show thee what these be. And the man that stood among the myrtle trees answered and said, These are they whom the Lord hath sent to walk to and fro through the earth. And they answered the angel of the Lord that stood among the myrtle trees, and said, We have walked to and fro through the earth, and, behold, all the earth sitteth still, and is at rest. Then the angel of the Lord answered and said, O Lord of hosts, how long wilt thou not have mercy on Jerusalem and on the cities of Judah, against which thou hast had indignation these threescore and ten years? And the Lord answered the angel that talked with me with good words and comfortable words. So the angel that communed with me said unto me, Cry thou, saying, Thus saith the Lord of hosts; I am jealous for Jerusalem and for Zion with a great jealousy. And I am very sore displeased with the heathen that are at ease: for I was but a little displeased, and they helped forward the affliction. Therefore thus saith the Lord; I am returned to Jerusalem with mercies: my house shall be built in it, saith the Lord of hosts, and a line shall be stretched forth upon Jerusalem. Cry yet, saying, Thus saith the Lord of hosts; My cities through prosperity shall yet be spread abroad; and the Lord shall yet comfort Zion, and shall yet choose Jerusalem."—ZECH. i. 7-17.

GOD, who "in divers manners" as well as "in many portions spake unto the fathers by the prophets," conveyed to the prophets themselves His communications by different means and through different channels. To Moses alone, the first and greatest of the prophets, did God speak mouth to mouth (Num. xii. 8; Deut. xxxiv. 10); to those that followed He made Himself known and communicated to them His message chiefly by dreams and visions, when He did not address them audibly or suggest to their minds by a Divine influence what He would have them to convey to others. The dream seems to have differed from the vision only in that it was sent to the prophet by night, whilst his senses were sunk in sleep; whereas the vision came to him by day, when he was physically awake, but when, being in an ecstacy or trance, his perception of the outer world was suspended, he was lifted above the sphere of his ordinary consciousness, and had presented to him a pictorial or scenic representation, in which sometimes the prophet himself appeared as an actor. Such, for instance, was the vision which Ezekiel saw as he sat in his house and the hand of the Lord fell upon him (viii. 1-4); such was the vision which Daniel saw when he was beside the great river which is Hiddekel (x. 1-9); such was the vision which Peter saw when about the sixth hour he fell into a trance on the housetop (Acts x. 9-18); and such probably was that which Paul had when he was caught up to the third heaven and heard unspeakable things which it is not for man to utter. From this the prophetic dream did not essentially differ. It was not an ordinary dream produced by physical causes; it was a state of entranced elevation divinely produced in which the man, taken out of himself, saw and heard things revealed to him by God. "The dream bore the most vivid and varied development of new surprising appearances, which passed before the eyes, so that the dreamer himself often knew not immediately what they were."* Hence they are called "visions of the night" (Gen. xlvi. 2; Job iv. 13; Dan. ii. 19; vii. 7). Such was the vision which Jacob had at Bethel (Gen. xxviii. 10–16); such the visions with which Daniel was repeatedly favoured (ii. 19; vii. 1, ff., &c.); and such the vision which Paul had when there appeared to him a man from Macedonia, and prayed him, saying, Come over and help us (Acts xvi. 9, 10), and when the Lord spake to him in the house of Justus at Corinth (Acts xviii. 9, 10).†

It was by means of such night visions that the Lord communicated to Zechariah certain messages of consolation, direction, and encouragement which he had to convey to the people of Israel. This prophet entered on the public discharge of his office in the eighth month of the second year of Darius Hystaspis, king of Babylonia. The time at which he appeared was when after a long cessation, during which Cambyses and the pseudo-Smerdis had occupied the throne of Cyrus, the permission given by that prince to the Jews to rebuild their temple at Jerusalem was renewed by Darius (Ezra iv. 5, 24; v.

---

* Ewald, "Propheten des A. B.," iii. 189.
† See Wardlaw's "Lectures on Zechariah," p. 23, ff.

1 ; vi. 1). This work the Jews, who went up from Babylon under the leadership of Zerubbabel or Sheshbazzar, had entered upon with ardour and enthusiastic devotedness; but in consequence of the troubles which arose from the hostility of the Samaritans, the work had been for some time abandoned, and the people had turned to provide houses for themselves, and were wasting their resources and energies in striving to adorn their dwellings with costly decorations of carved work, such, probably, as they had seen in the houses of the wealthy at Babylon. It was at this juncture that the prophets Haggai and Zechariah were sent to them with words of reproof, admonition, and encouragement, so as to stimulate them to resume the work they had intermitted, and at the same time to awaken in them a deeper spiritual interest, and rouse them to the anticipation of those grander results that were in store for them when the great spiritual temple should be built and should be filled with the glory of the Lord.

The message which Zechariah first bore to the people was of a general character. It is a message chiefly of warning. In it God, after reminding the Jews how He had been displeased with their fathers, exhorts them to take warning from their case, and by avoiding their evil courses escape the indignation and penalty that had fallen on them. God had sent to their fathers by the former prophets, the prophets who had prophesied before the captivity; by them He had summoned the people to repentance, calling on them to turn from their evil ways and doings; but the summons had been fruitless, the call in vain, and so there had come on the nation the punishment which God had threatened. By this experience of their fathers it would be their wisdom to profit. Men might pass away, but God's word remains; the prophet might cease, but the words of the prophet abide; and so, though their fathers were not and the prophets lived not for ever, the lesson which their fathers had been taught by bitter experience was still there for them to learn and lay to heart. If, profiting by this, they should not be as their fathers, but should turn to the Lord, He would turn to them and deal graciously with them (i. 1–6).

This first message which the prophet carried to the people may be regarded as the introduction to the series of prophetic utterances which are collected in the book of his prophecies; and in it we have the germ of what the prophet was specially commissioned to declare to the people. The series of visions which are narrated in the first six chapters of the book reiterate, expand, and illustrate what in this introductory section is more curtly and barely announced. In them we have, as has been justly remarked, "a complete picture of the future fate of the people of God."* They were all given in the same night,† the night between the 23d and 24th day of the

---

* Hengstenberg, "Christology," vol. iii. p. 304, Eng. trans.
† In the Hebrew the definite article is prefixed to "night," הַלַּיְלָה. "*the* night." Some regard this as equivalent to "this night," and suppose that some certain night is thereby indicated (Rosenmüller, Pressel, &c.). Others take the word as the accusative of continuance, and understand by it "throughout" or "during the night" (Keil, Lange, &c.). The rendering, however, in the Authorised Version is adequate, and sufficiently indicates the time during which the visions were seen by the prophet. The month Sebat or Shebat was the eleventh month in the Jewish calendar; it extended from the new moon in February to the new moon in March. It was, consequently, about the middle of March 519 B.C. that this series of visions was given.

eleventh month, which is the month Sebat, in the second year of Darius.

I. THE VISION OF THE RIDER AMONG THE MYRTLE TREES (Zech. i. 7–17). To the eye of the entranced prophet was presented the appearance of a man seated on a red horse, standing among myrtle trees planted in a hollow or deep valley; and behind him were horses red, reddish or tawny-coloured, and white, each with its rider; for though only the horses are mentioned in verse 8, it is evident from verse 11 that they had riders on them, who formed a band of which this man on the red horse was chief. There is some uncertainty as to the special colour of the second of these horses. The word by which it is expressed in the Hebrew (שְׂרֻקִּים) is used of the fruit of the vine (Isa. xvi. 8, A. V., "principal plants"), and seems to point to the reddish or purple colour of the grape. The Lexicons describe it as "fox-coloured;" as used of a horse it probably indicates what is commonly called bay, or, as it stands here between red and white, it may be roan; the ancient versions make it "vari-coloured." These colours are symbolical: the *red* of war and bloodshed, the *white* of peace and joy, and *the intermediate colour* of a mixed or transition state between these. There is no ground for the opinion that the colours here indicate different kingdoms against which the riders were sent, for they seem all to have gone in company; nor do they indicate the four quarters of the earth, for the fourth is wanting, and we have no right to suppose an omission in the text, as Ewald does, who would supply אֲמֻצִּים, "dark red," from vi. 3 to make up the four.

The word rendered "bottom" in the A. V. is by the LXX. taken as an adjective and rendered "shady," and so also the Syriac; and this some interpreters think is to be preferred ("in loco umbroso," Maurer; "loco uliginoso," Piscator; "in the shade," Henderson). But to speak of trees *in* a shady place seems absurd, seeing it is the trees that make the shade. The Vulgate renders by "in profundo," and this is preferred by most interpreters, מְצֻלָה being taken as another form of מְצוּלָה, "depth" or "abyss." Some recent interpreters (Hitzig, Ewald, Fürst, Bunsen) take מצלה here in the sense of "tent," and suppose the dwelling-place of Jehovah to be meant, before which, among the myrtles that grew in the forecourt, the rider stopped. But this meaning rests on a doubtful derivation of the word from the Arabic, and is altogether too far-fetched to be accepted. As the myrtle grove here symbolises the people of Israel, it is in keeping with the representation of their depressed condition that it should be planted in a low place. The LXX. seem to have read הָרִים "mountains," instead of הֲדַסִּים "myrtles," for they render by ἀναμέσον τῶν ὀρεών τῶν κατασκίων, and this some adopt as the true reading. There is, however, no reason for departing from the Massoretic text here. The prophet, seeing this group of riders, says to some one, "My lord, what are these?" To whom is this addressed? At first sight it might appear that it is to the man who was standing among the myrtle trees that the prophet here speaks. But it will be observed that as the prophet goes on with his description two persons appear, distinct from each other (see especially ii. 1–3), the one of whom he describes as the angel that talked with him,* the other as the angel of the Lord. Now the angel of the Lord is expressly said to be the man who stood among the myrtle trees, and, as he is not the same as the angel that talked with the prophet, it follows that it was not the man among the myrtle trees to whom the prophet addressed this question. The being to whom he spoke was the angel that talked or communed with him, the angel who was present with him throughout, and who acted the part of the *angelus interpres* to him. It is no objection to this that no other person has been mentioned as present than the angel of the Lord, the man among the myrtle trees; for in prophetic visions "on account of their dramatic character persons are very frequently introduced, either as speaking or as addressed by others, without having been previously mentioned." † It is true that the answer to the prophet's question was made by the man among the myrtle trees (ver. 10), and it may seem incongruous that his question should be addressed to one person and the answer to it be given by another. But it is to be observed that *two* answers were addressed to the prophet, the one by the angel that talked with him, the other by the man among the myrtle trees. The former, as the παράκλητος, the Helper and Guide of the prophet, said to him in reply to his question,

---

* הַדֹּבֵר בִּי. The LXX. render this by ὁ λαλῶν ἐν ἐμοί, and the Vulg. *qui loquebatur in me*. The Chaldee, on the contrary, has "with me" (עִמִּי), and this most interpreters adopt. There is a difference, however, between "דבר ב" and "דּ צם or עַל, which is not to be overlooked. The latter formula simply intimates that something is spoken to a person who may or may not attend to it; the former intimates that words are put into the mind of the hearer in order that they may be lodged there and abide. See Hengstenberg, "Christology," vol. i. p. 192.

† "Hengstenberg," *in loc.*

as immediately addressed to him, " I will show thee what these be ; " literally, " I will make thee to see," cause thee to understand, " what these be," what they import; and then the latter proceeded to expound the vision. The answer of the one had reference to the opening of the prophet's eyes, the clarifying of his mental vision so that he should perceive and understand what was about to be set before him ; the answer of the other had reference to the actual presentation of what he desired to see. We may well conceive, therefore, that two different persons are here introduced as speaking—the one the angel who communed with the prophet, the other the angel of the Lord who appeared as the man among the myrtle trees.*

To the prophet's question the man who stood among the myrtle trees replies, " These are they whom the Lord hath sent to walk to and fro through the earth " (ver. 10): in obedience to the Divine command they had gone forth as God's messengers to see what was doing on the earth, and to report to Him. And the report which they brought, and which in the hearing of the prophet they now repeat to the angel of the Lord, was, " We have walked to and fro through the earth, and, behold, all the earth sitteth still, and is at rest " (ver. 11). They had been out on their mission, they had fulfilled it, and now they appear before their chief and give in their report. They had gone through the whole earth and found all quiet; the nations were at peace and the tumult of war was stilled.

The fact that the nations were at peace while Judah was still exposed to unsettlement and disquiet seemed

* See Hengstenberg, "Christology," vol. iii. pp. 306-308.

to intimate that the wrath of God was still resting on His people. This moved the angel of the Lord, who here appears on the side of Israel, to cry to Jehovah on their behalf. "Then the angel of the Lord answered and said, O Lord of hosts, how long wilt Thou not have mercy on [wilt Thou not pity] Jerusalem and the cities of Judah, against which Thou hast had indignation these threescore and ten years?" (ver. 12). The prophet Jeremiah had foretold that the captivity of the people in Babylon should last for seventy years. If we compute from the final destruction of the temple and city of Jerusalem, in B.C. 588, there would be still nearly two years of the seventy to run in the second year of Darius. It would appear, however, that it is from an earlier terminus that the seventy years are to be reckoned, viz., from the time of the deportation of the king of Judah with the vessels of the temple to Babylon by Nebuchadnezzar, for they terminated in the first year of Cyrus (2 Chron. xxxvi. 21, 22; Ezra i. 1). They had expired, then, some years before the time of Zechariah's visions; but the people were still in a depressed condition, the temple was not rebuilt, and Jerusalem was not yet restored from its ruins; so that it seemed as if the captivity were still continued, and the promised period of release had not come. The angel of the Lord, therefore, as the intercessor for Israel, pleads with Jehovah that He would compassionate His people and restore their fallen state.

To this appeal the Lord replies, addressing His reply to the angel that talked with the prophet, as the medium of communication with the latter, and through him with the people; "Omnia ordine sunt: Deus angelo loquitur, angelus prophetæ" [*Grotius*]. "He answered with good words and comfortable words" (ver. 13); lit. "good words, words consolations" (דְּבָרִים נִחֻמִים); words designed to inspire hope in the minds of the people, and to give them comfort under trial, words that were themselves consolations. What the words were which the Lord spoke to the angel is not mentioned, but their substance may be gathered from what follows in the message which the prophet was enjoined to convey to the people. "And the angel that talked with me said unto me, Cry thou, saying, Thus saith the Lord of Hosts; I am jealous for Jerusalem and for Zion with a great jealousy. And I am very sore displeased with the heathen [the nations] that are at ease: for I was but a little displeased, and they helped forward the affliction." The prophet was to certify to the people that God had not ceased to regard His people, but, on the contrary, had towards them a great and burning zeal. And as He was zealous for them, so was He sore displeased with those who had oppressed them. They had indeed been used by Him as His instruments to chastise Israel, but they had exceeded their commission, and for their own ends had helped forward the calamity beyond what He willed. The prophet was further commanded to assure the people that God would again return to them and show them favour. "Therefore thus saith the Lord; I am returned to Jerusalem with mercies: My house shall be built in it, saith the Lord of Hosts, and a line shall be stretched forth over Jerusalem;" *i.e.* a measuring-line, such as builders use to measure the space they design their edifice to occupy, so that out of the ruins of the city fair buildings should arise. Still further, the prophet was commanded to assure the people that times of great prosperity and blessing should come to them. "Cry yet [still further], Thus saith the Lord of Hosts; My cities through prosperity shall yet be spread abroad;* and the Lord shall yet comfort Zion, and shall yet choose Jerusalem" (vers. 14-17). The blessing should be seen outwardly in the extension and increase of the cities of Judah, and experienced inwardly in the presence of God with His people, dwelling amongst them, and comforting them (comp. Joel ii. 18, ff.; Jer. xxxiii. 12, ff.). With the utterance of this message the vision ended and its scenery passed away.

Such was the vision: what is its significance?

The prophet saw a grove of myrtle trees in a hollow or low place. By the myrtle grove all are agreed is signified the covenant people, the nation of Israel; and by its being in a low place is indicated their then depressed and sad condition. The myrtle is a plant of unassuming appearance, a modest plant with no majestic branches or brilliant flowers, yet withal beautiful, and possessing the quality of perennial freshness. The Jewish maiden whom the Persians, who saw her in the brilliancy of her mature beauty, called Esther or Star,† was by her parents, who saw her first in the milder loveliness of infancy, called Hadassah or Myrtle (Esth. ii. 7). In the Hebrew mind the idea of modest beauty and freshness was associated with the myrtle; and hence we find this introduced as symbolical of the Church under the reign of the Messiah,

---

* Or shall overflow with good, *i.e.* shall enjoy the greatest prosperity.

† "Esther is without doubt to be collated with *stara*, new-Persian *sitarch*, ἀστήρ, *star*."—Bertheau, "Exeget. Handbuch zum A. T." *in loc.*

when "instead of the briar"—the symbol of the world under the curse—"shall come up the myrtle tree, and it shall be to the Lord for a name, for an everlasting sign that shall not be cut off" (Isa. lv. 13). A grove of myrtles would, therefore, appropriately represent in symbol to a Jew his nation, which was identical with the Church of God; and which, though at that time in a state of depression and affliction, was fair in the sight of God, was destined to endure and flourish, and was ere long to be visited by Him in mercy and restored to prosperity.

This is specially indicated here by the standing among the myrtle trees of the mounted rider. He, though in appearance as a man, is described as the Angel of Jehovah. By this appellation is designated in Scripture a being who on various occasions appeared to men, and who, though coming forth as the Angel or Messenger of Jehovah, is at the same time represented as a Divine being, having the power of God, receiving the honours due only to God, and exercising the proper functions of the Almighty (comp. Gen. xvi. 7–14; xxii. 11–19; xxxi. 11, ff.; xlviii. 15, 16; Exod. xiii. 2, ff; xxiii. 20, 21; Josh. v. 13–15, &c.). A comparison of these passages leads to the conclusion that the angel of Jehovah is none other than God manifest in human form, the Being who, as the Captain of the Lord's host, led up Israel to Canaan, the Being who came forth to execute vengeance on the enemies of the covenant people, and who was known to Israel as their Protector and Advocate.*

---

* See Hengstenberg, "Christology," vol. i. p. 107, ff.; Dr. Pye Smith's "Scripture Testimony to the Messiah," vol. i. p. 296, ff., 4th edit.; M'Caul's "Translation of Kimchi on Zechariah," p. 9.

That this Being is the same who in the fulness of time came to our world as the Angel of the covenant (Mal. iii. 1), who appeared in human nature made of a woman, made under the law for man's redemption, and who now in that nature sits on the throne of heaven and administers the affairs of the universe, the teachings of the New Testament lead us confidently to believe. Be this, however, as it may, there can be no doubt that the man among the myrtle trees whom the prophet saw was a Divine apparition; and that this was the understanding of the ancient Jewish Church may be gathered from the exposition in the Talmud: "This man is none other than the Holy One, blessed be He! for it is said, The Lord is a man of war."* With this the tone of his prayer to Jehovah is in keeping; it has in it "something superhuman, and reminds of the words, *Father, I will*" [*Lange*].

For the consolation and encouragement of the people, therefore, the prophet had to tell them that, depressed as was their condition, the Angel of the Lord, the Leader, the Protector, the Redeemer of Israel, was still in the midst of them. He was there, standing still and motionless, but ready to ride forth in their defence, and to send judgments on their adversaries; which was indicated in the vision by his being mounted on a red horse, the symbol of war and bloodshed (comp. Isa. lxiii. 1, ff.; Rev. vi. 4). The other riders are His subordinates, angels inferior to Him, and employed by Him as His emissaries and agents. The horses on which they ride are of different colours: red as the emblem of war, white

---

* "Babyl. Talm. Sanhedrin," fol. 93, col. i., quoted by Henderson, "Minor Prophets," p. 369.

as the emblem of peace, and a colour between these two to indicate a transition state, or a state in which war and peace alternate. In the vision these riders are represented as giving in their report to their chief. They report a state of general peace and quiet; which, however, had been reached through war and change. Before the white horse came the horse partly red and partly white, and before it the horse wholly red. The representation corresponds with the actual history of the time. After the death of Nebuchadnezzar the empire of Babylon was plunged in war, and this continued until the capital was taken and the throne seized by Cyrus. A season of unsettlement and change succeeded; but in the second year of Darius the nations were at rest, and through the then known world peace reigned.

The Angel of the Lord is not only the Protector and Vindicator of Israel, He is with them also as their Intercessor with God. Hence he appears in this vision as making intercession for them, beseeching God to have pity on Jerusalem and the cities of Judah; and now that the time of chastisement was at an end, that He would be gracious to them, and grant them full restoration and establishment in their own land. And through him also came the comforting answer to the people. The invisible God does not Himself speak. The speaker to men is the Angel of Jehovah, by whom alone He, "whom no man hath seen at any time, or can see," is manifested to men or speaks to them.

In the vision the Angel of Jehovah speaks directly and immediately to the invisible God; but to the prophet He speaks through the angel interpreter. So in the vision which Daniel saw: it was not Michael, the Great Prince, the Archangel, that spoke directly to him, but Gabriel, whom the other commanded to make Daniel understand the vision (Dan. viii. 16; ix. 21). The angel interpreter represents the Spirit of God by whom the ancient prophets spoke and wrote.

In the words which were conveyed to the ears of the prophet by the angel, God declares His zeal for His people, His indignation against their enemies, and His determination to do good unto His people and enrich them with His bounty. He is not an indifferent spectator of what happens to them. He watches over them with a constant jealousy, solicitous for their well-being, and ready to resent all attempts to injure them. Their enemies God may use as instruments by which He chastises them when they have sinned against Him; but when these enemies execute their commission without any thought of God, and are impelled merely by their own lust of conquest, of power, and of wealth, and in all the wantonness of cruelty aggravate the affliction to the utmost of their power, God will not hold them guiltless, but will avenge the wrongs of His people by punishing them (comp. Isa. x. 5–27).* His own He will never forsake. When the deepest abyss of calamity seems to be reached by them, when the darkest hour of their sorrow throws its shadows over them, the Angel of the Lord, He who ever encamps around them that fear Him, will suddenly appear on their side and will deliver them from all their enemies.

* See Wardlaw's "Lectures on Zechariah," p. 35.

II.

THE HORNS AND THE WORKMEN.

"Then lifted I up mine eyes, and saw, and behold four horns. And I said unto the angel that talked with me, What be these? And he answered me, These are the horns which have scattered Judah, Israel, and Jerusalem. And the Lord showed me four carpenters. Then said I, What come these to do? And he spake, saying, These are the horns which have scattered Judah, so that no man did lift up his head: but these are come to fray them, to cast out the horns of the Gentiles, which lifted up their horn over the land of Judah to scatter it."—ZECH. i. 18-21; in the Hebrew text, ii. 1-4.

AFTER a brief interval a second vision was presented to the prophet. That at the close of this interval the prophet was roused from sleep is not to be supposed; the phrase, " I lifted up mine eyes and saw" or "looked," is a formula used in introducing prophetic visions (comp. ii. 1; vi. 1; Ezek. viii. 5; Dan. x. 5), and implies merely, that the attention of the seer was aroused to what was presented to him. He saw "four horns." Whether these were seen by themselves, or as borne by animals, is not said; but the latter may be presumed to have been the case from the statement that they were frightened away or discomfited (ver. 21), which implies that the objects presented to the prophet's view were creatures susceptible of fear, and which could be driven away. As physical emblems of force, horns are in the prophetic visions representative of earthly powers or kingdoms (comp. Jer. xlviii. 25; Dan. viii. 3, 5–9, &c.);

B

the Chaldee Targum explains horns here as meaning kingdoms (מלכיות), and in answer to the prophet's questions, "What be these?" the angel interpreter said, "These are the horns—the earthly powers—that have scattered Judah, Israel, and Jerusalem." The number four, in its prophetic acceptation, is the signature of the world, and is used here to indicate powers coming on every side, or from all quarters. Many understand the four here specifically, of certain four great powers that were hostile to Judah; according to some, the Assyrian, the Babylonian, the Grecian, and the Roman; according to others, the Assyrian, the Babylonian, the Grecian, and the Persian. But it is improbable that reference would be made thus specially to the Assyrian and Babylonian empires, which were then virtually extinct; or, to such powers as Greece and Rome, with which the Jews did not become acquainted till long afterwards; and besides, neither the Grecian nor the Persian power can be regarded as hostile to the Jews, in the sense at least of tyrannising over them, and destroying them. As in the former vision the riders were represented as having gone over the whole earth, and found all quiet, so here, all the earthly powers hostile to the people of God are, in general, indicated by the four horns. In the answer to the prophet's question, "What be these?" the angel interpreter introduces Israel, between Judah and Jerusalem. That it is Judah alone that is in question, is evident from ver. 21; but there is no reason to suppose, as some have suggested, that the words "Israel and Jerusalem" are an interpolation. Jerusalem is expressly named, "because it was the head of the whole kingdom, and the seat of the sacred observances of the entire nation" [*Rosenm.*]. (Comp. Joel iii. [4], 6.) Israel cannot here designate the ten tribes as a nation, and the number of those, who from among these joined themselves to the Jews, was too small to be co-ordinated with Judah as a distinct body; they were incorporated with the Jews, and from the captivity ceased to have a separate existence. Hitzig takes Judah as the designation of the whole of which Israel and Jerusalem are parts, the former being the people of the country, the latter the metropolis; and with this Pressel agrees, only he thinks that Israel is not to be restricted to the country people. Lange suggests that "not only a scattering of the nation as a whole and externally may be intended, but also an internal scattering, —Judah dispersed, Israel and Jerusalem torn asunder." Ewald thinks that Israel is inserted between Judah and Jerusalem simply for the sake of honour, just as Benjamin is introduced along with Judah, in Ps. lxviii. 27; and this is probably the correct view.

As the prophet continued to look, Jehovah—the same who is called The Angel of Jehovah (ver. 12), and Jehovah (ver. 13),—showed him—rather caused him to see (יַרְאֵנִי)—four workmen or artificers. In the A. V. it is "four carpenters," but the Hebrew word means simply a workman; it is used of workers in stone and metal as well as in wood (comp. 2 Sam. v. 11; Isa. xliv. 11, 12); it is used frequently of one who works with the plough (Deut. xxii. 10; Ps. cxxix. 3; Isa. xxviii. 24, &c.); it is even used to designate those who work destruction (Ezek. xxi. 36) [A. V. 31, "skilful to destroy"]. As the horns which Zechariah saw were probably of iron (comp. 1 Kings xxii. 11; Micah iv. 13), the workmen in his vision would be smiths; and so Ewald renders the word here.* In answer to the prophet's question, "What come these to do?" the Lord repeats the explanation of the horns already given to the prophet by the angel that talked with him, telling him that "these are the horns which had scattered Judah, so that no man did lift up his head," an expression indicative of utter prostration and hopeless misery, as of persons under a yoke (comp. Job x. 15; Micah ii. 3); and in the close, passing from the symbol to the reality, he declares, that these are the horns of the peoples who had lifted up the horn against (that is, had proudly oppressed and tyrannised over) (Ps. lxxv. 5, 6) the land, *i.e.* the people of Judah, to scatter it; and informed him that the workmen had come to frighten away, or discomfit and cast down, these oppressors. "These are come to fray them." In modern usage the verb "fray" signifies to *rub* or *file down*, but in old English it is used in the sense of *terrify*, or *frighten*.† In this sense it occurs in the A. V. in Deut. xxviii. 26; and in Jer. vii. 33, as well as here: elsewhere the Hebrew word (הֶחֱרִיד Hiph. of חָרַד *to tremble*) is rendered by *make afraid*, except in Judg. viii. 12, where it is rendered by *discomfited*, with *terrified* in the margin. "Fray" is retained in the A. V. from the earlier versions,

---

* "Perhaps *plowers*, in the sense in which the same Hebrew word is used in Ps. cxxix. 3," Canon Drake in "Speaker's Commentary." But what special relation have ploughmen to horns?

† This verb is still in use in Scotland, and in some of the provinces of England, where it is sometimes pronounced *flay;* it is the root from which *afraid*, the participle of the obsolete verb *affray*, comes. It and the noun "fray" are probably connected with the root "frag," from which come Lat. *frango, fragor, fractura,* and our *fragment, fraction,* &c. "Fray," *to rub,* is from the French *frayer.*

the Genevan, Bishops' Bible, and Coverdale; Wicliffe has "to fere hem." Not only should they be frightened; they should also be cast down, flung down as a stone is from the hand (comp. Lam. iii. 53, the only other passage where the verb here used, occurs). The four workmen do not symbolise four special powers by which the enemies of Judah were to be discomfited and cast down; as the horns were four, so an equal number of workmen came to indicate the completeness of the overthrow of the enemies of Judah. Each horn has its destined destroyer.

This second vision may be regarded as supplementary of the first: there the restoration of Judah was indicated generally; here some of the means by which that was to be effected are presented. Though enemies from all quarters and on every side might assail the people of God, the Lord, their Protector, would raise up for them adequate defence, would bring into action powers sufficient to discomfit and cast down all their oppressors, however many or strong.

What was thus showed for the comfort of the people of God in the old time is no less for the comfort and encouragement of the Church in all ages and places. "The sum of the whole is, though the Church may not be exempt from many troubles, yet the Lord has in His hand resources by which He can restrain all assaults of the wicked, however impetuously and violently they may be impelled against the Church."* The Angel of the Lord, the Divine Redeemer, abides for ever with that Church which He hath purchased with His blood. And exalted as He is to the throne of His glory, and having all power

* Calvin, *in loc.*

in Heaven and on earth, He can send forth at any time agencies by which the power of the Church's enemies shall be broken, and all their forces routed. It behoves the Church, then, to have faith in her exalted Head, and patiently to wait for Him. In due time He will interpose on her behalf when she is afflicted; He will scatter and discomfit all her adversaries, and will "cause her righteousness to go forth as brightness, and her salvation as a lamp that burneth."

III.

THE MAN WITH THE MEASURING LINE.

"I lifted up mine eyes again, and looked, and behold a man with a measuring line in his hand. Then said I, Whither goest thou? And he said unto me, To measure Jerusalem, to see what is the breadth thereof, and what is the length thereof. And, behold, the angel that talked with me went forth, and another angel went out to meet him," &c.—ZECH. ii. 1–13; in the Hebrew text, ii. 5–17.

AFTER another brief interval the prophet lifted up his eyes and another vision was presented to him. He saw a man with a measuring line in his hand. Whether the man he saw was the same as the man among the myrtle trees of the first vision, the Angel of Jehovah, or some subordinate agent, is not said. Jerome, whom many recent interpreters (Hengstenberg, Keil, Pusey, &c.) follow, advocates the former view; Jarchi, Rosenmüller, Maurer, &c., think it is the angel interpreter whom the prophet saw; but the former of these views has nothing beyond a conjectural validity, and the latter seems directly opposed by ver. 4, where the angel interpreter is distinguished from the man seen in the vision. It is best to regard the man presented to the view of the prophet as a figure introduced merely to carry out the symbolical representation of the vision; it is needless to go so far as to suppose, with Kliefoth and Lange, that "it is the allegorical figure of the Israelitish idea concerning the new building up of Jerusalem." In answer to the prophet's question, "Whither goest thou?" the man replied, "To measure Jerusalem, to see what is the breadth thereof, and what is the length thereof." The measuring line in his hand was such as architects use to define the boundaries of their work; it was not merely to measure the extent of the city that he had it, but to lay the city out in order and proportion (comp. Ezek. xl.). The prophet's eager question was prompted, we may suppose, by his remembrance of the "good and comfortable words" of the first vision, in which, among other things, he was assured that God's house should be built and a line stretched forth on Jerusalem; and by his hope that now this was to be accomplished. In this he was not disappointed. The man whom the prophet saw had come to stretch out his line over the city, desolate and in ruins as it still was, to measure it, that he might lay out a plan as a necessary preliminary to its being rebuilt.

On this answer being given, the angel interpreter, who apparently had remained by the side of the prophet, stepped forward and advanced towards the man with the measuring line; or, it may be, simply went forward to receive any message that was to be conveyed to the prophet. He was met immediately by another angel, who may have been a subordinate angel commissioned by the Angel of the Lord to deliver the message, but more probably was the Angel of the Lord Himself, inasmuch as in delivering the message he does not use the language of one reporting the words of another, but speaks in his own person, and speaks as no mere creature could without impropriety speak as from himself (comp. vers. 5-9).

Seeing the angel interpreter coming forward, this other angel arrests him by commanding him to carry with haste a message: "Run," said he; "speak to this young man" (ver. 4). By the "young man" here, some understand the man with the measuring line, whom the angel is commanded to stop from measuring the city, seeing it was in the Divine purpose much more extensive than any city built on the basis of the ruined Jerusalem could be; while others think the "young man" is the prophet himself, who was then probably a youth just entered on the prophetic office. The latter seems the more probable view, partly because it was the special office of the angel interpreter to speak to the prophet, and partly because as the message was one to be conveyed by the prophet to the people, he, rather than the man with the measuring line, was the party to whom it was fitting that it should be announced. As the prophet was waiting, eager to know what this vision portended, and as the message the angel had to carry was a gladdening one, he is commanded to "run;" the bearer of good tidings must not delay or move with languid step.

The message conveyed had reference to the restoration of the Jews, and the re-occupation of Jerusalem, and that not within its ancient limits, but much beyond them: "Jerusalem shall be inhabited as towns without walls, for the multitude of men and cattle therein." The general meaning of this is obvious, but there is some uncertainty as to the signification of particular words. The verb rendered "shall be inhabited" properly signifies "shall sit" or "lie" (תֵּשֵׁב), though instances are not wanting of its being used with a passive acceptation (comp. Isa. xiii.

20; Ezek. xxvi. 20, &c.). The word rendered "towns without walls" (פְּרָזוֹת) derived from a root signifying *to spread abroad*, means properly the outlying or open country (comp. Esth. ix. 19, "towns of the country"; A. V. "unwalled towns"; Ezek. xxxviii. 11, "the land of open country"; A. V. "the land of unwalled villages"; and Deut. iii. 5; and 1 Sam. vi. 18; where a cognate word (פְּרָזִי) is used). The passage may, therefore, be rendered either by "Jerusalem shall be inhabited as open country," or "shall lie as open country," or (supposing an ellipsis of עָרֵי, *towns*), "shall lie as country towns." In any case the meaning is, that because of the multitude of occupants Jerusalem should not be confined within walls, but should spread abroad into the open country. Commentators compare with this Thucyd. i. 5, πόλεσιν ἀτειχίστοις καὶ κατὰ κώμας οἰκουμέναις, but the idea here seems to be not so much the dwelling in villages, as the spreading of the city over a wide space. "The new, better city should, on account of the multitude of inhabitants, have no limits, but (as is ever the case with all the great cities of the earth) should, without walls or gates, spread itself out indefinitely, hamlet-like" (*Ewald*).

The assurance thus given was ere long fully realised. After the rebuilding of Jerusalem under Nehemiah its inhabitants rapidly increased, and soon the ancient limits were passed, and large additions had to be made to the area of occupation from the surrounding country. Josephus, in his description of Jerusalem, says (De Bell. Jud. V. iv. 2), that King Agrippa built the third wall of the city "around that part of it which had accrued to the ancient city, which was before all unenclosed (γυμνή); for overflowing with numbers the city had gradually crept out beyond the walls; and including within the city the parts to the north of the temple on the ridge, [the people] went out not a little beyond, and covered a fourth ridge with buildings." This gradual increase of the population and extension of the city went on until "Jerusalem rose to a state of opulence, power, dignity, and splendour, which she had not known since the division of Israel and Judah" (*Stonard*).

What follows is in parallel lines after the manner of Hebrew poetry. The language rises into a higher strain, and the sentiment gradually ascends from the literal to the spiritual, from what belongs to the national Israel, to what appertains to that of which it was the type, the Church of God, and that in the times of the Messiah.

> 5. And I * will be to her, saith Jehovah, a wall of fire around,
> And for glory will I be in the midst of her.

How vivid and striking the imagery here employed! As a city surrounded by a wall of fire would be utterly inaccessible by any mortal foe, God would so surround and protect Jerusalem that any attempt to assail her, by whomsoever made, should not only prove fruitless, but involve those who made it in ruin. And as he would defend and protect her from assault from without, so would He dignify and glorify her within. The Targumist explains this latter expression thus: "And with glory will I place my Shekinah in the midst of her;" and this has led to the suggestion that the promise here refers to

---

* The "I" here is emphatic ואני. The Targum has for this מימרי *My Word*, i.e. the מימרא דיי *Word of Jah*, by which the Jews designated the Divine Personality as having intercourse with men.

the return to the temple of the visible manifestation of the Divine Presence in the Holy of Holies. But on this no stress can be laid, partly because the Rabbins use the word Shekinah frequently where there is no reference to the manifestation in the temple, and partly because there is no certain evidence that in the second temple there was, as in the first, the visible emblem of the Divine presence.* God Himself, in His glory and majesty, was to be in the midst of His people. He had chosen Zion for His rest, and there would He dwell; and where He dwells, His glory and majesty are displayed. This was to be the crowning honour and supreme privilege of the renovated City, and the restored State. (Comp. Isa. liv. 17; xxvi. 1; lx. 19; Zech. ix. 8.)

6. Ho! ho! [arise] and flee from the land of the North, saith Jehovah;
For, as the four winds of heaven, have I dispersed you, saith Jehovah.

The mimetic interjection at the beginning of this distich is of frequent occurrence in the Old Testament, though only here is it repeated. It is chiefly used with a denunciatory signification = woe!—also as an utterance of grief = oh! alas. Here and in Isa. x. 5; lv. 1; Jer. xlvii. 6, it is used hortatorily or keleusmatically. When repeated, as here, it may be regarded as including in it some such verb as "arise" or "hear," which will account for the "and" following it. The repetition may be also

---

* The word *Shekeena'* שְׁכִינָא, comes from the verb שָׁכַן *to inhabit, to dwell*, and signifies primarily *a dwelling-place*. By the Rabbins it is used of the Divine Presence wherever that is manifested or made known to men. See Buxtorf, Lex. Chal. Tal. et Rabb.; and Levy, Chald. Wörterbuch, on the word.

regarded as indicating the urgency of the call. By "the land of the north" Babylonia is intended. Strictly speaking, Babylon was to the north-east of Judea, but as travellers from Judea to Babylon would turn northwards, the Jews spoke of Babylonia as the land of the north or the north country (comp. Jer. vi. 22; xvi. 15). The meaning of the second part of the verse and its connection with the first are not very apparent. What, it may be asked, is meant by their being dispersed as the four winds of heaven?—and how could their being so dispersed be a reason for their fleeing in particular from the one quarter, the north? A few MSS. have "*by* the four winds" (בְּאַרְבַּע) instead of "*as* the," &c. כְּ; but even were this reading better supported, it would not relieve the difficulty, though it seems to have been a correction with that view. The phrase, the four winds, is used loosely to denote "all directions" (comp. Ezek. v. 10; xvii. 21; Matt. xxiv. 31); and as the Jews had been carried not only to Babylon but to other places, and many had fled in various directions, they might be said to have been dispersed as the four winds, *i.e.* separated from each other in all directions, as the four winds are separated from each other. Some think that there is rather an allusion here to the *violence* of their dispersion; they had been scattered as if the four winds had spent their combined fury on them. But the text will not bear this rendering, even though כְּ be read instead of בְּ. The call may be regarded as a call to return from all parts to which they had been banished, and Babylon is especially indicated, because that was the centre and chief place of their exile. The use of the "for" in the second line of the verse presents a difficulty. The particle might be rendered by *though* or *although*, as in Exod. xiii. 17; Josh. xvii. 18; Jer. iv. 30, &c.; *q. d.* "Though I have dispersed you, yet I call you to return." But this is a doubtful expedient. Better is it to suppose, that there is a tacit reference to the fact that as it was God who had dispersed them, so at His voice they might without fear of failure flee, so as to escape from their dispersion; *q. d.* As it was I who caused your dispersion, so it is I who now summon you to return, *wherefore*, arise, and flee, &c.

> 7. Ho! Zion, deliver thyself,
>   Thou that art dwelling with the daughter of Babylon.

This shows that it is especially the Jews who are here addressed, and not, as some have supposed, the ten tribes who were located farther north than Babylon. The interjection at the beginning of this clause is the same as that in the beginning of the sixth verse. "The daughter of Babylon" is a periphrasis for Babylon itself, or it may designate the population of that city (comp. "Daughter of Tyre," Ps. xlv. 12; "Daughter of Zion," "Daughter of Edom," Lam. iv. 22; "Daughter of Tarshish," Isa. xxiii. 10). The mass of the Jews were still at Babylon, and there probably they were for the most part content to remain. The Book of Esther shows how much the people generally had degenerated in spirit and religious feeling in the later years of the captivity; and it is probable, that for several reasons—indifference with some, the love of worldly ease and pleasure with others, and the possession of wealth and property in Babylon with others—the majority were little inclined to return to the land of their fathers, and share in the toils, privations, and perils of those who had availed themselves of the permission of Cyrus to go thither. Such are here addressed as dwelling with the daughter of Babylon, just as in Jer. xlvi. 19, those in Egypt are said to be dwelling with the daughter of Egypt (comp. also Jer. xlviii. 18, "dwelling with the daughter of Dibon," *i.e.* dwelling in Dibon). Whilst good days were coming on Jerusalem, the vengeance of God was about to fall on Babylon. The Jews there are therefore summoned to make their escape from thence, that they might not be involved in the impending calamity.

8. For thus saith Jehovah of Hosts,
   After glory hath he sent me to the nations that have spoiled you,
   For he that toucheth you toucheth the apple of His eye.

The speaker here is the Angel of Jehovah, sent by Him to execute His will (comp. Isa. xlviii. 16): it cannot be, as some suppose, the prophet himself, for the speaker in the 9th verse is the same as here, and the prophet could not say of himself what the speaker there says of himself. "After glory." Some take this as meaning "to acquire," or "obtain glory"; while by others it is taken in a temporal sense as meaning after the glory, *i.e.* after God had established His glory in the midst of Jerusalem (ver. 5). It is an objection to this latter view that there is no definite article in the original, which would seem to be required if the reference were to the glory specially announced before. We should expect also in this case that the verb following would be in the future and not the past tense—" will He send," not " hath He sent"; and, finally, if by the promise in ver. 5 we are to understand the presence of Jehovah in glory and majesty among His people, it could not be said that *after* that, posterior to that, God would send forth His angel to punish the nations, seeing the punishment of the nations is throughout represented as conducing to the manifestation of the Divine glory in the midst of Zion, and therefore prior to this. The other view is accordingly to be preferred. The preposition here (אַחַר) is used locally, as it often is after verbs of motion, and indicates the scope or end of the mission announced. God had sent forth His angel to get glory to Himself by taking vengeance on the enemies of His people (comp. Exod. xiv. 18). The reason of this is announced in what follows: " For he that toucheth you (*i.e.* with an evil intent so as to injure you) toucheth the apple of His eye." By the English phrase, "the apple of the eye," is designated the pupil of the eye, the small aperture through which the rays pass to the retina so as to excite vision. The Hebrew word, which occurs only here (בָּבַת), may be derived from the obsolete verb בוּב, to *hollow* (if there was such a verb), and like the Chaldaic בָּבָא may mean *gate* or *opening*; but it is more probably a mimetic word, expressive of the little image one sees of oneself when looking into the eye of another, or when looking on oneself in a mirror. The Hebrews delighted in varying their expression of this. In Deut. xxxii. 10 and Prov. vii. 2, the phrase used is, "the mannikin of the eye" (אִישׁוֹן עֵינוֹ); in Lam. ii. 18 it is, " the daughter of the eye " (בַּת עַיִן); and in Ps. xvii. 8, the two are combined, " the mannikin of the daughter of the eye." Here it is probably " the babe of the eye," which accords with our English phrase, "the pupil of the eye," *i.e.* the *pupilla* or little maiden of the eye.* So the Greeks used κόρη, "a girl," for the same object. The pupil of the eye is the most delicate part of one of the most delicate organs of the human frame, peculiarly sensitive to the touch, and hence guarded with special care. By no figure, then, could a more lively impression be conveyed of God's sensitively tender regard and care for His people than this.

> 9. For, behold, I wave my hand over them,
> And they shall become a spoil to their own servants,
> . And ye shall know that Jehovah of hosts hath sent me.

It needed but a wave of God's hand to overthrow those mighty powers that had enslaved Israel, so that they whom they had led into captivity should become their masters, "the spoilers should become the spoiled, and the oppressors the enslaved." And when this should be done, evidence should be afforded that it was indeed the Lord of hosts that had sent forth His messenger to convey to Israel these comforting assurances. These were glad tidings for Zion; therefore she is summoned to rejoice in receiving them.

> 10–13. Shout and rejoice, O daughter of Zion,
> For, behold, I come and dwell in the midst of thee, saith Jehovah;
> And many nations shall join themselves to Jehovah in that day,
> And shall be to Me for a people;
> And I will dwell in the midst of thee,
> And thou shalt know that Jehovah of hosts hath sent me to thee.
> For Jehovah shall take Judah as His portion in the holy land,
> And shall yet choose Jerusalem.

---

* The Heb. *Baba* is of kin to a whole host of words in other languages: Syr. ܒܒܐ *bobo*; Ar. بوبو *bubu*; Lat. *pupa*; Ital. *bambino*; Welsh, *baban*; and our own *babe*.

The daughter of Zion, the people of Jerusalem, is here addressed as a part for the whole, the call being to the entire Jewish nation to rejoice because God had returned to dwell with them in Zion, the place He had chosen: even in exile they had been His people, but now He would return to His own chosen portion and dwell with His people there (comp. Deut. xxxii. 8, 9). Nor should they alone share the blessing of His presence; many nations should be brought to join themselves to Him, and become a people unto Him. This cannot refer merely to an increase by means of proselytes to the Jewish nation. It is not said that many out of or from among the nations should come, but that many nations should come and join themselves to Jehovah and be His people. A promise like this cannot be held as being fulfilled by the addition of a few hundreds or thousands of converts from heathenism to Judaism during the progress of centuries. Something more befitting the grandeur of the promise than this must be intended, and this is confirmed by what follows,

>13. Hush all flesh before Jehovah.
>For He hath risen up out of His holy habitation.

The interjection at the beginning of this verse in the Hebrew, הס *hass*, corresponds in sound and meaning to our word *hush!* The call for silence intimates that a special manifestation of the Divine presence and majesty is about to be made. In other parts of the prophetic writings we find the same command in connection with an announcement of the presence of God in His temple, and exercising His power for the vindication and safety of His people (comp. Hab. ii. 20; Zeph. i. 7; see also

Rev. viii. 1). The call here is a summons to all flesh to wait in silent reverence and awe what should come to pass when God should arise as from sleep,* and manifest Himself from heaven, the habitation of His holiness (Deut. xxvi. 15; Jer. xxv. 30).

In this vision God presented to the prophet, and through him to the nation at large, the prospect and the assurance of the restoration of Jerusalem, and the re-establishment of the Jewish state as it had been before the captivity. The city should not only be rebuilt but greatly extended: the temple should be restored, and the worship of Jehovah resumed; His Presence should be with His people, and they should enjoy His protection; and whilst they were thus blessed judgment should come upon those nations that had oppressed them, and they should have supremacy over those by whom they had been enslaved. All this was literally fulfilled. But even in these promises there seems to be a reference to things of still higher import and of spiritual significancy. The speaker here is the Angel of Jehovah, and He, whilst He speaks of Himself as Jehovah's messenger, at the same time uses language which no mere created angel could use. In His own name He threatens to punish the nations, and that with a mere motion of His hand; and to Israel He promises for God that He would come and dwell among them as their God, and inherit Judah as His portion. Who can such a speaker be but that Being who in the fulness of time appeared in our world, uniting in His one person the Divine nature and the human; He

---

* The verb here used signifies properly, to be aroused from sleep or awakened (comp. ch. iv. 1; Job xiv. 12).

who came and dwelt among men, and was Emmanuel, God with us? May we not say, then, that there is here a promise of blessing to the Church through the advent of the Redeemer? Then certainly was glory brought to the temple of the Lord; then did God in a higher sense than of old make Zion His chosen rest and Judah His portion; then was the tabernacle of God with men, and men saw the glory of Him who tabernacled among them as the glory of the only begotten of the Father; and then was the season when the daughter of Zion, the true Church of God, rejoiced and exulted with all her heart.

It is in accordance with the general strain of prophetic announcement concerning the latter dispensation, when the speaker here announces that many nations should be joined to the Lord, and become His people. The conversion of individuals might take place under the ancient dispensation; a few proselytes might from time to time join themselves to the people of God; but it was reserved for the time of the Messiah for *nations* as such to be converted to the Lord. Only under Him on whose shoulder the government is laid, and who shall reign from sea to sea, and from the river to the ends of the earth, shall "the forces of the Gentiles" be brought into the Church, and the world be converted to God.

The Church of God, therefore, under the latter dispensation, may take to herself as her own the comfort and encouragement which those promises, given to the Church in the old time, were intended to convey. Security, protection, glory, grace, blessing, extension, and final triumph, are all here assured to her by the promise of Him whose Word cannot fail.

IV.

THE HIGH PRIEST AND THE ADVERSARY.

"And he showed me Joshua the high priest standing before the angel of the Lord, and Satan standing at his right hand to resist him. And the Lord said unto Satan, The Lord rebuke thee, O Satan; even the Lord that hath chosen Jerusalem rebuke thee: is not this a brand plucked out of the fire? Now Joshua was clothed with filthy garments, and stood before the angel. And he answered and spake unto those that stood before him, saying, Take away the filthy garments from him. And unto him he said, Behold, I have caused thine iniquity to pass from thee, and I will clothe thee with change of raiment. And I said, Let them set a fair mitre upon his head. So they set a fair mitre upon his head, and clothed him with garments. And the angel of the Lord stood by. And the angel of the Lord protested unto Joshua, saying, Thus saith the Lord of hosts; If thou wilt walk in my ways, and if thou wilt keep my charge, then thou shalt also judge my house, and shalt also keep my courts, and I will give thee places to walk among these that stand by. Hear now, O Joshua the high priest, thou, and thy fellows that sit before thee: for they are men wondered at: for, behold, I will bring forth my servant the BRANCH. For behold the stone that I have laid before Joshua; upon one stone shall be seven eyes: behold, I will engrave the graving thereof, saith the Lord of hosts, and I will remove the iniquity of that land in one day. In that day, saith the Lord of hosts, shall ye call every man his neighbour under the vine and under the fig tree."—ZECH. iii. 1-10.

THIS fourth vision seems to have been presented to the view of the prophet immediately, without any interval, after the preceding. The expression "he showed me" points back to the person who was commanded by the Angel of the Lord to speak to the prophet in the preceding vision (ii. 4). This was the angel-interpreter, whose it was to show to the prophet the visions, and to convey to him their meaning and the message of the Lord connected with each (i. 9, 13, 14, 19). Having delivered the message with which he was charged, the angel without pause showed to the prophet another vision, closely connected in purport with that which had just passed away. In the preceding vision the prophet had been assured that the Lord would return to Israel, would dwell again in His chosen heritage, and would enrich His people with blessing. But would God dwell with the unholy and impure? Assuredly not. Israel, indeed, had been guilty and vile, but their guilt and vileness should be taken away; and, purified and restored, they should again rejoice in the presence with them of their Redeemer God. This is what this fourth vision was especially designed to represent.

The prophet saw Joshua the high priest standing before the Angel of Jehovah, not in the proper attire of his office, the holy garments clean and white with which he had to come into the presence of God, but clothed in filthy garments. At his right hand stood the Adversary —Satan is not here a proper name, as is shown by the article being prefixed, הַשָּׂטָן, "the Satan"—to act the part of an adversary to him by resisting his plea. Nothing is said as to the *place* in which the high priest was seen, nor as to the *purpose* for which he stood before the Angel of the Lord. "To stand before the Lord" does not necessarily imply the performing of official service in the sanctuary, as some have supposed. The phrase "to stand before one" is used as well of the appearance of parties before a judge (Num. xxvii. 2, xxxv. 12; Deut. xix. 17;

Josh. xx. 6; 1 Kings iii. 16) as of the appearance of an inferior before a superior for the purpose of rendering service (1 Kings x. 8; Dan. i. 19). There is nothing, therefore, in the statement that Joshua was standing before the Angel of the Lord to determine whether he was seen in the temple engaged in official service, or appeared as a culprit before the judge; both of which views have found advocates among interpreters. Neither of them, however, is free from objection. In a vision the high priest might be seen officiating in the temple, though at the time the temple did not actually exist; but it is inconceivable that he should be represented as "in filthy garments" when so engaged. In such attire no priest would have dared to appear before God in the temple; and though in a natural dream nothing is too incongruous to be imagined, we cannot suppose that in a vision presented by God for instruction to His servant anything would be introduced which would violate all probability and savour of what to a Jew would appear the grossest profanity. The appearance of Satan at the right hand of Joshua has been regarded as conclusive in favour of the view that Joshua was represented as under trial at the bar of the judge, the position assigned to Satan being that ordinarily occupied by the accuser at a trial (see Ps. cix. 6). But it was not at judicial trials only, or for the purpose of urging an accusation alone, that one might be represented as at the right hand of another; the formula occurs where no such reference is intended. One may be at the right hand of another as a helper, adviser, or protector; or he may be there as an unfriend, to hinder or oppose. The context must in each particular case determine in what sense the phrase is to be taken. In the case before us it is undoubtedly as an enemy that the Adversary stood at the right hand of the high priest; but he was there simply to resist and oppose him; there is no intimation of any *judicial* process in which the parties were engaged; nor does the Angel of the Lord appear as seated on a throne of judgment. It may be doubted, indeed, if such a representation could have been given. The Angel of the Lord appears as the Messenger of Jehovah, as the Friend, Protector, and Guide of His people, and as the Destroyer of their enemies; but He nowhere is represented as acting the part of a Judge. This was not His function, and to represent Him in this capacity would have introduced into the vision a marked incongruity.

All that can be fairly gathered from the passage itself is that in the vision Joshua was seen standing before the Angel of the Lord, and the Adversary at his right hand to act the part of an adversary to him.* From the relation in which the Angel of the Lord stood to Israel, it may be inferred that Joshua appeared before Him to plead for His interposition on behalf of Israel, to deliver them from their enemies, and restore them to their former estate of peace and felicity. Such a plea might well be urged upon the Angel of the Lord, whose special function in relation to Israel was to encompass them as with a shield, and to deliver them. But if this was the special function of the Angel of the Lord, it was no less the function of the Adversary to resist such a plea, and, if he

---

* In the Hebrew the verb and the noun here are cognates: "And the Adversary" (הַשָּׂטָן, *Has-Satan*) "to oppose him" (לְשִׂטְנוֹ, *l' Sitno*).

might, to hinder the people from obtaining the protection and help they sought. Accordingly, in the vision Satan was seen at the right hand of the high priest, not as an accuser before a judge, but as an adversary who sought to divert from the petitioner the kind offices of a friend.

In presenting such a petition Joshua might appear in other dress than that which properly belonged to his office, seeing this was not an official act. But wherefore "in filthy garments"? To this a strange answer has been given. "The splendid attire of the high priest, studded with jewels, had been detained at Babylon, or at least could not be worn without special permission of the king; and until the accusations had been cleared away this became still more impossible." * Here is a series of assertions, every one of which is a pure assumption, without a shadow of evidence, historical or otherwise, to rest on; an outflow from the too lively imagination of Ewald, who evolved from his own inner consciousness the hypothesis of an accusation lying against the high priest at the Persian court which he had to meet, and pending which he had to wear the garments of mourning appropriate to one so accused—an hypothesis to which his English follower has lent the attractions of his pellucid and polished style. Ewald, it is true, appeals to Ezra v. 5 and vi. 13 as authorising his assertions, and to these Dean Stanley adds 1 Esdras iv. 54; but these passages lend him no support whatever. In none of them is there the least hint of any accusation being brought against Joshua personally; they simply intimate generally

* Stanley, "Lectures on the Jewish Church," iii. p. 103.

that a complaint was made against the Jews to King Darius by their enemies; and if any individual among the Jews had specially to answer to the king, it was Sheshbazzar, their political chief and prince, and not Joshua, who should have been called to account. The passage in Esdras merely tells us that Darius "wrote concerning the charges" [χορηγίαν, the stipend of the priests] "and the priests' vestments wherein they minister;" and as it was in response to the address of Zorobabel that this order was given, it is he rather than Joshua that comes into view here; all about the high priest's attire being detained in Babylon or withheld from him till he should clear himself from the charge brought against him is mere embellishment and fiction. Besides, as it is before the Angel of the Lord that Joshua was seen standing, how could this represent his standing at the bar of Darius or any other earthly judge?

The representation is symbolical, and must be so interpreted. Garments may be used to indicate the state or condition of the party wearing them; and in Scripture numerous instances of this usage are to be found. White garments were emblematical of joy, purity, and glory (Eccles. ix. 8; Dan. vii. 9; Mark xvi. 5: Rev. iii. 4); beautiful, admirable, and costly garments, of exaltation and triumph (Ps. xlv. 14; Isa. lii. 1, lxi. 3; Dan. v. 29; Esther viii. 15, 16); and mean, coarse, or defiled garments, of sorrow, depression, or moral impurity and guilt (2 Sam. xix. 24; Deut. xxi. 13; 2 Sam. iii. 31; Ps. lxix. 11; Lam. iv. 14, &c.). Josephus says that among the Jews persons who had to appear at the bar of a judge as accused usually, on such occasions, were habited in black garments. The garments, however, in which Joshua was seen were not black, but filthy; they may have been originally white or splendid, but they were unclean, sordid, or befouled (צוֹאִים, comp. the use of the cognate word צֹאָה, Isa. iv. 4, xxviii. 8). Now, as clean and white garments betokened purity and righteousness, garments dirtied and defiled indicated the opposite—a state of humiliation, impurity, and guilt. The filthy garments, therefore, in which Joshua was attired indicated his being in a state of moral impurity and sinfulness. Unlike the worthy few in the Church at Sardis "who had not defiled their garments," that is, had kept themselves free and blameless, he had come under sin, and appeared before the Angel of the Lord as one encompassed with iniquity. It was not, however, his own personal transgressions alone of which he bore the guilt. As the high priest, he represented the nation at large; and in him the people of Israel appeared before the Lord laden with iniquity. The question has been raised as to what special sin of the people reference is here made; but such a question is irrelevant. It was the sin of the nation, "the iniquity of the land" (ver. 9), the accumulated guilt of the whole people, which had brought on them God's displeasure, and led to their being for a season subjected to captivity and suffering. This the high priest bore as he stood before the Angel of the Lord to implore His favour for Israel; and of this the Adversary took advantage when he endeavoured to frustrate his plea, and prevent his obtaining what he sought.

In vain, however, was the Adversary's attempt.

"Jehovah said unto the Satan, Jehovah rebuke thee, thou Satan; yea, Jehovah that hath chosen Jerusalem rebuke thee: is not this a brand plucked out of the fire?" The speaker here is the Angel of the Lord before whom Joshua stood, and when He says "Jehovah rebuke thee," there is the same distinction made between Him, the manifested Jehovah, and the invisible Jehovah, that we find made in the account given of the destruction of the cities of the plain in Gen. xix. 24, where we read, "And Jehovah" [*i.e.* the Angel of Jehovah who had visited Lot] "rained upon Sodom and upon Gomorrah brimstone and fire from Jehovah out of heaven." There is a distinction between the two, and yet the incommunicable name Jehovah belongs to both, and both are on an equality in respect of attribute, power, and honour. The language of the Lord here is not that of petition or desire; it is that of performance. As "He rebuked the Red Sea and it was dried up" (Ps. cvi. 9), so here He rebuked the adversary, and he was silenced and rebuffed. Against the mercy and benevolence of God, Satan's malice and his pleading were in vain. The Lord had chosen Jerusalem, and though for a season He had apparently cast off His people, He had not forsaken them or forgotten them; they were still the people of Him "whose gifts and calling are without repentance" (Rom. xi. 29). And of Joshua, as representing the people, the Lord said, "Is not this a brand plucked from the fire?" The same expression occurs Amos iv. 11, where it is applied to the people of Israel rescued by God from amidst the terrible judgments which had been sent upon them, and by which they had been consumed as in a furnace. The expression is probably proverbial, and was used to convey the idea of unexpected deliverance from imminent calamity. Satan would have had the brand kept in "the furnace of affliction" (Isa. xlviii. 10) until it was utterly consumed; but the Lord would not have it so; His grace and power had interposed to rescue His people from captivity, and He would complete the deliverance He had begun. The brand had been plucked from the burning, and was not again to be cast into the fire.

It is the opinion of some commentators that it is to the scene here described that St. Jude refers when he says (ver. 9): "Yet Michael the archangel, when contending with the devil (he disputed about the body of Moses), ventured not to bring against him a railing accusation, but said, The Lord rebuke thee." By "the body of Moses," it is alleged, is intended the Jewish Church or State, and by Michael the archangel the Angel of the Lord who here speaks; and it is supposed that there was a contention between him and Satan which of them should possess that body: whether Satan to destroy it, or the angel to keep and preserve it. In support of this may be urged (1) the fact that the archangel Michael is undoubtedly the same being who appears here and elsewhere as the Angel of Jehovah, there being but one Angel of Jehovah and but one archangel mentioned in Scripture, and the archangel Michael being represented as having authority over other angels, and as the great prince that standeth up for the people of Jehovah (Dan. x. 13–xii. 1); and (2) the fact that the terms of reprimand used to Satan are the same in both cases: "The Lord rebuke thee." But whilst these considerations cannot be held as establishing the identity of the two, there are serious difficulties in the way of that conclusion. (1) Though the spiritual Church, including both Jew and Gentile, is called the body of Christ (Eph. iv. 12, &c.), there is no instance of the Jewish Church being called the body of Moses, and no authority for so calling it. Nor are the two cases parallel. The Church is the body of Christ because He is its living head, because all its members live in Him, because they are from their union to Him incorporated into one body. But in no sense could this be said of Moses in relation to the Jewish commonwealth, civil or sacred. He, as God's minister, gave laws and ordinances for the establishment and ordering of that body, but he was in no sense its head; nor was it in virtue of relationship to him that its members became incorporated with it. There is no ground, therefore, for the conclusion that by "the body of Moses" St. Jude meant the Jewish Church or State. Then (2) St. Jude represents Michael as contending with the devil for the body of Moses. But in the vision of Zechariah it is not the Angel of the Lord who is seen contending with Satan; the contention there is between the adversary and Joshua the high priest, whom Satan attempts to hinder in his suit. The Angel of the Lord takes no part in the strife. He sits supreme, and utters His rebuke as arbiter of the contest. Between the case here described, then, and that adduced by St. Jude there is no real parallel. The resemblance fails in the two *essential* points—the disputants, and that about which the dispute was. It may therefore be confidently concluded that it is not to the scene here described that St. Jude alludes.

At the rebuke of the Lord the Adversary seems to have retired abashed and discomfited. Joshua then stood alone before the Lord; in his filthy garments virtually acknowledging the iniquity of Israel, but hoping in the mercy of Him with whom is plenteous redemption, and who will redeem Israel from all his iniquities. His petition prevailed. "And He answered and spake unto those that stood before Him, saying, Take away the filthy garments from him." The speaker here is the Angel of the Lord; and when it is said "He answered," there is tacitly intimated that some petition or request had been preferred by the high priest, if not audibly, yet in his heart, for favour and blessing; in answer to which the Lord gave the command to those that stood before him, *i.e.* the attendant angels who waited to do His pleasure,* to remove from Joshua the filthy garments in which he had appeared. That this symbolised the remission of sins, and the acceptance into favour of Joshua and the people whom he represented, is seen from what follows. Addressing Joshua, the Lord says, "Behold, I have caused thine iniquity to pass from thee—I have taken it away, and delivered thee from it—and I have clothed thee with

---

* Ewald understands the command as given to the priests in attendance on Joshua, and he takes the לפניו "before him" as referring to Joshua. But (1) the ו in לפניו can be referred with propriety only to the subject of the preceding verb ויאמר; and (2) as no mention whatever is made of any priests as attendant on Joshua, it is gratuitous to bring such into the scene. It is true no mention either is made of attendant angels, but such are always considered to be waiting on the Lord, ready to do His will; and, as Hitzig remarks, when "one gives to servants a command, it is to be presumed that it is to his own servants, and not to those of another," that the command is given. That angels, however, were really seen to be in attendance may be inferred from ver. 7.

change of raiment" (festive garments, or rich dress, מַחֲלָצוֹת). The Targum explains this as meaning, "I have clothed thee with thy righteousness;" and such seems to be substantially the meaning.* The word used occurs only here and in Isa. iii. 22, where it is rendered in the A. V. by "changeable garments." This, however, is not a happy rendering; the idea of *change* is imported into the word from its being a formation from the verb חָלַץ, one of the meanings of which is *to put off* (a shoe, for instance—Deut. xxv. 9); but the verb also means *to equip, to gird*, and it is from this, rather than the other, that the meaning of the noun is to be derived. In both the passages where it occurs it is the putting on, not the putting off, of a garment that comes into consideration, and the kind of garment referred to is, from the connection, shown to be one of costliness and beauty. That this is the proper meaning of the word is further proved by the use of the cognate word in the Arabic خِلْعَة *chal'aton*, *pretiosa vestis* ("vestimentum quo a principe aliquis honoris causa donatur," Freytag). The word has no specific reference to priestly attire, as the usage of it in

---

* Hitzig objects to the rendering of the Targum here, that the proper symbol of innocence or guiltlessness is a white garment. But it is not so much the *whiteness* of the garment as its *cleanness*, its freedom from stain or smirch, that symbolises innocence; and it may be presumed that the garments put upon Joshua, whatever their colour, were without spot or stain. It was not merely, however, the removal of moral defilement from the high priest, as representing the people, but also his justification or restoration to acceptance, honour, and privilege that had to be indicated, and of this the rich and festive attire put on him was the fitting symbol. This the Targumist richly expresses by the word זְכִי, which means not moral purity so much as legal righteousness, acquittal, or establishment in the rights and immunities of citizenship; comp. Gen. xv. 6; Deut. vi. 25, &c.

Isa. iii. 22 shows; so the use of it here affords no reason for supposing that it was with his official garments that Joshua was seen in the vision to be clothed. He was clothed in rich and costly raiment to indicate his restoration to righteousness, and with that to favour.

Hitherto the prophet has been a mere beholder; but now, animated and excited by what he has seen, he can no longer, as it were, contain himself, but must needs take part in what he sees going on; just as St. John describes himself as affected by the visions which he saw, and as mingling in the action (Rev. v. 4, x. 9, xi. 1). "Let them," he exclaims, "set a fair mitre on his head." Some of the ancient versions in place of "I said" read "he said," which would make this a command of the Angel of the Lord; and this Ewald would adopt as the proper reading. But there is no sufficient reason for departing from the common reading; and that it is the prophet, and not the Angel of the Lord, who speaks here is rendered almost certain by the change in the mood of the verb from the imperative to the optative, יָשִׂימוּ, "let them put," "would that they put." The word rendered "mitre"—צָנִיף—means primarily something wrapped round the head, and so a turban, which rendering had better be adopted here; for though the high priest's mitre was a sort of turban, yet as it had a name specially appropriate to it, מִצְנֶפֶת, the rendering "mitre" should be reserved for that. The prophet's language is that of request, and what he desired was that the high priest's restoration should be shown to be complete, that the whole symbolical representation should be crowned by the putting of a fair, that is, a clean and comely, turban

D

on his head, so that he might stand forth, representing his people, as wholly accepted of the Lord.

Whilst the change in the attire of Joshua was being made, " the Angel of the Lord stood by," in silence, but with complacency, contemplating what was taking place. He then addressed the high priest, solemnly adjuring him to walk in the ways of the Lord, and assuring him that if he was faithful to his trust and charge, honour and blessing would be his, whilst to the nation a blessing still higher and more enduring should be secured.

"If thou wilt walk in My ways, and if thou wilt keep My charge." The "charge" of God is, as He Himself explained to Abraham (Gen. xxvi. 5), His commandments, His statutes, and His laws; and to keep this is to obey the injunctions and observe the institutions He has appointed. There is no real distinction between this and the walking in God's ways also enjoined on the high priest (comp. 1 Kings ii. 3). "Then thou shalt also judge My house, and shalt also keep My courts." The house of God and the courts of God here are synonymous, and this seems to fix the reference to the temple then in course of erection. It is not of the temple, however, as a building that this is said, "but as the spiritual dwelling-place of all Israel." God dwelt in the sanctuary as in the midst of His people, who are His real temple and house (Num. xii. 7; Jer. xii. 7; Hos. viii. 1, ix. 8; 1 Tim. iii. 15; Heb. iii. 2–6, x. 2; 1 Pet. iv. 7; Eph. ii. 22). The allusion to *judging* shows that it is in this point of view that it (the temple) comes into consideration here. The *keeping of the courts of the Lord* refers to the obligation which rested on the high priest to keep away every kind

of idolatry and ungodliness, first of all from the outward
temple (cf. 2 Chron. xix. 11, xxiii. 18; Jer. xxix. 26),
and then from the Church of God, of which the temple
was the central point.* This, which was binding on the
high priest as a duty, is here represented as a reward,
because it was an honour and a privilege to be intrusted
with such an office, and to be required to perform such
functions. "Activity in connection with the kingdom of
God is the highest honour and greatest favour which God
can confer on any mortal" (*Hengst.*). "And I will give
thee places to walk in among these that stand by." That
by "these that stand by" are intended the angels who as
ministering spirits stand ever before God, waiting His
behests and ready to do His will, all are agreed; but regarding the earlier part of the clause there is not the
same accordance among interpreters. It is not certain
whether the word (מַהְלְכִים) rendered "places to walk in,"
and "walks" in the margin, is to be taken as a noun or
as a verb. Those who take it as a verb suppose it is the
Chaldaised form of the Hiphil participle of the verb הָלַךְ
for מוֹלִיכִים the ordinary form; and they render it either
transitively by "leaders," "guides," or intransitively by
"walkers" (LXX ἀναστρεφομένους, Vulg. *ambulantes*).
Those who take the word as a noun suppose it is the
plural of מַהֲלָךְ or of an unused form מַהֲלָךְ, *a walk*
(Ezek. xlii. 4), *a journey* (Neh. ii. 6; Jonah iii. 3, 4). If
the word be taken as a verb, the causal force can alone
be retained, and the blessing promised to Joshua must be
taken to mean that the Lord would give him from among
the angels those who would cause him to go, *i.e.* would

* Hengstenberg, "Christology," iv. 327.

guide, direct, and help him in the discharge of his high functions. If it be taken as a noun, the meaning will be that God would give him walks or goings among the angels. The former affords the simpler meaning, but on philological grounds the latter must be preferred. No such form of the Hiphil participle as that assumed is anywhere to be found; and the use of the preposition "*between*" or "*amidst*" (בֵּין) is decisive against the interpretation, which makes God promise that helpers or guides *from among* the angels should be given him. The rendering in the margin of the A.V., " I will give thee walks," &c., is to be preferred. But to what does this refer? The Targumist explains it as meaning that in the resurrection Joshua should arise and walk amid the angels, his place should be among them in the enjoyment of heavenly life and in heavenly activity. It may be doubted, however, if any such meaning is intended here. As the other parts of the promise have reference to what is to take place in this world, it is not probable that the latter part should refer to what is to take place in the future state. Taken in connection with what precedes, this part of the promise may be understood to mean that Joshua, as a servant of the Lord, should have his sphere of activity among those who stand before Him as His ministers, that is, should continue as the Lord's high priest, to come before Him in the exercise of his lofty functions; the sin of Israel being forgiven, the institute which God had given to His people "for an ordinance for ever throughout their generations" (Num. x. 8) was, after a temporary suspension, to be restored and to continue in perpetuity; the high priest should have free access to Jehovah, should have an open way into His presence to serve Him along with those holy angels who stand continually before Him (comp. 2 Chron. xxix. 3–11). This seems better than the suggestion that God here promises to Joshua that he as high priest should have the rank of angel and bear that name, a suggestion which finds no real support from such usages as Hag. i. 13; Mal. ii. 7; Rev. ii. 1, &c.

The priesthood was thus to be retained in its integrity, and the succession in the family of Aaron to be preserved. But after all this was but a shadowy and typical priesthood; the reality was yet to come. Hence while assuring to Joshua the blessing and honour here promised, the Lord goes on to announce the advent of a far higher boon to Israel. "Hear now, O Joshua the high priest, thou and thy companions that sit before thee, for (or yea, verily) men of portent are they; for lo I am bringing My servant Branch." The "now" here is the "now" of entreaty, נָא, and adds intensity to the imperative. The companions of Joshua are the priests who attended with him in the service of the sanctuary; the reference to them does not necessarily imply that they were seen in the vision, as then attendant on the high priest; and as no mention is made of them as appearing with the high priest, it is to be presumed that he alone stood before the Angel of the Lord. He and his companions are called "men of portent" (מוֹפֵת, a wonder, something marvellous, the fore-sign or portent of something to be; comp. Isa. viii. 18, xx. 3; Ezek. xii. 6, 11, &c.), because they were signs portending something not yet revealed; they were types, divinely-appointed representations, prefiguring better things to come. "For"—this is why they are types or portents—"lo I am bringing forth My servant Branch." The reason of the type is found "in the appearance of the antitype; for if this is not real the type also falls away" (*Hengst.*). Two designations are here given of the Person referred to: "My servant" and "Branch." Both are designations of the Messiah in the prophetic Scriptures. The former occurs frequently in Isaiah, and reference may be had especially to Isa. lii. 13–liii. 11, which is closely parallel to the passage here, both having reference to the agency of the Messiah in the taking away of sin (ver. 9). The word rendered "Branch" (צֶמַח from צָמַח, *to sprout* or *grow up*) primarily means *sprout*. It is first used of the Messiah in Isa. iv. 2, where He is called צֶמַח יהוה, "the Branch of Jehovah;" in xi. 1 of the same book words of synonymous import—חֹטֶר, *rod* or *shoot*, and נֵצֶר, *sucker*—are applied to Him; and in Jer. xxiii. 5 He is called "the Righteous Branch," צֶמַח צַדִּיק, which in xxxiii. 15 is varied into "Branch of Righteousness," צֶמַח צְדָקָה. Zechariah uses the word as a proper name, both here and in vi. 12, which would seem to indicate that it had by his time come to be an appropriate and well-known designation of the Messiah. Primarily, it indicates the humility of His earthly origin; but, like many such designations, it gradually receded from its primary idea, and became a name of honour and dignity; the Sprout became the Branch.

The Messiah was the antitype of the ancient priesthood, inasmuch as He was to do really what they did only symbolically and typically. The proper priestly acts were sacrifice and intercession, and by these they made reconciliation and removed iniquity from the people as subjects of the theocracy. But these priestly acts and their effect merely shadowed forth and promised the sacrifice and intercession by which alone sin, as a transgression of the Divine law, could be atoned for and removed. Hence the Lord goes on to say to Joshua, "For"—here is the reason why the Lord will bring forth His servant Branch—"behold the stone that I have laid before Joshua; upon one stone shall be seven eyes: behold, I will engrave the graving thereof, saith the Lord of hosts, and I will remove the iniquity of this land in one day." It is not improbable that at this stage of the vision the prophet saw a stone lying at the feet of Joshua; but whether he saw this or not is of no moment; the important question is, What was the stone intended to signify? To this different answers have been given, only two of which need be mentioned here. The one is that the stone is the Messiah, the other is that it is the nation and kingdom of God. In support of the former such passages as Isa. xxviii. 16; Ps. cxviii. 22; Eph. ii. 20, 21, where the Messiah is undoubtedly represented under this designation, may be appealed to; and in support of the latter may be urged the representation in Dan. ii. of the stone cut out without hands which grew to be a great mountain and filled the whole earth, which is usually understood to represent the Church or kingdom of God. Both interpretations are thus seen to be allowable so far as the word is concerned, nor is it easy to determine which is to be preferred. On the whole, however, the latter is that which seems most to commend itself. It is a serious objection to the former that the stone is laid before Joshua, which not only indicates something already existing and done, but also that in some sense it is under the superintendence and management of the high priest; neither of which will apply to the Messiah, who had not then come, and who, when He came, was to rule in His own house. It is difficult also on this supposition to understand what is meant by the words, "I will engrave the graving thereof." This means that God would grave and polish the stone,* so that, no longer a rude block, it should become beautiful and admirable; and this can hardly be understood of the Messiah, who, though in Himself fairer than the children of men, was to be wounded and bruised for man's iniquity and transgression. Of the kingdom of God on earth this may be readily understood; small and mean to outward view in its beginning, it should be so dealt with by God that in due time it should appear worthy of all admiration; He would "make it a praise in the whole earth." Of it also might it be fitly said that it was already laid, for it then existed, and that it was laid before the high priest, for on this functionary devolved the management and care of it until He should come who is its proper Head and Lord. "Upon one stone shall be seven eyes." This may mean either that on the stone seven figures of eyes should be engraved, or that seven real eyes should look on it, and, in looking, as it were, rest on it. In the former case the stone, like the wheels in Ezekiel's vision which were "full of eyes round about," is represented as instinct with in-

---

* For this sense of the verb פתח see 1 Kings vii. 36; 2 Chron. ii. 7, iii. 7.

telligence and full of knowledge; in the latter case it is represented as the object of God's watchful care and providential solicitude. Both of these will apply to either of the interpretations of the stone above noted, for in Scripture both the Messiah and the Church are represented as endowed with intelligence, and as watched over and cared for by God. From the reference, however, in the next chapter to "the seven eyes of the Lord which run to and fro through the whole earth," it would seem that the latter interpretation and application are to be preferred. On His Church God's watchful and all-seeing eye would rest; it should be ever under His providential care.

When God adorns His Church, it is with "the beauty of holiness" that she is decorated. Therefore says He, "I will remove the iniquity of the land in one day." For "iniquity" some would read "punishment" here; but though the Hebrew word עָוֹן is sometimes found in this sense, it properly means *sin, crime, guilt,* and has the secondary meaning of punishment very rarely. "To take away iniquity" is the proper counterpart of "to bear iniquity;" and as the latter means to be held guilty, the former means to absolve from guilt, to pardon. God will pardon, cleanse, and restore Israel (comp. Jer. xxxiii. 7, 8). "In one day." This is emphatic. "Year by year came *the day of atonement;* its yearly repetition showed that nothing lasting was effected. *On one day* that removal should be which needed no renewal" [*Pusey*]. Comp. Heb. viii. 27, x. 10–14.

With pardon and cleansing God will send peace and felicity. "In that day, saith the Lord of hosts, shall ye call every man his neighbour, under the vine and under the fig-tree." To sit under the vine and under the fig-tree was a proverbial expression for a state of tranquillity and happiness (comp. Micah iv. 4). So here the people are represented as inviting each man his neighbour to come and sit in peace and quiet, free from tumult, discord, danger, or fear—a picture of peace and social enjoyment. So doth God cause peace to be upon Israel; a blessing to be fully realised under the reign of Him who is our Peace.

Pardon, acceptance, purity, blessedness: this is the order of the kingdom of God both for the Church at large and for each individual member of it.

V.

THE CANDELABRUM AND OLIVE TREES.

"And the angel that talked with me came again, and waked me, as a man that is wakened out of his sleep, and said unto me, What seest thou? And I said, I have looked, and behold a candlestick all of gold, with a bowl upon the top of it, and his seven lamps thereon, and seven pipes to the seven lamps, which are upon the top thereof: And two olive trees by it, one upon the right side of the bowl, and the other upon the left side thereof. So I answered and spake to the angel that talked with me, saying, What are these, my lord? Then the angel that talked with me answered and said unto me, Knowest thou not what these be? And I said, No, my lord. Then he answered and spake unto me, saying, This is the word of the Lord unto Zerubbabel, saying, Not by might, nor by power, but by my Spirit, saith the Lord of hosts. Who art thou, O great mountain? before Zerubbabel thou shalt become a plain: and he shall bring forth the head-stone thereof with shoutings, crying, Grace, grace unto it. Moreover the word of the Lord came unto me, saying, The hands of Zerubbabel have laid the foundation of this house; his hands shall also finish it; and thou shalt know that the Lord of hosts hath sent me unto you. For who hath despised the day of small things? for they shall rejoice, and shall see the plummet in the hand of Zerubbabel with those seven; they are the eyes of the Lord, which run to and fro through the whole earth. Then answered I, and said unto him, What are these two olive trees upon the right side of the candlestick and upon the left side thereof? And I answered again, and said unto him, What be these two olive branches which through the two golden pipes empty the golden oil out of themselves? And he answered me and said, Knowest thou not what these be? And I said, No, my lord. Then said he, These are the two anointed ones, that stand by the Lord of the whole earth."—ZECH. iv. 1-14.

IT would appear that after the preceding vision the prophet had sunk into a sort of lethargic state, whether overwhelmed by the vision he had just witnessed, or depressed by a sense of the greatness of the difficulties which lay in the way of a realisation of the issue to which that vision seemed to point. Apparently, also, Zerubbabel had yielded to despondency at this juncture, and in consequence of the great opposition which he had to encounter had begun to fear lest he should be compelled to relinquish altogether the work on which he had entered. Under these circumstances the vision described in this chapter was given; the design of which is to rouse the prophet and his friends from torpor and despondency, and send them to their work with the energy and earnestness which the certainty of success is fitted to communicate.

The prophet tells us that the angel that spake with him, the angel interpreter, came again and waked him as a man that is wakened out of his sleep. It is supposed by some that the prophet needed to be thus roused because he was so intent on observing the vision that had just been presented to him, and so utterly absorbed by it, that he was not prepared to attend to anything else. But the expression that the angel came *again* to him, would indicate that for a season the angel had left him; and his being wakened as one is wakened out of sleep, would seem to show that he had passed out of the state of ecstatic quickening, in which he had seen the visions, into a state of mental depression and torpor.* We are

---

* It is true that שׁוּב, "according to a common Hebrew idiom, when used before another verb, merely indicates the repetition of the action expressed by such verb" (Henderson, "Min. Proph.," p. 384). At the same time there is always implied an interval, more or less extended, between the earlier act and the repetition of it (cf. Gen. xxvi. 18, xxx. 31, &c.).

to suppose, therefore, that a short interval elapsed after the preceding vision had passed away, during which the prophet was in a state of mental somnolency, the natural result, probably, of a reaction from the state of abnormal excitement into which he had been brought. That he was not really asleep is evident from the form of the expression in which he describes his wakening; it was *as* a man is wakened out of sleep that he was wakened by the angel—like, but not the same. He was roused from the torpor into which he had sunk, into a state in which he could behold anew " the visions of the Lord."

In answer to the question of the angel—" What seest thou?" the prophet describes what met his view. There was presented to him a large candelabrum of gold, on the top of which was a bowl or basin, whence proceeded seven pipes through which oil flowed from the reservoir at the top to supply the seven lamps of the candelabrum. He saw also by the side of the candelabrum, and rising above the basin at the top, two olive trees, one on the right side of the basin and the other on the left, and from these depended two fruit-bearing branches from which oil passed through two channels or conductors into the bowl (ver. 12).*

In the latter part of ver. 2 the A.V. follows the LXX rather than the Hebrew. According to the latter the passage reads thus : " And its seven lamps upon it, seven and seven pipes to the lamps which are on its top." The number of pipes is thus made to be fourteen in all, two for each lamp. The LXX reads: " And seven lamps

* See this excellently explained and illustrated in Mr. Wright's recently published " Bampton Lecture," p. 81, ff.

upon it, and seven conduits * for the lamps that are upon it." This is probably the correct reading; two pipes for each lamp would seem to be superfluous; and the first seven in the Hebrew may be an interpolation through a *lapsus calami* on the part of some transcriber.

The candelabrum seen by the prophet was, in its main features, the same as that which Moses was directed to make and place in the tabernacle; the only difference being that the reservoir from which the lamps were supplied was in the tabernacle arrangement placed apart from the candelabrum, whilst in what was seen by the prophet it formed part of the candelabrum itself, and was fed with oil by means of the branches of the two olive trees, without the intervention of any human agency, whereas the candelabrum in the tabernacle had to be daily tended and supplied with oil by the priests. Being thus in its main features identical with that with which the prophet was familiar, he did not need to ask an explanation of its meaning. It was otherwise, however, with the two olive trees; this was something novel, and he inquired of the angel, "What are these, my lord?" Instead of directly answering this, the angel proceeded to give him the message which the vision as a whole was designed to shadow forth, and which the prophet was to convey to Zerubbabel; nor was it until the prophet had repeated his question again and again, uttering it three times in all, that the angel told him their significance.

---

* The word here, ἐπαρυστρίδες, properly means *pitchers* or *buckets*, vessels in which water is drawn up; but it may also designate vessels by which a fluid is conveyed, or from which it is poured out: Schleus. *infusoria, infundibula.*

"These," he at length said, "are the two sons of oil that stand by the Lord of the whole earth" (ver. 14).

Before examining the symbolic part of this vision it will be of advantage to consider the purport of the message which the prophet was instructed to convey to Zerubbabel. In this lies the key of the whole representation; and hence when we have seen what it imports we shall be the better fitted to inquire into the meaning of the symbols by which it was presented to the view of the prophet.

"This is the word of Jehovah unto Zerubbabel, saying, Not by might, nor by power, but by my Spirit, saith Jehovah of hosts" (ver. 6). This is a general assertion of the utter inadequacy of mere human power and strength to accomplish any great work such as that in which Zerubbabel and his coadjutors were engaged, and the necessity for Divine agency ere it can be accomplished. The Spirit of God is the great Divine operator both in the physical and in the moral world (cf. Gen. i. 2; Job xxvi. 13, xxxiii. 4; Ps. li. 12; Exod. xxxi. 3; 1 Sam. x. 10; Neh. ix. 30; Ezek. i. 12, iii. 14, xi. 24; Matt. iii. 16, iv. 1; Rom. viii. 11, xv. 19; 1 Cor. ii. 10, vi. 11; Eph. iii. 16; Rev. i. 10, iv. 2, &c.); and whether it be such work as Zerubbabel had then in hand in the building of the temple at Jerusalem, or the higher work of erecting the great spiritual temple of which that at Jerusalem was but the type, it is only as the Spirit of the Lord influences and energises in the work that it can be successfully accomplished. Human agency must be employed in the work; human might and power must be put forth on it, alike the might of thought and the might of effort, the power of skill and the power of material resources; but these will be exerted in vain unless that might and power that come from above, the might and power of the eternal and omnipotent Spirit, be put forth to direct, sustain, effect, and crown the whole.

The work to which Zerubbabel was called was great and arduous; and there was much to discourage him not only in the difficulties of the work itself, but also in the temper and disposition of those by whose exertions it was to be carried on, and in the watchful and uncompromising hostility of the adversaries by whom he was surrounded. Under the pressure of these influences his spirit seems to have succumbed. It appeared to him as if a huge mountain had risen up before him which he could neither remove nor surmount. But God, by the prophet, bade him not be discouraged, assuring him that the difficulties, however great, should be made to disappear. "Who art thou, O great mountain before Zerubbabel? To a plain down!" (or, Be for a plain!) was the cheering utterance which the prophet was commissioned to bear to his chief. A mountain is a figure common among all peoples for an accumulation of difficulties; and the removal of it, so that the place it occupied shall become a plain, obviously indicates the overcoming or the smoothing away of the obstacles created by such difficulties. Thus our Lord said to His disciples, "Verily I say unto you, If ye have faith as a grain of mustard seed, ye shall say to this mountain, Remove hence to yonder place; and it shall remove; and nothing shall be impossible unto you" (Matt. xvii. 20). Among the Jews an eloquent teacher is called עֲקַר הָרִים—one who tears up mountains. This now Christ takes as a figure and example of any miraculously powerful effort of faith, when He immediately goes on to say in general: "Mountains shall remove out of their place if ye bid them, all things will be obedient to what you say, nothing will be impossible to you,—to you even as to God" (chap. xix. 26 ; Luke i. 37).* So also of our Lord's advent it was said: "Every valley shall be exalted, and every mountain and hill shall be made low," and thereby a way be prepared for Him (Isa. xl. 3, 4; cf. Matt. iii. 3 ; Mark i. 3 ; Luke iii. 4). Many and great were the obstacles which lay in the way of the Messiah when He came to get for Himself a kingdom on earth ; but these were all to be overcome, a plain path should be made along which He might travel, He should gain His end, and all nations should behold His glory and submit to His sway. In like manner the mountain of difficulty that was before Zerubbabel should, at the Divine command, sink down into a plain; and an open path should be made for him by which to go on to the accomplishment of his work. Let him, then, have faith in God and not be discouraged.

The words, "to a plain," are to be taken as a command (cf. for a similar construction 2 Kings iii. 23).

"And [yea] he hath brought forth (וְהוֹצִיא) the chief stone with shoutings, Grace, grace be to it!" (ver. 8). The "he" here is by some understood of Jehovah, but the following verse shows it is Zerubbabel who is intended; all obstacles being surmounted, he should complete the work he had begun ; as conductor of the building he had already brought forth from his stores the stone on which

* Stier, "Words of Jesus," ii. p. 379, English translation.

E

the whole edifice should be made securely to rest. By
"head-stone," lit. *the stone the head* (הָאֶבֶן הָרֹאשָׁה), many
understand the top-stone, the stone which completes and
crowns the building. But it is impossible to determine
what is the top-stone of a building like the temple, for in
the uppermost course of masonry in such an edifice, no
stone is higher than another; the only edifice that can
have a top-stone is a pyramid. It is better, therefore, to
understand the phrase here as designating the chief stone,
that is, the corner-stone at the foundation by which the
walls of the building are bound together, and on which it
virtually rests; what the Greeks called λίθος ἀκρογωνιαῖος,
the stone "which holds together the walls and foundations" (Chrysostom on Eph. ii. 20). The Hebrews and
the ancients generally attached much importance to the
corner-stone (Job xxxviii. 6; Ps. cxviii. 22; Isa. xxviii.
16; Zech. x. 4); the name was applied to chiefs and
leaders as those on whom the rest depended (cf. Judges
xx. 2; Isa. xxix. 13); and in the New Testament this
is applied to Jesus Christ, inasmuch as He is the foundation on which the whole Church rests, and because
"through the one faith He binds together in a spiritual
oneness both peoples" (*i.e.*, Jews and Gentiles; Cyrill.
Alex. on Isa. xxviii. 16); cf. Eph. ii. 20; 1 Pet. ii. 6, 7.
It is true the Hebrews had a special term by which to
denote the corner-stone (פִּנָּה), but seeing they attached
so much importance to it, they might very well also
describe it as the stone the chief. This chief stone Zerubbabel, notwithstanding all difficulties and opposition, had
been privileged to lay; and when it was laid the attendant multitude hailed the event with shoutings of " Grace,

grace be to it!" The reduplication here is for effect; equivalent to abundant grace; comp. Isa. xxvi. 3, "perfect peace," lit. peace, peace; lvii. 19. The purport of the exclamation may be either a petition that God's favour may rest on the building, the chief stone of which had been brought forth; or an assertion that grace or favour belongs to it; that the temple, that is, is the place where the Divine grace is specially and abundantly manifested. It is difficult to say which of these interpretations is to be preferred, for both are in accordance with the tenor of exclamations of this sort in Scripture. "Hosannah to the Son of David!" is a prayer for salvation and blessing (Matt. xxi. 9; cf. Ps. cxviii. 25); "Salvation to our God, which sitteth upon the throne, and unto the Lamb" (Rev. vii. 10), is an ascription of honour to those to whom it specially belongs. It is probable, however, in the circumstances, that the exclamation of the multitude on the laying of the chief stone of the temple, is to be regarded as an expression of desire and hope, rather than as an ascription of quality. It is the utterance of their earnest wish that He, by whose favour the chief stone had been laid, would so abundantly manifest his favour that the whole building should ere long be completed, and stand for ever as a monument of His favour to His people (cf. Ezra iii. 11).

In what follows the angel repeats explicitly what he had, in a more figurative manner, already enunciated. "The hands of Zerubbabel have laid the foundation of this house; his hands shall also finish it; and thou shalt know that the Lord of Hosts hath sent me unto you" (ver. 9). The speaker in this verse is most probably the angel of the Lord, who in the name of Jehovah promises that as Zerubbabel had been privileged to lay the foundation of the temple, so should he, in spite of all opposition and of every difficulty, assuredly complete the work he had thus begun. And by this should assurance be given that He was indeed the angel of the Lord, sent forth by Him, and commissioned to speak in His name. By some the speaker, in the latter half of the verse, is assumed to be the prophet himself, while the speaker in the former part is the Lord; but so sudden a change of persons is hardly to be supposed. In any case the utterance is to be regarded as a message from Jehovah to be conveyed to Zerubbabel and the people for their encouragement in the work of rebuilding the temple.

Something had been already done in respect of that work, but it was little as compared with what yet remained to be done ere the whole should be accomplished. It was not, however, on that account to be lightly thought of. The people are cautioned against this: "Who hath despised the day of small things?"—who will regard with contempt this small beginning as if it were not the prelude and pledge, under God's blessing, of a completed work? If any have so regarded it let them no longer do so; for they shall yet see the work finished, the temple rebuilt, and the worship of God in it restored. And whence came this certainty? It came from this, that Jehovah had determined that the work should be done, and would watch over, direct, and further it till it was completed. "For these seven rejoice and see (= rejoicingly see) the plummet in the hand of Zerubbabel; the eyes of Jehovah are these which range over the whole earth" (ver. 10). This rendering is according to the Masoretic accentuation, which directs the words, "these seven," (שִׁבְעָה־אֵלֶּה) to be taken as the subject of the verbs "see" and "rejoice." The A. V. follows the Vulgate and the Targums in making the despisers of the day of small things the subject; but if we read, with the Vulgate, "et laetabuntur et videbunt lapidem stanneum in manu Zorobabel. Septem ipsi oculi sunt Domini qui discurrunt in universam terram," we disjoin the last clause wholly from what precedes, and make it idle and irrelevant; and if to avoid this we join the words "these seven" to the preceding clause, as in the A. V., we have to do this by adding to the text the preposition "with," for which there is no authority. The meaning of the passage is, that in contrast with those who might be despising the day of small things the eyes of the Lord were beholding with joy the beginning of the work in the hand of Zerubbabel. By "the eyes of the Lord" is intended His omniscient providence, by which, knowing all things, He orders all events so as to accomplish what He designs; a representation more fully brought out by the addition in the close of the verse (comp. Deut. xi. 12; 2 Chron. xvi. 9; Prov. xv. 3; Jer. xvi. 17, xxxii. 19). From God's sight nothing can be hid, so that whatever was needful for the success of the work should be provided, and whatever might hinder it would be detected and prevented. As "the eyes of the Lord are upon the righteous" (Ps. xxxiv. 15), so He beheld with complacency the plummet in the hand of Zerubbabel, betokening the commencement of the work. The rendering "plummet" has been called in question by some, but it seems the only proper rendering of the original. The Hebrew is הָאֶבֶן הַבְּדִיל lit. *the stone, the tin,* i.e., *the stone* (the weight) *made of tin* (comp. Exod. xxxix. 17, *the two wreaths, the gold* = two wreaths of gold; 2 Kings xvi. 14-17, *the altar, the brass* = the altar of brass; *the oxen, the brass* = the oxen of brass); and this can only mean the plummet which was in the hand of Zerubbabel, as director of the building.

Having received this explanation of the general import of the symbolical vision presented to him, the prophet repeats his request for a more special explanation of certain parts of it. The significance of the candelabrum he, as a priest familiar with the furniture of the Mosaic tabernacle, did not need to be informed of; and he would also at once perceive the significance of the oil with which it was fed and by which its light was sustained; but the meaning of the two olive trees beside it, and of the branches that yielded the oil, he did not see. He therefore " answered, *i.e.*, resumed or continued the discourse," and said unto Him (the angel of the Lord), " What are these two olive trees upon the right side of the candelabrum, and upon the left side thereof?" To this inquiry no answer was given by the angel, probably, as has been suggested, " to invite closer attention and a more definite question " (Pusey). The prophet, therefore, asks again, indicating precisely the part of the vision he wished explained, " What are these two ears (dependent things or clusters like ears of corn, שִׁבֲּלֵי) of the olive trees, which by means of two golden channels (or tubes) pour out (or convey) from themselves the gold (*i.e.*, the golden oil, so called from its colour). The only word here regarding which there is any dispute is that rendered "channels" or "tubes" (צַנְתְּרוֹת). This word occurs only in this passage; but there can be little doubt that it is the same word which in the Chaldaic form צַנְתְּרִין appears in the Targum to II. Esther i. 2, and is allied to צִינוֹרָא, which in the sense of "channels" occurs in the Targum on Eccl. i. 7, and to the Heb. צִנּוֹר, "an aqueduct" (2 Sam. v. 8); all being referable to the root צָנַר, *to hold*. The LXX have here μυξωτῆρες, *noses*, and the Vulgate has *rostra, beaks*. Hengstenberg says the word must be rendered "presses;" but for this there is no good reason or authority. The objects indicated were evidently conduits of some sort, by which the oil was conveyed into the pipes which fed the lamps on the candelabrum. Dr. Pusey affirms that these conduits "were symbols of living agents;" but his only reason for this is that "Zechariah's expression, *in the hand of*, or if so be, *by the hand of*, is nowhere used except of a living agent, or of that which is personified as such." That such was the primary and proper usage of the phrase is unquestionable; but as the hand is the instrument or medium through which something is effected, the phrase, *in the hand of*, came to mean generally, *by means of*, and so it is used frequently, chiefly indeed of persons, but sometimes also of things, as *e.g.*, Isa. lxiv. 7 [6]: "For thou consumest us (causest us to pine away) by the hand of our iniquities," *i.e.*, by means of them; where there is no personification. Nor is there any personification in the passage before us.

Into these conduits the oil came from two branches of the olive trees laden with fruit. These are called *Shibbolîm, ears of corn*, probably, as Kimchi suggests, "because they were full of olive-berries as the ears are full of grains of wheat" ("Comment. on Zechariah," translated by McCaul, p. 45); or it may be simply to indicate their fruitfulness. They formed the reservoir whence oil was supplied to the lamps on the candelabrum, and this source was seen to be copious.

To the prophet's inquiry the angel replied, "These are the two sons of oil, that stand by the Lord of the whole earth" (ver. 14). The phrase, "sons of oil," may mean either "objects anointed with oil," or "objects possessing oil," which they may minister to others. The idiom is used in both ways; comp. בֶּן הַכּוֹת son of smiting, deserving to be smitten, Deut. xxv. 2 ; בֶּן חַיִל son of might, possessing might, a mighty man. It is in the latter of these ways that the phrase is to be taken here: (1) this is the ordinary usage when a *quality* or *property* is predicated; comp. *Ben Belial*, "son of wickedness," *Ben 'avlah*, "son of iniquity," *Ben Shamen*, "son of oil" (Isa. v. 1, A. V. ",very fruitful"); (2) the word used here for "oil," יִצְהָר, designates the natural produce of the olive, and is not the word generally used where anointing is predicated; (3) in this vision it is as the instrument of *light*, and not of *anointing*, that the oil appears. "Sons of oil," therefore, we explain here as meaning "possessors of oil," oil-bearers, channels through which the oil plentifully flowed. The phrase, "that stand by," meaning that stand as ministers or attendants (lit. "that stand over," or "above," the person waited on being supposed seated, and the attendants standing near him so as to rise above him; comp. Exod. xviii. 13; Job ii. 1; Isa. vi. 1, 2), indicates that the objects here referred to are symbols of agents. Who the agents intended are hardly admits of question, though more than one conjectural answer has been suggested. Thus, some say they are Moses and Christ; others, they are the Old and New Testaments; others, they are Haggai and Zechariah. But, as Hengstenberg says, "We cannot be left to that species of conjecture in which some indulge;" if we would interpret safely we must look to the context and interpret according to it. Now the whole purport of this vision is to assure the accomplishment by the Divine power, through the agency of God's appointed servant Zerubbabel, of the great work in which the people were engaged. But Zerubbabel was not alone; Joshua the high priest was associated with him, was equally with him an instrument in God's hand for the accomplishment of the work, and in the preceding vision had been represented as standing before the Lord as His accepted servant. From an early period, accordingly, these two have been regarded as symbolically represented in this vision by the two conduits, the possessors of oil, through which the oil flowed to the pipes of the candelabrum; and this interpretation, which is that of Kimchi, has been generally accepted by commentators. Zerubbabel and Joshua, however, were not mere individual agents; they were representative men, the one of the royal and the other of the priestly office in Israel. It is the office, then, rather than the individual, that is here represented. "It is with justice," says Hengstenberg, "that it has been assumed that the two sons of oil denote the two offices of priest and king (or rather the sacerdotal and civil authorities in general), which were principally employed in the economy of the Old Testament as instruments of the grace of God, and of which Joshua and

Zerubbabel were the existing representatives" ("Christology," vol. iii. p. 340).

We may now look at the whole symbolic representation, and ask the meaning of it and its separate parts. That by the candelabrum was symbolised the Israelitish community, the nation of the old covenant, the people of the theocracy, may be regarded as generally conceded. But Israel was itself a symbol and type; it was the visible manifestation of that invisible spiritual community, the Church of the living God, which embraces the faithful of all ages and places. It is represented as made of the most precious of metals, pure gold, to indicate the worth and excellence of that which God hath chosen for Himself as His special treasure; and it is represented as having seven lamps, to indicate that the Church is a luminous body, having light in itself, and appearing as the luminary from which proceeds light to the world. So our Lord said to His disciples as representing His Church, "Ye are the light of the world;" and comparing them to a candelabrum or lamp-stand ($\lambda v \chi v i a$), on which the lighted lamp is placed that it may give light to all who are in the house, He exhorted them to let their light so shine before men (Matt. v. 14, 16); so also in the Apocalypse our Lord is represented as "walking in the midst of the seven golden candlesticks" ($\lambda v \chi v\iota \hat{\omega} v$ $\tau \hat{\omega} v$ $\chi \rho v \sigma \hat{\omega} v$), the New Testament Churches over which He presides and for which He cares (Rev. i. 13; ii. 1).

But the light which the Church possesses is not from herself; it is light communicated and sustained by influences from above. Hence in the vision which Zechariah saw, the lamps were supplied with oil, not by human ministration, but through channels and pipes from the olive trees which stood beside and were over the candelabrum. Oil is the proper symbol of the Holy Spirit's influences. Hence under the ancient economy men were consecrated to office by the anointing of oil, to indicate not merely that they were Divinely appointed thereto, but that Divine influences would rest on them and fit them for the office to which they were appointed; and so the Messiah, the Priest and King of His Church, appears in prophecy as saying, "The Spirit of the Lord is upon me, because the Lord hath anointed me to preach good tidings unto the meek," &c. (Isa. lxi. 1); where the anointing is identified with the resting on Him of the Spirit. This, then, is the oil by which the Church is sustained, is made to shine, and is enabled to accomplish the work she has to do in the world. Apart from the Divine Spirit the Church is dark and cold and feeble; but through the visitation of the Spirit she is animated and invigorated, becomes luminous and glorious, and is crowned with success as she labours to erect God's temple on earth. The work which Israel had in hand in the time of Zechariah was hard, and it had to be done amid reproach and in spite of bitter opposition on the part of their enemies; but they were taught by this vision not to be discouraged, for it was not by human might or power that the work was to be done, but by the Spirit of the Lord. Through His grace the light should be sustained in them; their hands should be strengthened for their work; and ere long they should see the consummation of that which had been so auspiciously begun.

God sustains His Church by His grace. But this grace

comes to men through certain appointed media. This was symbolised in the vision by the fruit-bearing branches of the olive trees and by the conduits and the pipes through which the oil was conveyed to the lamps. The branches, as we have seen, represented the sacerdotal and civil authorities in Israel. These were in the old time the channels through which God conveyed His grace to His Church on earth; and as they operated through means of subordinate functionaries, the branches were represented in the vision as emptying themselves into the conduits and pipes by means of which the oil was conveyed to the lamps.

The Israel of God, for whose encouragement and comfort this vision was designed, no longer exists as a visible community. But the Church of God of which it was the envelope and the type still exists, and to her the same lesson is conveyed by this vision as was conveyed by it to the ancient Israel. Not indeed in the same outward form does the Church exist now as it existed then. The visible Church is no longer one great outward organisation, but rather a number of separate organisations, all holding the Head and all united by spiritual bonds, but no longer appearing to the eye of man as one body or state. Accordingly, when the symbol was again exhibited, it was not one candelabrum with seven lamps, but seven candelabra each with its light or lights that appeared (Rev. i. 12). Nor were symbols of sacerdotal and royal authority as channels of Divine grace then displayed. The Great Head of the Church Himself, in proper person, then was seen in the midst of the seven golden candelabra. Through Him, as the great Priest and King, uniting in Himself the two offices and discharging the functions of both to His Church, "the oil of Divine grace is poured into the candlestick of the Church in infinitely greater abundance than through any of the previous servants of God" (Hengstenberg). He is ever present with all the Churches of the saints; He walks amidst them; He sees their condition, knows their wants, and stands ready to supply their needs. "Out of His fulness they all receive, and grace for grace." Let the Church then strengthen herself in the Lord, and go forth determinately and courageously to do the work which the Lord hath given her to do.

VI.

THE DRIVEN PARCHMENT.

"Then I turned, and lifted up mine eyes, and looked, and behold a flying roll. And he said unto me, What seest thou? And I answered, I see a flying roll; the length thereof is twenty cubits, and the breadth thereof ten cubits. Then said he unto me, This is the curse that goeth forth over the face of the whole earth: for every one that stealeth shall be cut off as on this side according to it; and every one that sweareth shall be cut off as on that side according to it. I will bring it forth, saith the Lord of hosts, and it shall enter into the house of the thief, and into the house of him that sweareth falsely by my name: and it shall remain in the midst of his house, and shall consume it with the timber thereof and the stones thereof."
—Zech. v. 1-4.

THE two visions contained in this chapter are closely connected with each other, the latter being the fitting sequel of the former. Both are of a character different from those that preceded them. The design of these was to encourage the people by the assurance of God's continued regard for them, and of the favour He would show them. But here the utterance is, in the first instance, at least, one of warning and threatening, designed to deter the people from sin, by showing God's abhorrence of it, and the certainty of its being punished. God would remind His people that it was not enough that they should be restored to their own land, that the temple should be rebuilt, and its worship re-established; there must also be the careful observance of the moral precepts of His law, the neglect of which would bring down His judgments on the nation.

After a brief interval indicated by the phrase, "I returned" (וָאָשׁוּב see on iv. 1, *ante*, p. 60), the prophet lifted up his eyes and saw a roll of vast dimensions flying through the air. In answer to the angel who asked him what he saw, he describes the roll as 20 cubits in length, and 10 cubits in breadth. Taking the cubit as = 18 inches, this would give a superficial area of 450 square feet. Of what material this roll was composed the prophet does not say; but as the Jews used for literary documents not only parchment, papyrus, and other more fragile substances, but also leather prepared for the purpose, it is probable that the roll which the prophet saw was of this material, as none of the others could be supposed capable of bearing the strain to which a roll of such dimensions as those here given would, when distended and flying before the wind, be exposed.* The great size of the roll has been supposed to indicate the number and gravity of the curses which it contained. But something more than this seems to be intended. It is to be observed that the dimensions assigned to the roll are exactly those of the porch of the temple (1 Kings vi. 3); and as there

---

* Aquila and Theodotion both give διφθέρα, prepared skin or leather, as the rendering of מגלה here. The LXX seem to have had another reading, as they render by δρέπανον, *hook* or *sickle*; probably reading מגל for מגלה. It has been suggested that the object seen by the prophet was rather in the form of one of our books, and was composed of papyrus leaves bound together, on which the curses were written. But whilst, on the one hand, there is no evidence that books such as ours were known to the Jews in the time of Zechariah, it is, on the other, certain that the term מגלה can only mean a roll.

must be a reason for a specific measurement being given, when the prophet might have contented himself with merely saying that the roll was of vast size, it is probable that the dimensions specified were designed to correspond with those of the temple porch. If so, the reason may be sought in this, that as the temple was the place where God held intercourse with His people, and whence He sent forth His blessing or His curse, the people are reminded that in rebuilding the temple they were not necessarily securing to themselves blessing, but might find a curse coming forth from it if they were rebellious, disobedient, or ungodly. It has been suggested that as the dimensions of the roll are also those of the sanctuary in the tabernacle, what is signified is, that " the measure by which this curse upon sinners will be meted out, will be the measure of the holy place" (*Kliefoth*). If by this is meant that the curse was to be measured, not by any human standard, but by that of God, the suggestion is futile; for, though men may estimate *sin*, or measure *their own actions*, by another standard than that of God, the curse of God uttered against sin can be estimated only by one standard, that of God Himself; it is as He means it to be, and can suffer no detraction, let men think of it as they may. If, on the other hand, it means, as Keil has it, "that with this measure would all sinners be measured, that they might be cut off from the congregation of the Lord which appeared before God in the holy place," one does not see how a roll containing a curse could be in any sense a measure by which sinners should be measured so as to be cut off from the congregation. The essential thing is that the curse should be seen coming forth from the temple; that it should be seen to be a Divine curse; and this is indicated by the special size and form of the roll, whether the measurement be that of the porch of the temple or that of the sanctuary.

The prophet saw this roll open, by which was indicated that the vision was not one that was to be sealed up or kept undivulged (comp. Rev. x. 4), but was to be made plain so as to be open to the knowledge of all (comp. Hab. ii. 2); and he saw it "flying," to indicate that it was *general* in its application; that it did not relate to one spot or locality alone, but had reference to all alike (see ver. 2). The flying may also indicate "the velocity with which the judgments denounced in the volume would come upon the wicked" (*Henderson*).

When the prophet had in answer to the angel described what he saw, the angel proceeded to give the explanation. "This is the curse," *i.e.*, the utterance of the Divine denunciation of sin and the announcement of the penalty that shall come on those by whom sin is committed, "which goeth forth over the face of the whole land." The roll is said to *be* the curse because the curse was inscribed upon it; a metonymy of frequent occurrence in Scripture, where the thing containing is put for that which it contains.* It may be also said that the utterance of the curse is the curse, for it comes from Him who "saith and it is done, who commandeth and it standeth fast." By the "land" here is intended the land of Israel,

---

* See Glassii Philol. Sac., p. 686. Henderson compares our Lord's words, "This is my body," Matt. xxvi. 26, &c. But the metonymy there is not the same as here; there it is *signatum pro signo*, here it is *continens pro contento*.

over the whole of which the curse was to be imminent; not that it actually came on the people of that land in any special calamity, as some suppose,—Hengstenberg, for instance, who would understand it of "a new and terrible judgment from God which was to fall upon Judæa, when the ungodliness that already existed in the germ, even in the time of the prophet, should have taken root, and put forth branches,"—but simply that it was suspended over the land, ready to take effect on any or all who should incur it by their transgressions.

Two descriptions of crime are here denounced, stealing and swearing; that is, as is indicated by what follows in ver. 4, false swearing or perjury. As these sins are taken, the one from the first, the other from the second table of the law, and as the command forbidding each is the central command of the table to which it belongs, it has been suggested that these are selected as examples of the breach of *any* of the laws which God had given to Israel in the Decalogue; so that in fact it is the whole of that code which the people are here warned against transgressing. This is not improbable. At the same time it is to be noted that the two crimes specified are precisely those to which the Jews who had returned from the Captivity were most liable to be enticed. In Babylon they had, from the necessity of the case, become a race of traffickers, and when they returned to their own land they brought with them the habits and tendencies which such pursuits are apt to engender. Against nothing, therefore, did they more need to be warned than against covetousness, dishonesty, and falsehood. One can easily believe that these sins might cleave to the people whilst other breaches of the Decalogue were no longer common among them. Since the Captivity the Jew has been noted for his abhorrence of idolatry, for his observance of the Sabbath, and for his regard for human life; but he has nowhere acquired a reputation for honesty and veracity, however much individuals of the race have displayed these virtues.

Against these sins God's curse goes forth. They that commit them are to be cut off, and the land is to be cleansed from them: "Every one that stealeth shall be cleansed off hence according to it; and every one that sweareth shall be cleansed off hence according to it." The word rendered by "cut off" in the A. V. (נִקָּה) is part of a verb which signifies primarily to be pure or clean; and which in the form which occurs here has the general meaning of being cleared, as *e.g.* by being freed from any charge of guilt, or by being delivered from the bond of an oath or obligation, or as when a city is rendered desolate (Isa. iii. 26) by being cleared of its inhabitants. By some, this meaning is retained here. Jarchi interprets thus: Omnis fur ab hac poena immunis fuit. Luther has: Alle Diebe werden fromm gesprochen, "All thieves shall be pronounced innocent." Piscator has: Der da stielet wird für unschuldig gehalten, "He who steals shall be held as blameless." By others the verb is taken with a reflexive meaning, as in the margin of the A. V., "Every one of this people that stealeth holdeth himself guiltless." But it is not probable that this is the meaning here; for in this latter part of the verse it is evidently not the condition of the people as exempt from blame, nor the perverse judgments they might form of themselves or of one another, but the purport and direction of the curse that is intended to be set forth. Among recent interpreters there seems a general consent to take the verb with the transferred sense of *cleansing off*, so that the meaning here would be: " Every one that stealeth shall be cleared away or purged out"; *i.e.* shall be extirpated or destroyed. The only objection to this is that no instance can be adduced of the Hebrew verb being used in this sense. But the analogy of other Hebrew verbs (כָּרַת for instance, by which Kimchi explains the word here, and which signifies both to cut and to cut off, or extirpate); of the Greek, ἐκκαθαίρειν (1 Cor. v. 7); and of the Latin, *purgare*, may be held to justify the assigning to נִקָּה of this transferred signification here.

Another question arises as to the word rendered by "on this side" and "on that side" in the A. V. Some take this to indicate that the roll was written on both sides, and that the two sides represented the two tables of the Law against violations of which the curse was denounced. That the word may be so rendered, and that this may be the meaning of the statement, cannot be questioned; but had the prophet intended this, it is presumed he would have arranged his words differently. Instead of מִזֶּה כָּמוֹהָ—" on this side according to it," " and on that side according to it,"—he would have written כָּמוֹהָ מִזֶּה—" according to it on this side," &c.; in other words, he would have arranged his words so as to connect the verb immediately with כָּמוֹהָ and not with מִזֶּה. It may be added, that whilst it is perfectly easy to understand how a roll could be *written* on this side and on that, it is not easy to understand how one sinner could be *cut off* on this side and another on that side, according to the roll. It seems better, therefore, to take מִזֶּה here in the sense of *hence, i.e.* out of this land (comp. Gen. xxxvii. 17, xlii. 15; Exod. xi. 1): so Targum, De Wette, Maurer, Köhler, Drake, &c. כְּמוֹהָ—*according to it,* as prescribed in it, the roll; Vulg., sicut ibi scriptum est. The verb is here the prophetic perfect.*

The curse thus denounced was to go forth from Jehovah; and God is represented as bringing it forth, and causing it to go so as to enter into the house of the transgressor, there to abide. It should come, not as a passing blast that might sweep over the house and be gone, but as a visitant that comes to tarry; it should lodge there (לָנָה) and abide until it had accomplished that for which it was sent forth, until the house was utterly consumed, the stones of it as well as the wood; just as when the fire of the Lord fell on the altar of the prophet, it consumed not only the sacrifice but also " the wood, and the stones, and the dust, and licked up the water that was in the trench" (1 Kings xviii. 38). So terrible should be the curse of God on the transgressors of His law.

The prophet was thus furnished with a message of warning to the people. They were reminded that God's ancient law was still in force; that He was as jealous over it as ever He was; and that " every transgression and disobedience should receive a just recompense of reward." He whom none can elude, from whom none

---

* It is objected to this that the reduplication of מזה implies a contrast, as in Exod. xxxii. 15; Num. xxii. 24; Ezek. xlvii. 7. But this is only when this word is repeated in the same clause. Here the two are in different clauses, and the word is required in both to complete the sense; as in Exod. xi. 1, where the מזה is of necessity repeated.

can escape; He "who seeth in secret," and "whose eyes run to and fro through the whole earth;" He who will not suffer His law to be broken with impunity—would be sure to detect the transgressor, and would be swift to punish his transgression. "God will not endure the practice of immorality in the midst of those that are His people. The justified must also be sanctified. His people must be righteous. He sits to purify and to refine the house of Israel. Visibly or invisibly He ever separates the chaff from the wheat, and executes judgment in the midst of his people." *

* Wright, "Zechariah and his Prophecies," p. 110.

VII.

THE WOMAN AND THE MEASURE.

"Then the angel that talked with me went forth, and said unto me, Lift up now thine eyes, and see what is this that goeth forth. And I said, What is it? And he said, This is an ephah that goeth forth. He said moreover, This is their resemblance through all the earth. And, behold, there was lifted up a talent of lead: and this is a woman that sitteth in the midst of the ephah. And he said, This is wickedness. And he cast it into the midst of the ephah; and he cast the weight of lead upon the mouth thereof. Then lifted I up mine eyes, and looked, and, behold, there came out two women, and the wind was in their wings; for they had wings like the wings of a stork; and they lifted up the ephah between the earth and the heaven. Then said I to the angel that talked with me, Whither do these bear the ephah? And he said unto me, To build it an house in the land of Shinar: and it shall be established, and set there upon her own base."—ZECH. v. 5–11.

IT is not enough that men should be deterred from sin by fear of punishment, nor that those who sin should be cast out; sin itself, the principle of evil dwelling in man (1 Sam. xxiv. 13), must be wholly banished from the kingdom of God. To indicate this another vision was brought before the eye of the prophet. The Angel-interpreter, who had apparently retired for a little, came forth, probably, as Rosenmüller suggests, from the ranks of the other angels, and roused the prophet to observation by the summons: "Lift up thine eyes, and see what is this that goeth forth"—that comes into view. "To this the prophet—to whose vision, perhaps, the object was only indistinctly presented—replied by asking, 'What is it?' Or his question may mean, What does this import? The reply of the Angel was: 'This is the ephah that is coming forth.' The definite article stands before ephah, because it is alone of its kind, is thereby determined, and by the Angel who has knowledge is recognised" (*Hitzig*). The ephah was one of the largest measures of quantity used by the Hebrews; it contained about an English bushel. Having told the prophet what the object which he saw was, the Angel goes on to tell what it meant: "This is their eye in the whole land." Different explanations have been offered of the word "eye" here. Jerome explains it as "ostensio peccatorum," the exhibition or show of the sinners—the spectacle, as it were, of them in their sin and misery as a warning to others; and this Rosenmüller, Ewald, and others follow. Others prefer taking "eye" here in the sense of image or resemblance, as in the Authorised Version. But though "eye" may be used for that which the eye sees, the appearance (comp. Lev. xiii. 55; Num. xi. 7; "colour," A. V.), or the image of an object such as is formed in the eye, this can hardly be the meaning here, for how could the sinners in Israel be represented or imaged by the ephah or by what it contained? The LXX have ἀδικία here, from which it is supposed they had in their copies עֲוֹנָם "their wickedness," instead of עֵינָם "their eye;" and this Hitzig and some others regard as the true reading. It is not, however, sanctioned by any adequate MS. authority; nor does the meaning thus brought out approve itself, for it is not the ephah, but the woman in the ephah, that is "wickedness," as appears from verse 8. A preferable explanation is that which Umbreit, Hengstenberg, and Pressel adopt, viz. that by "eye" here is intended that to which the eye is directed; that which the eye regards; that which, as is commonly said, one has in his eye. The meaning would thus be: "This is what they regard; what they set their eyes on; the object of their affections and aim." The ephah being the principal measure in use among the Hebrews, has been regarded as standing here as a symbol of commercial transactions generally; and as it was to these that the affection not only of thieves and perjurers but of men of worldly minds and carnal inclinations generally would be chiefly directed, these may be said to be what they set their eye on. It may be doubted, however, if this is what is intended here. It does not appear that it is against any especial class of sinners that the curse in the former vision is denounced; and at any rate in this latter vision it is wickedness in general, and not any especial form of it, that is in view, as that which is to be utterly cast out of God's kingdom on earth. It seems better, therefore, to retain the *general* reference here, and to suppose a metonymy in the phraseology: this is (*i.e.* contains) what they have an eye to; what they affect and desire.

As the prophet looked on the ephah "there was lifted up a weight of lead, and there was one woman sitting in the midst of the ephah." The word rendered "talent" in the A. V. (כִּכָּר) designates primarily something round and flat, such as, *e.g.* a cake of bread (Exod. xxix. 23; 1 Sam. ii. 36; Prov. vi. 26); a tract of country appearing to the eye as a flat circle (Gen. xiii. 12); a talent of metal round and flat. Here it means simply, as expressed in the margin of the A. V., "a weighty piece." This was of lead, and lay apparently on the ephah as a covering or lid. On its being lifted up a woman was seen sitting in the ephah. The pronoun זאת *this*, has here an adverbial force, and is best represented in English by "there." As an ephah was not large enough to contain a woman of average size, the figure that the prophet saw must be conceived of as a miniature resemblance of a woman, and this for symbolical purposes would answer as well as one of full size. "One" here (אַחַת) is not for the indefinite article, but is emphatic; sin is represented in the aggregate as one mass, "as a unity; *i.e.* as *one* living personality, instead of forming an atomistic heap of individuals" (*Keil*). The woman thus seen the Angel pronounced to be "wickedness," *i.e.* the personified concentration of iniquity; just as Athaliah is called "The Wickedness" (2 Chron. xxiv. 7, A. V. "that wicked woman"). As the prophet saw the woman she was sitting up in the ephah, or perhaps attempting to rise out of it: but presently the angel thrust her down into the ephah, and then cast the leaden weight upon the mouth of the ephah so as to shut her in. Those who think that it is still to thieves and perjurers specially that reference is had here put a somewhat different interpretation on this part of the vision. Taking כִּכָּר in the sense of talent as a measure of weight, and regarding the talent and the ephah as emblems of traffic, they suppose that the woman represented wickedness in the form of dishonesty and false swearing; and that she was thrust down into the ephah, and the talent was dashed upon her mouth; that the instruments with which she had plied her iniquitous trade might become the instruments of her condign punishment. But besides the objection already urged that this latter vision has reference to wickedness as such in the general, and not to any special forms of it, there is also to be said: (1) that as the ephah and talent were properly the instruments of honest traffic, there could be no fitness in representing them as the instruments of wickedness; (2) that if the wickedness specially in view was that of stealing and false-swearing, the ephah and talent would not be the instruments of that; men neither steal nor swear by means of an ephah or a talent; and (3) it is not the condign punishment of wickedness that is intended to be represented by this vision, but the utter removal of it. If, in support of this interpretation, it be urged that the pronominal suffix in פִּיהָ *her* mouth, being feminine, is most naturally understood of the woman, it may be replied that as אֵיפָה also is feminine, the suffix may with equal propriety be taken as referring to it. The ephah being a well-known vessel, was presented in the vision for the sake of precision and force, just as our Lord specifies the bushel and the bed (Matt. v. 15) where He might, but with less effect, have merely used the general term "cover." The weight laid upon the ephah was of lead, to indicate the security with which the woman was shut up and imprisoned.

The woman being thus enclosed in the ephah, the prophet, as he continued to look, saw two women with outspread wings as of a stork carried before the wind, who came and lifted the ephah and bore it away through the air. In answer to his inquiry, Whither do these bear the ephah? the Angel-interpreter told the prophet that these were carrying away the ephah that there might be built for it a house in the land of Shinar, where it should have its permanent abode; for when it (the house) should be prepared, she should be set there upon her own base [or place]. The two women with stork-like wings have been supposed by some to represent the Assyrian and Babylonian powers; by others, to typify two evil powers, allies of the woman, who come to deliver her, and carry her to a place where for a season at least she should be safe from the vengeance that would destroy her. But the former of these suppositions is inconsistent with the *ideal* character of this entire representation; and the latter introduces an element foreign to the general idea of the vision, which is not the rescuing of wickedness from vengeance, but the deliverance of the kingdom of God from wickedness. There does not appear to be any special significance belonging to the two women; they are merely adjutatory parts of the representation: *women*, because it was a woman that was to be carried; *two*, because the ephah was heavy, and required more than one to carry it; and both with wings like a stork, as emblematical of the power and rapidity of their flight. The ephah was to be carried with its content to the land of Shinar or Babylon, the land of ungodliness, where was its proper place, and where it should permanently abide. "The picture is simply an ideal one. The land of Shinar is an ideal land contrasted with the land of Israel. The former was the land of unholiness, the latter was the holy land (chap. ii. 12). The picture represents sin and transgression as removed from the land of Israel, the land of the people of God, driven to find its resting-place in the land where Babylon had once been built, driven into the land of the world-power, which was antagonistic to God" (*Wright*, p. 118).

The main design of both these visions is to show the utter incompatibility of iniquity with the kingdom of God. All ungodliness, profanity, falsehood, and covetousness are put under a ban; and wickedness of every kind is to be for ever banished from it. The people of the Lord are to be all righteous, and only such shall inherit the land (Isa. x. 21). Wickedness is to be shut up and banished to its own proper place, where it is to remain [comp. the representation in Rev. xx. 1–3]. If the former of these visions is one of threatening and warning, the latter has a bright as well as a dark side. For when all wickedness is banished from the congregation of the Lord, the beauty of the Lord shall be upon it, and His people shall be glad, and rejoice in His salvation.

VIII.

THE FOUR WAR-CHARIOTS.

"And I turned, and lifted up mine eyes, and looked, and, behold, there came four chariots out from between two mountains; and the mountains were mountains of brass. In the first chariot were red horses; and in the second chariot black horses. And in the third chariot white horses; and in the fourth chariot grisled and bay horses. Then I answered and said unto the angel that talked with me, What are these, my lord? And the angel answered and said unto me, These are the four spirits of the heavens, which go forth from standing before the Lord of all the earth. The black horses which are therein go forth into the north country; and the white go forth after them; and the grisled go forth toward the south country. And the bay went forth, and sought to go that they might walk to and fro through the earth; and he said, Get you hence, walk to and fro through the earth. So they walked to and fro through the earth. Then cried he upon me, and spake unto me, saying, Behold these that go toward the north country have quieted my spirit in the north country."—ZECH. vi. 1-8.

THIS is the last of the series of visions with which the prophet was favoured on the memorable night of the 24th of the month Sebat in the second year of King Darius. These visions were designed partly to animate and encourage the Jews in the work of rebuilding the temple and restoring the worship of Jehovah, partly to warn them against transgression, and especially against rebelliousness and apostasy from Him. As, however, all God's dealings towards His ancient people bear an analogy to His dealings towards His spiritual Church, and especially as in these visions there is reference more or less immediate to the Messiah, they convey instruction and counsel profitable for the people of God as such in all ages. This book of prophecy has, consequently, engaged much of the attention of students of Scripture at all times in the Christian Church. Luther says of it: "The Prophet Zechariah is a paragon (Ausbund), to my thinking the most excellent. For he appeared at a time when it was supremely needful to comfort and encourage the people, and along with that to keep them for the coming reign of Christ and under training."—(*Werke,* vi. 3300.)

In the vision described in chap. v. the prophet saw what was designed to convey warning to the people by showing that God would not suffer wickedness among them to pass unpunished, and that from His inheritance all iniquity must be purged out and driven away. In the vision which follows in the beginning of chap. vi. reference is had to the judgments which God would bring on the enemies of Israel, on the enemies of His Church. The symbols in this vision are not difficult to explain; but over the special reference of the vision itself considerable obscurity hangs.

The prophet saw four chariots coming forth from between two mountains of brass (rather of copper, *nehosheth*). That to the eye of the prophet were presented two mountains apparently formed of copper need not be supposed; all that is intended by the description is that the mountains were impregnable and undecaying, copper or brass being to the Hebrews symbolical of strength and durability; hence such phrases as "gates of brass" (Ps. cvii. 16; Isa. xlv. 2), "brazen wall" (Jer. i. 18, xv. 20), and "hoofs of brass" (Mic. iv. 13). In the Hebrew the definite article is prefixed, "*the* two mountains;" and this has led to the supposition that two well-known mountains appeared to the view of the prophet. As to what mountains are intended various conjectures have been hazarded; some suggesting Mount Zion and Mount Moriah, others Mount Zion and the Mount of Olives. But such a supposition is incompatible with the symbolical character of the representation; two actual, material, localised, and well-known hills of no great magnitude could not be described as mountains of brass, whether that be understood literally or tropically. More probable is what Hengstenberg suggests, that by *the* mountains are intended the mountains in general that were round about Jerusalem, and which were constituted a symbol of the Divine protection extended over Israel; though in this case one does not see why *two* mountains should be specially mentioned. The adhibition of the article, however, does not necessarily determine that two well-known mountains are intended; for it may only be used to specify the particular mountains that were before the prophet in vision, *q. d.* " the two mountains that were there;" these mountains forming the background of the picture, or, as Hitzig suggests, the side-scenes (*coulissen*) of the representation. A recent expositor proposes "to regard the mountains in the vision as referring to Mount Zion and the Mount of Olives viewed as ideal mountains."* But how can actual well-known mountains be viewed as "ideal mountains?" What *is* an ideal mountain? The prophet saw *something*:—was it the figure of

---

* Wright, "Zechariah and his Prophecies," p. 125.

a mountain or the idea of a mountain? and if the latter, what *did* he see?

It is certainly going to the opposite extreme to say that " the two brazen mountains may be merely an ornamental part of the vision " (Newcome). The older interpretation is to be preferred, viz., that " the two mountains of brass denote the immovable decrees of God, His steady execution of His counsels, and the insuperable restraints that are upon all empires and counsels, which God keeps within the barriers of such impregnable mountains, that not one can start till He open the way" (Cruden, " Concord." s. v. *Brass;* comp. also Calvin *in loc.*). This may be too definitely expressed, but this seems to be unquestionably in the right direction. The prophet saw two mountains, strong and impregnable; these were symbols of Jehovah's mighty containing and restraining power; not any mountains in particular, but mountains simply as symbols of strength, support, and defence. " The powers symbolised by the four chariots are pictured as closed in on either side by these mountains, strong as brass, unsurmountable, undecaying, ' that they should not go forth to other lands to conquer until the time should come, fixed by the counsels of God, when the gates should be opened for their going forth' (Rib.). The mountains of brass may signify the height of the Divine wisdom ordering this, and the sublimity of the power which putteth them in operation: as the Psalmist says, *Thy righteousnesses are like the mountains of God*" (Pusey).

From between these two mountains the prophet saw the four chariots rushing forth. These were probably war-chariots drawn, it may be, as Kimchi suggests, each by four horses, more probably by two, though neither is said. The horses, whatever their number, were of the same colour for each chariot, but of different colours for the different chariots; of the first chariot the horses were red, of the second black, of the third white, and of the fourth grisled or piebald. The horses in the fourth chariot are in the A.V. described as also "bay." But the same horses could not be both grisled or piebald, and bay. In the margin, the rendering "strong" is proposed instead of "bay;" and this is undoubtedly to be preferred. The Hebrew word means *strong, active, powerful*, (אֲמֻצִּים from אָמֵץ to be alert, active, strong); and is added to the description of the horses in the fourth chariot to indicate that they were specially vigorous and powerful. Hengstenberg, indeed, supposes that it applies to all the horses; however different in colour they were all strong and active, and therefore fitted for the work they had to do; but whilst this is in itself improbable from the position of the word in close apposition to the word rendered "grisled," it is shown to be untenable by the consideration, as has been pointed out by Pressel, that had this been intended the phrase would have been, "strong all of them" (אֲמֻצִּים כֻּלָּם). It may be added that as a wider sphere was to be occupied by the fourth chariot (see ver. 7), and a harder service rendered consequently by the horses by which it was drawn, it was fitting that these should be especially signalised as "strong."

It will be seen that whilst there are points of resemblance in this symbol to that of the first vision, there are also marked points of difference. In both visions there are horses of different colours, and in both there are red horses and white. Here the resemblance ends. In the first vision there were only horses, with probably riders on them; here there are horses yoked to chariots: in the former vision, the horses with their riders had been sent forth to walk to and fro through the earth on an embassy of inquiry; in this the chariots are war-chariots sent forth to execute God's judgments: in the former vision the horses are red, speckled (roan ?), and white; in the latter they are red, black, white, and grisled: and the order in which the horses proceed is different in the two visions. These differences sufficiently indicate that the two visions are entirely distinct, and each is to be interpreted by itself without reference to the other.

The colours of the horses must be regarded as symbolical. Hitzig throws doubt on this; but if there be no significance in the different colours, for what purpose are they so carefully specified? It can hardly be merely "to distinguish one chariot from another." As four are mentioned, it would have sufficed to distinguish them had they been numbered first, second, third, and fourth, without the colour of their horses being so expressly described. Of the symbols in Scripture none are more frequent and none more distinctively significant, than those which have to do with colour;* and in such a connection as that of a prophetic vision, where all else is symbolical, congruity seems to require that the colours specifically described should be viewed also as symbolical. *Red*, as the colour of blood, is the symbol of war and bloodshed (comp. 2 Kings iii. 22; Isa. lxiii. 2; Neh. ii. 3; Rev. vi. 4, xii. 3, 7); *black* is the symbol of desolation, sorrow, and

* See Bähr, "Symbolik des Mosaischen Cultus," i. 316.

mourning (comp. Isa. l. 3; Jer. iv. 28, viii. 21, xiv. 2; Ezek. xxxi. 15; Joel ii. 6; Rev. vi. 5, 12 ff.); *white* is the symbol of victory and gladness (Eccles. ix. 8; Rev. vi. 2, xix. 11). The significance of the fourth colour in this vision is uncertain, as the word occurs only here and in Gen. xxxi. 10, 12, where no symbolical meaning can be supposed. That the colour was not simple but of a mixed character seems to be generally admitted; and this being accepted we may safely conclude thus much, that it symbolised a combined condition, or an infliction of a twofold character. Hengstenberg takes the word as meaning "literally *hail-like*," deriving it from בָּרָד, *hail*, and regards it as a figurative representation of the Divine judgments which fall upon the ungodly, inasmuch as "hail" is frequently so employed in Scripture. But even if we admit his etymology, his explanation cannot be accepted; for it is not hail but a colour like hail (according to his rendering) that has to be explained; and it by no means follows that because *hail* is used in Scripture as a figure of the Divine judgments, a *colour* like hail is of the same significance. Keil regards the colour as indicating famine and pestilence; and this seems better than with Henderson to take it as indicating a mixed dispensation of joy and sorrow, or, with others, of peace and war.

In answer to the prophet's request the angel-interpreter proceeds to explain the vision. "These," says he, "are the four winds of heaven that are going forth from standing before the Lord of all the earth." In the A.V. it is the "four spirits of the heavens." But the only spirits in heaven of whom Scripture knows anything are the angels, and there are none of them who are by way of eminence "the four spirits of the heavens." The four winds of heaven is a phrase frequently used, and used with reference to the wind as an instrument to execute God's will on the earth in the punishment of the wicked. "Upon Elam," says God by the prophet Jeremiah (xlix. 36), "will I bring the four winds, from the four quarters of heaven, and will scatter them towards all those winds." In the vision which Daniel saw he beheld the four winds of the heavens bursting forth on the great sea (vii. 2); the emblem of the judgments to be executed by the great conquerors whose advent the prophet foresaw. And in Rev. vii. 1 St. John tells us he saw four angels "holding the four winds of the earth that they should not blow on the earth, nor on the sea, nor on any tree," restraining, but ready to let loose when commanded, the judgments of God upon the earth. With this symbol, then, the Jews, it may be presumed, were familiar; and accordingly here this more familiar symbol is employed by the angel to explain the less familiar and more obscure.

These four winds of heaven the angel describes as "going forth from standing before the Lord of all the earth." This is probably what led to the translation "spirits" rather than "winds" in the preceding clause. How, it may be asked, can winds be said to go forth from standing before the Lord? To this it may be replied—
1. That we read elsewhere of God sending out a wind (Jonah i. 4), and of His bringing the wind out of His treasuries (Ps. cxxxv. 7; Jer. x. 13, li. 16); from which it may be inferred that the Hebrews conceived the wind to be kept by God in His repositories, and sent forth as from His presence when He saw meet; and, 2. As we

read that God "maketh the winds His ministers," it is only a carrying out of the same figure when these are represented as standing before Him, His servants awaiting His behest. As in nature it is at God's command that the wind ariseth, and as it is His word which the stormy wind fulfils, so in this vision the mighty agencies here symbolised are represented as standing before the Lord, to indicate that they were entirely under His control, and that they could act only as He willed and appointed.

The angel goes on to indicate to the prophet the *destination* of these instruments of the Divine vengeance. "That in which are the black horses [they] are going forth to the land of the north; and the white are gone after them; and the grisled are gone to the land of the south." There are some peculiarities of construction in this verse which have to be noted. In the first clause there is an anacolouthon; where we should expect a verb in the singular agreeing with "that" (אֲשֶׁר), we have a participle in the plural agreeing with "horses" (יֹצְאִים סוּסִים); and whilst in the first clause we have a present participle, in the other two the verb is in the perfect. Ewald proposes to change the verb in both these clauses from the perfect (יָצְאוּ) to the imperfect (יֵצְאוּ), so as to read "the white go," or "will go," &c. But the alteration is unnecessary. The angel passes from the present to the perfect, because as the chariots were seen rushing at full speed, the white horses and the grisled had already passed and gone whilst he was describing the destination of the chariot with the black horses.*

* Wright, p. 557.

"The land of the north," to which the chariot with the black horses was seen going, is undoubtedly Babylonia (cf. ii. 10, 11). By this was indicated that on Babylon, the bitter and cruel enemy of Israel, heavy judgments were about to come. Following this chariot came that with white horses hastening to the same destination; to indicate the complete triumph which was to be obtained over the enemy that had ravaged the land and led captive the people of Israel. Instead of "after them" or "behind them" (אֶל־אַחֲרֵיהֶם), Ewald proposes to render "to the back part" (nach hinter sich), *i.e.*, to the west; but to the west of what? To the west of Palestine there are no peoples, but only the Great Sea, the Mediterranean; and besides, had the west been specified, we should have expected the east to have been also mentioned, just as the south is set over against the north. Pressel renders the words by "farther behind," and understands them of the region lying beyond Babylonia, the Medo-Persian territory. But this overlooks the pronominal suffix "them" appended to the preposition, which indicates the black horses in the second chariot as what the chariot with the white horses followed; and besides, as the phrase אֶל־אַחֲרֵי with verbs of motion properly means "after" in the sense of following, it may be doubted if it may legitimately be translated "behind" in the sense of lying beyond. The chariot with the grisled or piebald horses was seen rushing to the land of the south, that is, towards Egypt (Dan. ii. 5 ff.), also the enemy of Israel. Inasmuch, however, as Egypt had not oppressed and injured Israel as Babylon had, only one of the judgment chariots was seen going thither; but that carried famine and pestilence as a scourge from the Lord on the inhabitants of that land. Nor was the infliction confined to that land. The strong horses that drew the fourth chariot impatient of restraint sought a wider sphere through which to roam; and so were permitted to go thence and walk to and fro through the earth. If by the colours of these horses be symbolised famine and pestilence, their walking to and fro through the earth agrees with the character of these visitations as apt to occur at all times and in all countries, and as coming unexpectedly and mysteriously (Ps. xci. 5, 6; Jer. xxxiv. 17, xlii. 17; Ezek. vii. 15, &c.), as arrows shot from the hand of God (Ezek. v. 16) on the objects of His displeasure.

In this detail no mention is made of the chariot with the red horses; and this presents a difficulty which has much exercised the ingenuity of interpreters. Were it allowable to suppose that the word translated "bay," and which is properly "strong," in ver. 3, had slipped into that verse from the second, and was originally appended as a further description of the horses in the first chariot; or if Hengstenberg's suggestion, that the epithet "strong" is meant to apply to the horses in all the chariots, could be accepted, the difficulty would be easily removed; for we could then regard ver. 7 as giving the description of the destination of this first chariot, reserved to the last because of its more general reference and wider field of operation. But as neither of these expedients can be adopted, the solution must be sought elsewhere. Ewald, following Kimchi, suggests that for אמצים, "strong," in ver. 7, we should read החמצים, *shining, bright, scarlet* or *red*, as a bright and sharply-defined colour. Gesenius pronounces this "omnino inconcinnum" (Thes. i. 5); but as אָמֵץ and חָמֵץ are fundamentally the same word, the only difference being that the guttural in the one is less pronounced than in the other (probably a dialectical peculiarity), there is nothing absurd or unbefitting in the suggestion. But in *usage* the words have different meanings; for starting alike from the primary idea of "sharpness," the one passes on to the secondary idea of fleetness, vigour, strength, while the other passes on to the idea of brightness and redness as a sharply-defined colour. It is not probable, therefore, that the one word would be used where the other would have been more appropriate; nor is there any reason to suppose an error of transcription here. Saint Jerome suggests that the rest is passed over because "when the prophet related this the Babylonian empire had passed, and the power of the Medes possessed all Asia." But this proceeds on the assumption that the red was destined for Babylonia, whereas it is the black which is expressly said to be so destined; and besides, if the fact that the Babylonian empire had passed away was a reason for not mentioning the destination of the red, this would have equally been a reason for not mentioning the destination of the black. The truth is that no satisfactory solution of this difficulty has been advanced; and it is best, therefore, to leave it without any attempt to remove it. Keil justly remarks, that in all the visions there are things which are not expressly explained; and where, consequently, the main purpose of the vision is ascertained it is not necessary to insist on an explanation of all the accessory details. All, therefore, that can be safely said on the point in hand is, that for some reason not specified, the chariot with the red horses was passed over, and no account of its destination given by the angel.

From the time of Jerome there have been interpreters who have maintained that by the horses in the chariots are represented the four empires of Daniel, as instruments of the Divine judgments. But in the vision itself, as explained by the angel, these empires, at least some of them, are represented as the *objects* of the Divine judgments, which the chariots are represented as instrumentally bringing upon them; and as the same thing cannot represent both the object and the instrument of judgment, to interpret these chariots and horses of the empires, to which they were sent, is to introduce utter confusion into the picture. Besides, as these chariots were seen by the prophet as rushing forth *simultaneously*, they cannot represent agencies that came into operation at intervals separated widely, in some instances by many generations. And in fine, whilst there is no difficulty in the way of understanding how Babylonia and Egypt, as the enemies of Israel, should be the objects of the Divine vengeance, and the whole earth should be visited with calamity because of the sins of its inhabitants; it is not easy to perceive in what sense Babylonia and Egypt were, after this date, the instruments of the Divine judgments on others; while to represent the whole earth as such an instrument is simply absurd.

The enemies of God's people are the enemies of God Himself, and the wrongs done to them He regards as done to Him. "He that toucheth you," he had already said to Israel by this prophet, " toucheth the apple of his eye "

(ii. 8). Hence He takes up the case of His people as His own, and becomes the avenger of the wrongs done to His Church. It is to this that the language in ver. 8 refers: "Then cried He unto them and spake, saying, Behold, these that go toward the north country have quieted my Spirit in the north country." The speaker here is not the angel who was by the side of the prophet and interpreted to him the visions, but "the other angel," the Angel of Jehovah, who in these visions appears speaking and acting as God. Not being by the side of the prophet He cried to him, called aloud to him, so as to arrest his attention to what He was about to utter, as of importance. The phrase, "have quieted My Spirit in the north country," or, as the words may be rendered, "have caused My Spirit to rest on the land of the north," has been variously understood and explained. Kimchi takes it as meaning that the black horses which went forth to Babylon to destroy it had by destroying it caused a quieting of God's Spirit; and this is substantially adopted by Hengstenberg—"this Spirit of God is quieted in the north country with regard to its operations and the manifestations of its power, namely, the judgments which it executes there" —by Hitzig and by Henderson, only these two take "Spirit" in the sense of "wrath." Calvin explains it as meaning that "God began to be quieted after that second chariot had been sent forth, for then He showed that He was reconciled to His chosen people; forthwith redemption followed." Ewald renders it, "they leave my Spirit in the land of the north," and understands the meaning to be that the people of Israel still in Babylon would receive an accession of spirit and courage from the Spirit of the Lord. Not a few, among whom are Dr. Pusey and Mr. Wright, taking "Spirit" in the sense of wrath or anger, understand the utterance as declaring that the wrath of God would rest, *i.e.*, abide, on the land of the north until the final execution of his judgments upon that cruel enemy of Israel. Of these interpretations the first and the last alone seem worthy of consideration. So far as the language is concerned either interpretation may be accepted; only there is less certainty that רוּחַ means anger than that it means Spirit, the latter being the common meaning of the word, while the former is at least doubtful.* It may be questioned also whether, had the thing to be expressed been the abiding of God's wrath on Babylon, another formula and one less ambiguous would not have been employed, such *e.g.* as that in Ezek. xxiv. 13. On the other hand, it may be said that "the idiom ' to cause to rest upon' a person involves that that person is the object on whom it abides" (Pusey); but this is not always the case, as may be seen from Ezek. xiv. 42; indeed it might rather be said that where the verb is followed by the prep. בְּ and not by עַל, the meaning conveyed is that the subject of the verb finds satisfaction, appeasement, and so rest and quiet in respect of the object; comp. Ezek. v. 13, xxiv. 13; also Ezek. xxi. 22 [A.V. 17], and Isa. xxv. 10. On the whole, the interpretation of Kimchi is to be preferred. By the judgments executed on the enemies and oppressors of His people satisfaction was rendered to God, His just anger was

---

* The instances usually adduced of this meaning, viz., Judg. viii. 3; Eccl. x. 4; Ps. xxv. 4, xxxiii. 11, are by no means decisive, for in none of them is it certain that רוּחַ means *wrath*.

appeased, and His Spirit roused against them was quieted. The statement is in harmony with what He elsewhere says, " Ah, I will ease Me of mine adversaries; I will avenge Me of mine enemies " (Isa. i. 24).

This vision had reference primarily to the judgments with which God would visit those nations that had oppressed and wronged Israel. But there are here involved general truths which are for all times and for all places. One thing plainly taught here is, that all agencies are under the Divine control, and operate only as God directs or permits. War, pestilence, and famine are His servants that wait His bidding, and go forth only as He wills. It may be possible to trace their outbreaks to secondary causes; wars may arise from human ambition, passion, covetousness, or vanity; famine may ensue on certain atmospheric conditions, or as the consequence of some misconduct or negligence on the part of man; and pestilence or disease may ravage a country through neglect of proper sanitary precautions on the part of its inhabitants. But no event or effect is the result of any one isolated cause; and in the great chain of causes and effects on which all events hang the ultimate link is ever in the hand of Him " of whom, and to whom, and through whom are all things." The forces and powers of nature, and the influences that affect the condition or determine the conduct of individuals and communities, are alike under His control. Nothing can happen except as He permits or appoints; and " if He cut off, and shut up or gather together, who can hinder Him?" (Job xi. 10).

We are reminded here also of the deep interest, the quick and living interest, which God takes in His people,

His care for them, and His intense displeasure with all who injure and oppress them. Babylon and Egypt stand in the prophetical Scriptures, both of the Old Testament and the New, as the types and emblems of the enemies of God's Church; and both in the Old Testament and the New, the Divine displeasure is emphatically expressed against those who are thus hostile to that cause which is dear to Him. Because of this trouble and calamity, desolation and ruin come upon peoples and upon dynasties. If the inner history of nations could be deciphered—if we could see all the minute relations of events as God sees them—we should in many cases discover that calamities which have come upon countries and kingdoms, and which the ordinary historian traces to this or that secondary cause, were in reality the outcome of Divine judgments on the oppressors or persecutors of God's people. "Thus saith the Lord, Even the captives of the mighty shall be taken away, and the prey of the terrible shall be delivered: for I will contend with him that contendeth with thee, and I will save thy children. And I will feed them that oppress thee with their own flesh; and they shall be drunken with their own blood, as with sweet wine: and all flesh shall know that I the Lord am thy Saviour and thy Redeemer, the mighty One of Jacob" (Isa. xlix. 25, 26).

IX.

EVIL DENOUNCED.

"And it came to pass in the fourth year of king Darius, that the word of the Lord came unto Zechariah in the fourth day of the ninth month, even in Chisleu; when they had sent unto the house of God Sherezer and Regem-melech, and their men, to pray before the Lord, and to speak unto the priests which were in the house of the Lord of hosts, and to the prophets, saying, Should I weep in the fifth month, separating myself, as I have done these so many years? Then came the word of the Lord of hosts unto me, saying, Speak unto all the people of the land, and to the priests, saying, When ye fasted and mourned in the fifth and seventh month, even those seventy years, did ye at all fast unto me, even to me? And when ye did eat, and when ye did drink, did not ye eat for yourselves, and drink for yourselves? Should ye not hear the words which the Lord hath cried by the former prophets, when Jerusalem was inhabited and in prosperity, and the cities thereof round about her, when men inhabited the south and the plain? And the word of the Lord came unto Zechariah, saying, Thus speaketh the Lord of hosts, saying, Execute true judgment, and shew mercy and compassions every man to his brother: and oppress not the widow, nor the fatherless, the stranger, nor the poor; and let none of you imagine evil against his brother in your heart. But they refused to hearken, and pulled away the shoulder, and stopped their ears, that they should not hear. Yea, they made their hearts as an adamant stone, lest they should hear the law, and the words which the Lord of hosts hath sent in his spirit by the former prophets: therefore came a great wrath from the Lord of hosts. Therefore it is come to pass, that as he cried, and they would not hear; so they cried, and I would not hear, saith the Lord of hosts: but I scattered them with a whirlwind among all the nations whom they knew not: thus the land was desolate after them, that no man passed through nor returned; for they laid the pleasant land desolate."

—ZECH. vii. 1-14.

THE series of visions recorded in the preceding chapters took place on the night between the 23d and 24th of the eleventh month, the month Tebat, in the second year of king Darius. What is recorded in this 7th chapter and the chapter following occurred about a year and three quarters later, in the fourth year of Darius, on the 4th of the month Chisleu, the ninth month of the Jewish year. It is not to be supposed that during this interval the prophet's work was suspended; on the contrary, he was doubtless actively engaged in encouraging and admonishing the people who were employed in the rebuilding of the temple; for it is in reference to this time that it is said that "the elders of the Jews builded, and they prospered through the prophesying of Haggai the prophet and Zechariah the son of Iddo" (Ezra vi. 14). But during the interval no special vision or message from the Lord was given to the prophet to communicate to the people; at least none that it seemed meet to the Holy Spirit to cause to be committed to writing, and preserved as part of the sacred canon.

According to the rendering of ver. 1 in the A.V., the entire reckoning is of the time when the word of the Lord came to the prophet, and this is as directed by the Masoretic accentuation. It will be observed, however, that here the date of the day and month is not, as in previous instances, connected immediately with the date of the year, but is separated from it by the words, "the word of the Lord came unto Zechariah." This has led to the suggestion that the last clause of the verse should be read with ver. 2, thus: "On the fourth day of the ninth month in Chisleu, then sent," &c., thus giving the date of the mission here described, rather than that of the giving of the word to the prophet. But the position of the verb in ver. 2 with vau conversive (וַיִּשְׁלַח) seems to preclude such a rendering; this is dependent grammatically on the הָיָה of ver. 1, and must be taken as beginning a new clause. Notwithstanding, therefore, the unusual arrangement of the clauses, the rendering given in the A.V. is to be preferred. There is no need, however, for rendering the verb as a pluperfect "had sent," for which there is no sufficient authority in the usage of the language; the ו may be rendered by "for" or "now."

As to the further rendering of this second verse, and as to its meaning, opinion is much divided among interpreters. Four different renderings and explanations have been proposed: 1. "They sent unto the house of God Sharezer and Regem-melech, and their men," &c. (A.V., Vulg., Grotius, Rosenmüller, &c.); here the verb is regarded as impersonal, and "the house of God" (Bethel) is taken as an accusative local, and is understood of the temple at Jerusalem then in course of being restored. 2. Bethel (*i.e.* the people of Bethel) sent Sharezer, &c. (Keil, Henderson, Pusey, Drake, &c.); here Bethel is taken as the subject of the verb, and Sharezer, &c., as its object. 3. Bethel, *that is* Sharezer, Regem-melech, and their men sent, &c. (Ewald, Hitzig, Wright); here Sharezer, &c., are viewed as the senders of the deputation and their names as in apposition to Bethel. 4. The house of God (*i.e.* the congregation of Israel, whether those still in Babylon or those in Palestine) sent Sharezer, &c. (Hengstenberg, Maurer); here Bethel is assumed as the subject, the sender, and Sharezer, &c., as the object, the parties sent. Of these renderings the second seems that most naturally suggested by the words as they stand in

H

the text. It has, indeed, been said that for this there must have been a preposition (אֵת) before the noun in the accusative; but this by no means holds; cf. Zech. i. 10, and many other places where the accusative follows שָׁלַח without the preposition. The third of these renderings has in its favour the support of eminent scholars; but it is not in itself very probable; for if the inhabitants of Bethel as a community were the senders, why should two of their number with their attendants be specially named; and if these men were themselves the senders, why should it be said that Bethel was the sender? It is altogether more probable that Bethel was the sender, and that these men are named with their attendants because they were the parties who, thus attended, came forth as the deputation from the town; and this is strengthened by the use of the singular "I" (ver. 3), which, as not referring to any individual, points to a community as collectively the sender of the deputation. The first of these renderings, which is that of the A. V., is objectionable on the ground that Bethel is nowhere used as an appellation of the temple, which is properly designated בֵּית יְהוָֹה, "the house of the Lord," as in ver. 3; and that had the writer intended to represent Bethel as the place to which the deputation was sent he would have made this certain by prefixing אֶל to בֵּית אֵל or putting this name after that of the men. The last of the renderings has not found much favour among interpreters, but it has been rejected generally for a reason which does not seem to have much weight, viz., that the appellation "house of God" is nowhere in the Old Testament used of the people of Israel. This is true; but at the same time, as this phrase appears in the New Testament as a designation of the spiritual Israel (Heb. x. 21; 1 Pet. iv. 17), and as such designations are usually transferred by the New Testament writers from those in use among the Jews for the national Israel, the probability is that this was a well-known designation of the latter, though it does not appear in the Old Testament. Moreover, though this exact phrase does not elsewhere occur in the Old Testament of the national Israel, the equivalent phrase "My house," as used by God of that people, is found in this book (ch. iii. 7). It is worthy of notice also, that the answer which the prophet was directed to make is addressed primarily to "the people of the land;" from which it seems fair to conclude that it was from the people as such that the inquiry came, and not from a single town, and that one of no prominent importance in the nation. The view, therefore, that by "the house of God" here is meant the Israelitish community, "the congregation of the Lord," is not to be rejected as wholly improbable. The question was one for the nation at large, and the parties who were sent to propound it to the priests may with great probability be regarded as commissioned by the whole community to represent what was a national feeling and a national want.

Bethel, then, whether the people of that town or the people of Israel generally, was the sender of the deputation, and the parties sent were "Sharezer, Regem-melech, and their men," *i.e.* the persons sent with them as their attendants, their "suite," to use a modern phrase. The former of these names is apparently Assyrian. Sharezer was the name of one of the sons of Sennacherib (2 Kings

xix. 37; Isa. xxxvii. 38), and the name Nergal-Sharezer appears as that borne by one of the princes of Nebuchadnezzar (Jer. xxxix. 3, 13). It has been identified with the Assyrian "Sar-usur, contracted from Asur (Bil, Nirgal)-sar-usur, *i.e.*, *May Asur* (Bel or Nergal, Assyrian gods) *protect the king*. (See Schrader, 'Die Keilinschriften und Das Alte Testament,' p. 206)."* Roediger regards the name as Persian, a compound of Zend *çara*, prince, and *athar*, fire; while others think it may be a compound of Heb. *Sar*, prince, and *eçar*, treasure.† Regem-melech is explained by Gesenius and Fürst as a Hebrew name meaning "friend of the king." If Sharezer is Assyrian or Persian it is probable that the person here named was born in Babylonia during the exile. There is nothing, however, in this to support the opinion of some of the Jewish writers that the deputation was sent from the Jews who were still in exile.‡

The deputation was sent "to pray before the Lord" (margin, to entreat the face of the Lord). The verb here used signifies primarily to smooth by rubbing; but in the Piel, in the phrase חִלָּה פָּנִים this primary signification is lost in that of paying court to one (Job xi. 19; Ps. xlv. 13; Prov. xix. 6), entreating or beseeching favour of one (Exod. xxxii. 11; 1 Sam. xiii. 12; Ps. cxix. 58; Dan. ix. 13: Zech. viii. 21, 22, &c.). When the phrase is employed in reference to God, it is in the latter sense invariably that it is used. Render here, "To entreat the favour of Jehovah." Whether these men carried with

---

* Wright, "Zechariah," p. 168.
† In many MSS. the reading is Sarezer in place of Sharezer.
‡ "The senders were the children of the captivity."—Kimchi.

them gifts and offerings to present before the Lord does not appear; but as it was usual in such cases for this to be done (Exod. xxxiv. 20; 1 Sam. ix. 7; 2 Sam. xxiv. 24; Jer. xli. 5), the probability is that the usage was observed on this occasion also.

The priests and the prophets were the proper medium through which the suppliant could approach Jehovah and obtain an answer to his petition (2 Kings iii. 11 ff.; Jer. xviii. 18, xlii. 1 ff.; Ezek. vii. 26; Hag. ii. 13; Mal. ii. 7, &c.). The priests were the authorised expositors of the law to the people, and the prophets were the medium through which special messages were conveyed to them from God. These men were accordingly sent to address their request to the priests that were in the house of the Lord, and to the prophets at Jerusalem, saying (לֵאמֹר at the beginning of ver. 3 is repeated in the next clause because of the intervening words, as תֹּאמַר is 2 Sam. xiv. 4), "Should I weep in the fifth month, separating myself, as I have done these so many years?" The body or community by which the deputation was sent is here introduced as speaking in the singular.

To understand the purport of this inquiry, we must observe that during the exile the Jews seem to have set apart certain days as seasons of fasting and mourning in commemoration of calamities that had befallen their nation. Here, in this third verse, only one of these is mentioned, but in the next verse two are named, and in ch. viii. 19 four are specified, viz., "The fast of the fourth month, the fast of the fifth, the fast of the seventh, and the fast of the tenth month." No certain information is attainable as to the origin of these institutions; nor do we know for certain the occasion which each of these fasts was designed to commemorate. They may have been, and probably were, self-imposed ordinances adopted by the Jews in their exile, as there is no evidence that they were instituted by command from heaven. It has been supposed that the events designed to be commemorated by them were—the breaking down of the wall of Jerusalem by the fast of the fourth month, the burning of the temple by that of the fifth month, the slaughter of Gedaliah the son of Ahikam by that of the seventh, and the beginning of the final siege of Jerusalem by that of the tenth. This is probably correct, and it enables us to find a reason why the fast of the fifth month alone should have been the object of inquiry by the deputation from Bethel. What they desired to know was, whether the fast they had been in the habit of observing in the fifth month should continue to be observed with mourning and lamentation as formerly. Now, as the deputation was sent in the ninth month it might have been expected that it would have been as to the fast of the tenth month, the one still remaining to be observed in that year, rather than to one already observed and past, that inquiry would be made. But if the fast of the fifth month was commemorative of the destruction of the temple, there was an obvious reason why it should specially be selected as the object of inquiry, seeing as the temple was now in course of being restored it might appear incongruous and unseemly to keep up a mournful commemoration of its former destruction. This fast also was the most important of all, as commemorating what to the Jews was of all the calamities that had befallen their nation the most conspicuous and deplorable. A decision regarding it, therefore, would be applicable to all the rest; whereas a decision regarding any one of them might not be held as reaching to it.

The people had, even after their return to their own land, continued to observe these fasts. But now a difficulty had occurred to them in regard to this. Now that the temple was nearly rebuilt, and the city to a great extent restored, was it needful or desirable or fitting to keep up those days of sorrowful remembrance? Should they continue to mourn and fast now that the cause of their sorrowing had been removed by the restoration of that the loss of which they had deplored? With this difficulty pressing on them they sent to God for counsel and direction through His priests and prophets.

The direct answer to their inquiry was not immediately given. The prophet was first instructed to denounce in the name of the Lord the wrong and pernicious notions which had crept into the minds of the people regarding the use and meaning and value of such observances. As the inquiry of the man of Bethel concerned not them alone but the nation at large, the prophet was instructed to address his message to "the people of the land and to the priests." The message is in two parts; the one (vii. 3–14) of rebuke and warning; the other (viii. 1–17) of promise and encouragement, followed (18–23) by an answer to the inquiry regarding the fasts, and a prediction of the great number of proselytes that should be drawn to the Jews by the manifestation of God's goodness to them. The former of these parts is also subdivided into two, each introduced by the formula: "Then came the word of Jehovah of hosts unto me."

These people had observed these fasts during the seventy years of the exile; but God by the prophet calls in question the spirit and motive of their observance. "When ye fasted and mourned . . . did ye at all fast unto Me, to Me?" The Hebrew here is peculiarly emphatic; not only is the finite form of the verb used after the infinitive, הֲצוֹם צַמְתֻּנִי, *fasting, fasted ye to Me*, but the nominative of the personal pronoun אָנִי, is appended to the suffix for the sake of greater emphasis (cf. Gen. xxvii. 34; Hag. i. 4). As the suffix is appended immediately to the verb, it has been maintained by Ewald and others that the prophet here uses the intransitive verb as a transitive to which its object is subjoined: "When ye fasted . . . fasted ye Me?" *i.e.* as they explain it: "Did your fasts impose any constraint on Me, exert any effect on Me, or in any way benefit Me?" But this surely is doing violence to the passage. How can an intransitive verb like "fast" be construed as a transitive? and how can "fast me" be made to mean "constrain or influence Me by your fast?" This is to put a forced meaning on the words, not to bring out the meaning they properly contain. The construction, it is admitted, is somewhat peculiar; but it is easily resolved by regarding the possessive suffix as in the dative after the intransitive verb (צַמְתֻּנִי for צַמְתָּם לִי), a not unusual construction (cf. Job xxxi. 18; Isa. lxv. 5, xliv. 21; Gesenius, "Heb. Gr.," § 119, 7th ed.; Ewald, "Ausf. Lehrb.," § 305, 5th ed.). By this question God denounces the self-righteousness of the people. He neither condemns nor commends the fasts themselves. But He censures the motive from which, and the spirit in which, they were observed. It was not for the sake of serving and honouring God that they fasted when they mourned and wept, it was not that they really humbled themselves before Him, confessing with contrite hearts the sins which had caused the calamities they deplored, and in the spirit of sincere devotion and penitential sorrow seeking forgiveness and restoration to favour. No; it was not thus to God that they fasted and mourned. It was wholly to themselves in a self-righteous spirit and reliance upon their own good doings that they acted. They had fasted and mourned in the belief that by mortifying of the body they were accumulating merit in the sight of God, by which they might, as it were, buy back what had been lost through the sins of their fathers. Their fasting and mourning had been, no less than their feasting and rejoicing, wholly for themselves, to procure advantage to themselves: "And when ye eat and when ye drink, is it not ye that eat and ye that drink?" In either case there was no respect to God in what they did. Observed in this spirit and with this intent, their fastings and mournings were utterly unmeaning and worthless; they were nothing to God, and profitless to themselves in His regard.

God further reminds them that not now for the first time had such admonitions been addressed to their nation. "Should ye not hear the words?" (or as in the margin with the Vulgate and LXX, "Are not these the words?" or as Ewald and others propose, "Do ye not know the words?" אֶת הַדְּבָרִים being either an accusative following a verb, or a nominative preceding a verb, the verb in either case having to be supplied), "Are not these the words which Jehovah proclaimed by the former prophets when Jerusalem was inhabited and in serenity (שַׁלְוָה), and her towns round about her, and the South country (Negeb) and the Lowland (Shephelah) were inhabited?" This is a description of the whole land of Judah; the towns round about Jerusalem being those in the mountain district of Judah surrounding Jerusalem as their centre, and more or less dependent on it, and the Negeb and the Shephelah comprehending the rural districts which belonged to the kingdom of Judah. Whilst this territory was as yet undisturbed by foreign invasion, God had spoken to its inhabitants by the prophets, warning them against self-righteousness and against trusting in mere outward observances, in a mere empty ritualism, for acceptance with Him. And as God thus spoke to their fathers so did He speak now to them. Whether they continued to observe these fasts or not mattered little; the all-important thing was that they should not regard these as something done to God, whereby they secured a title to His favour, whilst they were "omitting the weightier matters of the law, judgment, mercy, and faith."

In order further to enforce on the people this lesson, the prophet was commissioned to convey to them an additional message from the Lord, in which the substance of what He had before spoken to their fathers is given; ver. 9: "Thus spake Jehovah of hosts" (the verb here is to be taken as a preterite, the reference being to what the Lord had spoken to the people before the captivity), "saying," &c. The message which God has thus sent by the prophets sets forth what He would have His people to be and to do, and by the being and doing of which they should approve themselves to Him far more than by fastings and ritual observances. He enjoins the executing of true judgment—literally, judgment of truth (*mishpat' emeth*)—a judgment which proceeds on a correct apprehension of the actual facts of the case, and is in accordance with rectitude; the showing of loving-kindness (*chesed*) and compassions to one another, each man to his brother; the avoiding of all injustice or violence towards those who are poor and helpless, especially those who belong to the classes which God has marked out as specially the objects of His regard and care—the widow, the fatherless, and the stranger. He forbids also the indulgence of revengeful feelings or malignant and evil purposes against others; none was to imagine in his heart evil against his brother; literally, imagine evil of a man, his brother, *i.e.*, of any man. Injunctions to this effect God had frequently given to Israel of old. They are but an expansion of that which is the sum of the whole law—Love.

Thus God had by His prophets admonished their fathers, commanding them to " do justly, to love mercy, and to walk humbly before Him," and giving them to understand that this was more acceptable to Him than any amount of fastings or sacrifices. They had, however, refused to hearken to this admonitory voice; had impiously flung themselves free from the Divine control, and had become obdurate in their rebellion (vers. 11, 22). The successive stages, so to speak, of their revolt are here indicated; (1) they refused to listen, simply treating with neglect God's voice to them; (2) they pulled away the shoulder—literally, they gave (exhibited) an intractable shoulder; they refused to bear what was laid upon them, or they fretfully and angrily freed themselves from the grasp by which, as it were, God sought to hold them and urge them to obedience (cf. Neh. ix. 29, where the same phrase occurs); (3) they stopped their ears—literally, they made their ears heavy that they should not hear; they sought to rid themselves of God's urgent entreaties by turning a deaf ear to all that He said. (4) As a natural consequence, they became utterly hardened in their rebellion; they made their hearts as an adamant stone, as the diamond (שָׁמִיר), the paragon of hardness ("duritia inenarrabilis est," Plin. "Nat. Hist.," xxxvii. 15), so that they became inaccessible to all entreaty, and ceased to be under any right impression either of obligation or of gratitude, and accordingly would no longer regard either what was enjoined on them in the law, or the message God had sent to them by His Spirit through means of His prophets. Thus, through their own obstinacy and rebellion, all that God had done in the way of showing them their duty proved fruitless, and they went on their way to ruin in spite of all that had been done to save them. Refusing to submit to an authority they were bound to obey, and turning petulantly and insolently away from a hand that sought to direct them for their good, they drew down on them great wrath and righteous retribution from Jehovah. As He had called, and they had refused to listen, so when they in their distress called on Him, He declared He would not hear them. As they would not submit to His hand for guidance, they were made to feel the weight of His hand in punishment. "Therefore it came to pass that, as He cried and they did not hear, so they cried and I would not hear, said Jehovah of hosts. And I scattered them with a whirlwind (violently tossed them) among all the nations whom they knew not (people foreign to them and strange), and the land was desolate after them, so that no one passed through nor returned" (so that there was no passing to and fro; no travelling through the land). The phrase מֵעֹבֵר וּמִשָּׁב lit. "from passing over and returning," occurs again (ix. 8); it seems to have been proverbial, and to refer to the going to and fro of persons for traffic or for social intercourse (cf. Ezek. xxxv. 7). A land so utterly forsaken that no one goes through it either on business or for pleasure is indeed desolate. The concluding clause is apparently the prophet's own remark: "And they made that pleasant land to be a desolation." Or the verb may be taken indeterminately, and, as it were, impersonally, and the phrase rendered, " So the pleasant land was made desolate;" thus Ewald and Maurer.

Thus while on the one hand the people were reproved for their formalism, and taught the vanity of all mere outward service, they were on the other warned against neglecting God's word, refusing to obey Him, casting off His control, and in sinful pride and self-willedness indulging their own tastes and passions, instead of following those courses which God had commended to them by His word.

X.

ISRAEL CHEERED.

"Again the word of the Lord of hosts came to me, saying, Thus saith the Lord of hosts; I was jealous for Zion with great jealousy, and I was jealous for her with great fury. Thus saith the Lord; I am returned unto Zion, and will dwell in the midst of Jerusalem: and Jerusalem shall be called a city of truth; and the mountain of the Lord of hosts the holy mountain. Thus saith the Lord of hosts; There shall yet old men and old women dwell in the streets of Jerusalem, and every man with his staff in his hand for very age. And the streets of the city shall be full of boys and girls playing in the streets thereof. Thus saith the Lord of hosts; If it be marvellous in the eyes of the remnant of this people in these days, should it also be marvellous in mine eyes? saith the Lord of hosts. Thus saith the Lord of hosts; Behold, I will save my people from the east country, and from the west country; and I will bring them, and they shall dwell in the midst of Jerusalem: and they shall be my people, and I will be their God, in truth and in righteousness. Thus saith the Lord of hosts; Let your hands be strong, ye that hear in these days these words by the mouth of the prophets, which were in the day that the foundation of the house of the Lord of hosts was laid, that the temple might be built. For before these days there was no hire for man, nor any hire for beast; neither was there any peace to him that went out or came in because of the affliction: for I set all men every one against his neighbour. But now I will not be unto the residue of this people as in the former days, saith the Lord of hosts. For the seed shall be prosperous; the vine shall give her fruit, and the ground shall give her increase, and the heavens shall give their dew; and I will cause the remnant of this people to possess all these things. And it shall come to pass, that as ye were a curse among the heathen, O house of Judah, and house of Israel; so will I save you, and ye shall be a blessing: fear not, but let your hands be strong. For thus saith the Lord of hosts; As I thought to punish you, when your fathers provoked me to wrath, saith the Lord of hosts, and I repented not: so again have I thought in these days to do well unto Jerusalem and to the house of Judah: fear ye not. These are the things that ye shall do; Speak ye every man the truth to his neighbour; execute the judgment of truth and peace in your gates: and let none of you imagine evil in your hearts against his neighbour; and love no false oath: for all these are things that I hate, saith the Lord. And the word of the Lord of hosts came unto me, saying, Thus saith the Lord of hosts; The fast of the fourth month, and the fast of the fifth, and the fast of the seventh, and the fast of the tenth, shall be to the house of Judah joy and gladness, and cheerful feasts; therefore love the truth and peace. Thus saith the Lord of hosts; It shall yet come to pass, that there shall come people, and the inhabitants of many cities: and the inhabitants of one city shall go to another, saying, Let us go speedily to pray before the Lord, and to seek the Lord of hosts: I will go also. Yea, many people and strong nations shall come to seek the Lord of hosts in Jerusalem, and to pray before the Lord. Thus saith the Lord of hosts; In those days it shall come to pass, that ten men shall take hold out of all languages of the nations, even shall take hold of the skirt of him that is a Jew, saying, We will go with you: for we have heard that God is with you."—ZECH. viii. 1-23.

IN this chapter we have the second part of the message which the prophet was commissioned to bear to the people, in answer to the application of the deputation from Bethel for advice as to the observance of certain fasts. In the former part the language is that of reproof and warning; in this it is that of consolation, exhortation, and encouragement. Having rebuked the people for their insincerity and formalism, and having reminded them of the sad consequences of neglecting God's messages and disobeying His commands, the prophet proceeds to depict the blessed effects of obedience, and conveys to the people God's gracious promise and assurance of a renewal of His favour to them; after which a direct answer is given to the question, the putting of which had given occasion for this message, and a prediction is uttered regarding the future glory of the kingdom of God, and the eagerness with which heathen nations should press into it. The chapter thus falls into two main divisions, each introduced by the phrase—" The word of Jehovah came to me ; " the former extending from ver. 1 to ver. 17 inclusive, the latter from ver. 18 to the end of the chapter. The former is again, after the introductory clause, subdivided into sections, each of which is marked by the words, " Thus saith Jehovah of hosts." The repetition of this formula at the beginning of each section is designed, doubtless, to assure the people that the great things here promised will surely come to pass, being certified to them by the word of Him whose covenant shall stand, and who will do all His pleasure.

The message begins by announcing the continued regard of the Lord for His chosen people, His return to dwell among them, and their return to Him in truth and purity. "Thus saith Jehovah of hosts, I am zealous for Zion with great zeal, and with great fury am I zealous for her." The verb here (the root-signification of which is apparently "to be red with heat") is used in Scripture —1. With an accusative of object, or with the preposition בְּ, in the sense of being jealous of another, as of a wife (Num. v. 14), or of a rival (Gen. xxx. 1), which meaning easily passes into that of envying; 2. With לְ in the sense of being ardently affected towards any object, either from loving regard (Num. xxv. 11–13 ; 2 Sam. xxi. 2 ; 2 Kings xix. 10), or in anger and displeasure (Gen. xxvi. 14 ; Ps. cvi. 16). The construction here is with לְ, and therefore it is better to render the verb by "zealous" than by "jealous." Because of the apostasy and iniquity of the people, God had suffered them to come under the power of the enemy ; but He had not utterly forsaken them; on the contrary, He still, as before, was zealously affected towards them, and His zeal for Zion, the place of His chosen habitation, was ardent and intense. The verb is in the perfect, but is more properly rendered in the present—" I am zealous," or with the force of the Greek perfect—" I have been and still am zealous."

God's zeal for Zion was His intense affection for His chosen people—His zeal for them and against their enemies. This He had towards them even whilst chastising them for their sins; and this He now especially showed in restoring them from captivity and returning to dwell among them. The expression, "I was jealous for her with great fury," as it is in the A. V., has been pressed by some to support the view that it is zeal against Zion that is here intimated, that wrath which the sins of the nation had excited, and which had brought on them the severe chastisement under which they had suffered. But the form of the phrase shows that it is zeal for Zion, not zeal against her, that is here in view, and the fury or wrath is that which God in His zeal for Zion directs against her enemies.

Zion had been polluted by the sins of the nation, and God had forsaken for a time His chosen place of rest. Ezekiel had seen in prophetic vision "The glory of the Lord depart from the temple, and from the midst of the city, and rest upon the mountain which is on the east side of the city" (Ezek. xi. 23), thereby indicating God's removal from Zion. But this was only for a season, and the end for which He had withdrawn having been accomplished, He had again returned to Zion. "Thus saith Jehovah: I am again returned unto Zion, and will dwell in the midst of Jerusalem" (ver. 3). And as He had returned to her, so should she be in sincerity and truth turned to Him. "And Jerusalem shall be called a city of truth; and the mountain of the Lord of hosts the holy mountain." In Scripture phraseology, "to be called" is "to be." As God creates when He calls, and as He calls only according to truth, so the name by which any thing or person is designated by Him expresses what that thing or person really is. Thus when it is said of the Messiah that His name shall be called Wonderful, Counsellor, &c., the meaning is that He shall really be what these epithets express; and so of the name Emmanuel, by which both the Prophet Isaiah and the Evangelist Matthew say the child born of the Virgin should be called—a name which our Lord never actually received, but which expresses what He really is—"God with us." Accordingly, when here Jerusalem is said to be called the city of truth, the meaning is that it shall really be the city of truth, that is, the place where truth shall dwell, the city of which truth shall be the characteristic. So elsewhere it is said of Jerusalem that she should be called "the city of Jehovah, the city of righteousness, the faithful city" (Isa. i. 26, lx. 14), and "the throne of Jehovah" (Jer. iii. 17) —appellations at no time really used of that city, but which express what was to be her peculiar character and dignity. As the city of truth, there should reign in her "everything opposite to untruth; faithfulness as opposed to faithlessness; sincerity as opposed to simulation; veracity as opposed to falsehood; honesty as opposed to untruth in act; truth of religion or faith as opposed to untrue doctrine" (Pusey). God is the God of truth, and the place where He dwells must be a place of truth. He had departed from Zion because of the falsehood and iniquity that had come to be there; when now He returned, it should be to a city in which truth should reign, and where He should be served in sincerity and truth. That such should be the character of the restored people had been announced by an earlier prophet: "The remnant of Israel shall not do iniquity, nor speak lies; neither shall a deceitful tongue be found in their mouth" (Zeph. iii. 13). And as God is the Holy One, so the place where He dwells is a place of holiness. "The mountain of the Lord"—the place where His temple stands, Mount Moriah, "shall be called—shall be the holy mountain." Such had ever been the appropriate designation of "the mountain of the Lord's house" (see Ps. ii. 6, iii. 4, xv. 1, xliii. 3, lxxxvii. 1; Isa. xi. 9, lvi. 7; Joel iii. 17, &c.); and what it had thus been called it should really be when Israel was restored. As had been foretold, "Upon mount Zion there should be holiness" (Obadiah 17), and when the Lord "had brought again this captivity" they should "use this speech in the land of Judah and in the cities thereof, The Lord shall bless thee, O habitation of justice, and mountain of holiness" (Jer. xxxi. 23). "Then should Jerusalem be holy, and no strangers ('aliens from the commonwealth of Israel, strangers from the covenants of promise,' unconsecrated and unclean) should pass through her any more" (Joel iii. 17; comp. Isa. xxxv. 8; Jer. li. 51; Zech. xiv. 21; Eph. ii. 12–19; Rev. xxi. 27).

As consequent on restored sanctity and spiritual privilege, an accession of temporal blessings is promised (vers.

4-6). "Thus saith the Lord of hosts, There shall yet old men and old women dwell [sit] in the streets of Jerusalem, each man with his staff in his hand from very age (lit. from multitude of days). And the streets of the city shall be full of boys and girls playing in the streets thereof" (vers. 4, 5). These words graphically depict a scene of peaceful serenity and happy enjoyment. Along the sides of the streets—on the shady side if the sun be hot, on the sunny side if the air be cool—sit the aged engaged in pleasant talk or resting in quiet meditation; while the children fill the open space, and make the street ring with their merry laugh or jubilant shouts. The aged here are represented as very aged, so aged that they cannot sit without leaning each on his staff; the design of the representation being to heighten as much as may be the picture of security which the scene presents. In all countries longevity, when it is found exceeding the ordinary average, may be regarded as indicating a healthful climate and a peaceful and prosperous state of society; and in Scripture longevity is frequently included among the special blessings which God promises to those who obey His law and keep His covenant. It is in accordance with this that the prophet here, in depicting the happy state of restored Jerusalem, introduces the old men and the old women as sitting (the verb is ישׁב, which means primarily *to sit*, only secondarily *to dwell*) in peace and quiet in the streets of the city; while the children, in the exuberance of their young life, pursue their sports without fear of interruption or harm. The "playing" here is to be taken in this sense, not as it has by some been interpreted, as a playing upon instruments in religious worship ("Targ. Jon."). This is not childlike, it is not true to nature; it introduces an uncongenial element into the picture, which is that of social serenity and joyousness, not that of religious service. The sports of childhood are the native and spontaneous outcome of the young, fresh life that is buoyant in those who have not yet felt the burden of life's cares, or been depressed by life's sorrows; and as St. Jerome remarks, "When cities are in security and profound peace, it is wont to happen that this sportive age celebrates the gladness of communities by plays and dances." A serene old age and a happy, joyous youth alike attest the goodness of God to men; "The tottering limbs of the very old and the elastic, perpetual motion of childhood are alike far distant chords of a diapason of the Creator's love" (Pusey).

When God promises blessing to His people they are entitled and bound confidently to expect a rich effusion of favour when He shall see meet to bestow what He has promised. But their highest anticipations are apt to come far short of what actually is brought to pass; so that to those who witness it the doing of the Lord is marvellous, and fills them with surprise. So God here says, "If it shall be marvellous in the eyes of the remnant of this people in those days, shall it be marvellous in My eyes? saith Jehovah of hosts" (ver. 6). By "the remnant of the people" is meant those who should be alive and remain at the time when this promise should be fulfilled, the time referred to as "those days" (בַּיָּמִים הָהֵם, not as in A. V., "in these days"; cf. Gen. vi. 4; Ex. ii. 11, &c.) To them the blessing received would appear so great as to excite their surprise; they would be ready to say, "We never expected it to be like this; we are like them that dream; the Lord hath done great things for us, whereof we are glad." But what should be thus wonderful in their eyes would be no marvel to God. To infinite wisdom and knowledge nothing can be strange; to infinite power nothing impossible or difficult. To Him who saith and it is done all things are easy; and whatever He purposes comes to pass as a matter of course in His own time. Events which fill men with wonder are to Him but the commonplaces of His omnipotence.

By some the latter part of this verse is taken not interrogatively, but as an assertion. Hitzig, who says that to construe this as a question is a mistake, interprets the whole thus: "If then when ye see it actually done it will appear to you still impossible, I also will hold it for impossible." But it is hardly possible to attach any tenable meaning to this. We cannot suppose that God means to say that if His work shall appear wonderful to men, it will also appear wonderful to Him, for to Him to whom all things are possible nothing can be wonderful; and however He may astonish men by what He does, His doings can never astonish Himself, being only what He has ever purposed to do. Nor can the meaning be, As it is impossible for Me to wonder at My own acts, so when this comes to pass it will be also impossible for those who witness it to wonder at it; for this is too insipid, not to say absurd, to be accepted. The interrogative rendering is the only one that gives a tolerable meaning; and though the sign of interrogation is wanting in the Hebrew, this is not of moment, for though interrogations are usually introduced by the particle ה, this is not indispensable;* and in one other passage (1 Sam. xxii. 7) we have גם in place of הגם in an interrogation.

Still further to assure the minds of the people, God reiterates His promise that He would restore the nation from their exile: "Behold Me! I am saving My people from the land of the rising, and from the land of the going down of the sun; and I will bring them, and they shall dwell in the midst of Jerusalem: and they shall be to Me a people, and I shall be to them a God, in truth and righteousness" (vers. 7, 8). As yet only a small portion of the people had returned from their state of exile. Zechariah prophesied in the earlier years of the return, and at least a century elapsed before the great body of the nation was brought back. God had showed His grace to them in that He had brought back those who were then engaged in repairing Jerusalem and rebuilding the temple; but this was not all that He would do for the nation. He was still carrying on the work of recovery,—this seems to be the force of the participle here after "behold," הִנְנִי מוֹשִׁיעַ, behold me saving,—and in due time He would complete it; the nation should be restored, and Jerusalem inhabited as of old. There is no reference here, as some have supposed, to a restoration of the Jews to Palestine from their present dispersion. The phrase, "from the land of the rising of the sun to the land of his going down," is a poetical expression for "from every place" (cf. Ps. l. 1; cxiii. 3). Wherever

---

* "Interrogative sentences require no interrogative particles specially to distinguish them" (Müller, "Outlines of Heb. Syntax," translated by Professor Robertson, 1882, p. 97).

the people had gone in their exile, thence should they be gathered and brought back to their own land. This promise was fulfilled when the mass of the nation came back from Babylonia and reoccupied the places from which their fathers had been driven—a people purified by trial, never again to apostatise from Jehovah. When Israel was subdued and carried captive to a strange land, and made to endure long years of exile and bondage, it might seem as if God had utterly cast them off and dissolved for ever the relation between Him and them as His chosen people. But when He should bring them back, it would be seen that this relation still subsisted: "They shall be to Me a people, and I will be to them a God, in truth and righteousness." These concluding words are to be connected with both parts of the preceding clause, and are meant to apply to both sides of the relation. On both sides there should be reality and sincerity. God is the God of truth and righteousness, and in relation to those whom He chooses to be His people He ever acts in truth and righteousness; and they on their part are required to be faithful to all their obligations to Him, and to be to Him in reality all that they profess to be. Before the exile they had as a nation sadly failed in this; God upbraids them by the prophet as a people that "swore by the name of the Lord and made mention of the God of Israel, but not in truth nor in righteousness" (Isa. xlviii. 1). But when they should be restored it would not be so. As He would be to them all that He engaged to be as their God, so should they be to Him a true and faithful people, serving Him in righteousness and truth.

In the verses that follow the prophet continues the strain of encouragement by reminding the people how God had already dealt graciously by them, and had fulfilled the promises He had given them by the prophets. "Thus saith the Lord of hosts: Let your hands be strong, ye that hear in these days these words from the mouths of the prophets, who were in the day of the founding of the house of Jehovah of hosts, the temple, that it might be built" (ver. 9). The prophets here referred to are Zechariah himself and Haggai, both of whom had spoken to the people words of admonition and encouragement at the time referred to, viz., the time when, after a pause and a season of inactive despondency, the work was resumed and the building of the temple from the new foundation was vigorously prosecuted. The words of these prophets the people whom Zechariah now addressed were hearing. Haggai, indeed, was now dead, but his words lived and were still sounding in their ears, and they were substantially the same as those which Zechariah now spoke (as may be seen by comparing Haggai i. 7 ff, ii. 15 ff, with Zech. vii. 8 ff). Both declared to the people that so long as they neglected the work of the Lord nothing prospered with them; but when they cast off indolence and ceased to care only for themselves, and applied themselves to the work to which they were called, all went well with them, and they prospered even in their material interests. While they allowed the temple to lie waste God did not smile upon them or bless them. "There was no hire for man nor any hire for beast;" their fields produced so little that neither man nor beast was hired to gather it in. They were so beset and encompassed with enemies that no one could with safety pass, for either business or pleasure, from one part to another; "there was no peace to him who went out or came in because of the adversary" (הַצָּר). They were torn also by internal dissension and strife; God had set all men every one against his neighbour. So it had been, but now it was different. "Now," says God by the prophet, "I will not be to the residue (the remnant, שְׁאֵרִית) of this people as in the former days." Now there should be the seed of peace, *i.e.*, not as the Chaldee paraphrast gives it, "the seed shall be safe," shall suffer no damage from any noxious influence; but that that from which peace springs should be sown in their land, so that peace (according to Hebrew conception the complex of all good) should be there not casually or transiently, but permanently, and not as an exotic brought in from without, but as the native product of the land; in contrast to the state of things in the former days, when there was no peace to him that came in or that went out because of the adversary. By most recent interpreters the phrase, "the seed of peace," is read in apposition with what follows—"the seed of peace, the vine," &c. But how can the vine be the seed of peace? Is it not rather the fruit of peace, seeing it is only in times of peace that its culture is attended to? If it be said, "This is precisely what the phrase means: the vine is the seed of peace because it is only in times of peace that it is sown," the reply is obvious: The vine is not raised from seed, but is propagated from suckers, or by cuttings, and therefore cannot even by metonymy be described as a seed. It is best to take the words,

"There shall be the seed of peace," as an independent clause, and what follows as illustrative of the condition thus affirmed. Seeing peace should be radically established in the land, the vine should give her fruit, and the ground should give its increase, &c. Now that the people were heartily engaged in the work of the Lord, the time to favour Zion had arrived; God would now give prosperity to the nation, and the remnant of the people should possess all the riches of that "goodly land" to which they had been restored.

Still further to encourage the people, God declares by the prophet that whereas the house of Judah and the house of Israel had been a curse among the heathen, they should be delivered and made a blessing (ver. 13). The house of Judah and the house of Israel are here joined together as partakers in common alike of the curse and of the blessing. As both had been carried into exile, and thus had been united in calamity, so both should be united in the restoration and be made to partake together of the blessing. One good effect of the captivity was that it reunited the severed portions of the chosen nation. They were no longer two peoples, but one. Many belonging to the ten tribes from time to time returned to Palestine from Babylon, and were amalgamated with the tribes of Judah and Benjamin as one nation. Thus united, as they had been a curse among the heathen, so were they to be a blessing. This does not mean that they had been a curse *to* the nations among whom they had been dispersed, for as they were commanded to seek the peace of the place whither they had been carried captive (Jer. xxix. 7), their residence among the heathen had been a source of advantage to the latter rather than the opposite; but the meaning is, that in the eyes of the heathen so miserable seemed the condition of the captive Hebrews that when imprecating evil upon any they were wont to wish that it might be with them as it was with the Hebrews. This is the force of the phrase, "to be a curse," or "to be taken up as a curse," as elsewhere used in Scripture (cf. 2 Kings xxii. 19; Isa. lxv. 15; Jer. xxiv. 9, xxvi. 6, xxix. 22, xlix. 13). So, on the other hand, their being a blessing among the heathen is to be understood not of their being a source of blessing to the nations, but of their becoming the norm or paradigm according to which blessing should be invoked (cf. Gen. xlviii. 20): they should be so prospered that it would become a common imprecation among the nations, May you be happy as these Jews are!

The assurance that God would deliver His people and give them prosperity and peace was well fitted to encourage those to whom it was addressed to persevere in the work to which they were called, notwithstanding the difficulties they had to encounter and the hostility of the adversaries by whom they were surrounded. To impress upon them more deeply this effect, the Lord by the prophet adds: "As I thought (purposed) to do evil to you [the nation as such (cf. Haggai ii. 5)], when your fathers provoked Me to wrath, saith the Lord of hosts, and I repented not: so again have I thought in these days to do good unto Jerusalem and to the house of Judah; fear ye not" (vers. 14, 15). Because of the sins of their fathers God had brought calamity upon the nation as He had purposed and threatened. To this purpose He had adhered; "He repented not." He had not retired or turned back from what He had purposed (cf. Jer. iv. 28); and they had been made to feel that His threatenings were not mere empty words of menace, but that He would certainly do what He had threatened. But no less certainly would His promise of blessing be fulfilled now that He had purposed to do them good. As He had threatened punishment and had punished, so now that He had promised blessing He would bless. Let them then take courage and fear not. With God as their Benefactor and Helper, they could not fail of success if they courageously and diligently prosecuted their work.

This assurance, however, like all similar promises, was conditioned by the people's being obedient and acting as God required. "These," says God, "are the things that ye shall do;" these are the things which, as to your fathers of old (see ch. vii. 9 ff.), so now to you I command. "The demonstrative אֵלֶּה intimates that what the prophet now proposes are instead of those fasts which of their own accord the Jews had appointed" (Rosenmüller). What is here supremely inculcated is *truth*—truth in the general in all their intercourse with each other, truth specially in judicial proceedings. Every man is to speak truth to his neighbour, both in common conversation and in their commercial transactions they are to say to each other exactly what is accordant with fact. And in the administration of justice, perfect equity is to regulate their decisions; those who act as judges in the gates of the cities where justice was wont to be administered are in all their proceedings to have regard to truth, and to seek to promote peace, striving to bring together those who are at variance, discouraging all merely litigious strifes, repressing all vexatious suits, and doing even-handed justice to all. They are enjoined also to bear no malice to others, and not to plan evil in their hearts to others, to make conscience of an oath, under no temptation to swear falsely, but to abhor all false oaths. It is noticeable how often at this time the prophet was commissioned to inculcate on the people a regard to the claims of truth and equity in their dealings with each other (cf. chap. i. 2–6, v. 2–4, vii. 8–13). These are the things that God requires, and the opposite of which He hates.

The prophet has now finished the message of reproof, warning, and encouragement which he was commissioned to bear to the people. He proceeds to answer the question about the fasts, the putting of which had been the occasion of this message. The answer he had to give is substantially that these fasts should not be any longer observed, but should rather be turned into occasions of rejoicing and thanksgiving; the fast should become a festival, the day of mourning a day of gladness, and the painful reminiscences of the past be exchanged for joyful recognition of blessing in the present, and anticipation of still higher blessing in the future. (For the fasts themselves, see chap. ix., pp. 117, 118.) Occasion is taken at the same time to press on the people still further attention to the Divine requirements, alike from a sense of obligation for good already received, and from a regard to their own welfare, inasmuch as only as they sought truth and peace could they hope to secure enjoyment of the Divine favour and blessing. The prophet goes on to assure them that thus continuing in obedience they should receive so rich a blessing that surrounding nations should earnestly desire to participate in their felicity. Notwithstanding the desolation that had come on Jerusalem, and the low estate to which the people had been reduced, there should yet (עד emphatic) be seen many of other nations hastening to join in the observance of those sacred festivals that had come in the place of the fasts they had kept during the season of calamity. The inhabitants of one city should be found saying to those of another, "We will go indeed ('omnes uno et magno studio,' Ros.) to entreat the Lord (cf. chap. vii. 2), and to seek the Lord; and in response another will say, I also will go." Ten—*i.e.*, many (cf. Gen. xxxi. 7; Lev. xxvi. 26; Num. xiv. 22)—men of all languages of the nations (from all parts of the world) should take hold of the skirt of one that is a Jew, one who was going up to the feast, and to worship, saying, We will go with you, for we have heard that God is with you. "As one who desires to go with another, and will not allow himself to be easily put off, is wont to seize hold of the garment of that other, so also men of all nations should determine to be associated with the Jews" (Ros., cf. 1 Sam. xv. 27; Haggai ii. 12 for the figure).

That this refers in the first instance to the fact that proselytes should come from all parts to join themselves to the people of God, and to worship at Jerusalem, hardly admits of a doubt. But it is only in gospel times, and under the reign of the Messiah, that this prediction in its full import can be fulfilled. As the Prophet Isaiah had foretold that "the mountain of the Lord's house should be established on the top of the mountains, and all nations should flow into it" (Jer. ii. 2; cf. chap. lxvi. 20 ff.); and as Micah had foretold that "many nations should come and say, Come, let us go up to the mountain of the Lord and to the house of the God of Jacob, and He will teach us of His ways, and we will walk in His paths" (Mic. iv. 2); so here the prophet represents the nations as eagerly seeking admission into that kingdom of God, and men of every nation as stimulating each other to the pious quest, and eagerly laying hold of the Jew, that along with him and by his help they may obtain the blessing of God's favour. "The literal fulfilment of such passages," it has been justly remarked, "is a sheer impossibility."* During the centuries succeeding the restoration of the Jews to their own land, there were indeed multitudes of proselytes who came out of heathendom and joined themselves to the God of Israel; but nothing corresponding to the descriptions of these prophets ever happened so long as the Jewish state lasted. Nor is any literal fulfilment of these predictions to be desired. What the prophets teach us to desire and expect is the conversion of the nations by a spiritual turning unto the Lord, through the proclamation among them of the glad tidings of salvation. Then in the one possible sense shall men of all nations lay hold of the Jew ("for salvation is of the Jews"), and then shall the nations be gathered with the ancient

* Wright, "Zechariah and his Prophecies," p. 194.

people of God into one fold under one Shepherd. It is but an idle conceit of St. Jerome that by the Jew here, on whom many were to lay hold, is meant the Lord Jesus Christ, who, when He appeared here on earth, was of the seed of Abraham. Our Lord, it is true, was in outward relations a Jew; but it was not as a Jew, but as the Man, who "forasmuch as the children are partakers of flesh and blood, also himself likewise took part of the same," that Jesus, Incarnate God, being lifted up, is to draw all men unto Him. "He is our peace," the Shiloh of the race, and to "him shall the gathering of the nations be."

XI.

ENEMIES REBUKED.

"The burden of the word of the Lord in the land of Hadrach, and Damascus shall be the rest thereof: when the eyes of man, as of all the tribes of Israel, shall be toward the Lord. And Hamath also shall border thereby; Tyrus, and Zidon, though it be very wise. And Tyrus did build herself a strong hold, and heaped up silver as the dust, and fine gold as the mire of the streets. Behold, the Lord will cast her out, and he will smite her power in the sea; and she shall be devoured with fire. Ashkelon shall see it, and fear; Gaza also shall see it, and be very sorrowful, and Ekron; for her expectation shall be ashamed; and the king shall perish from Gaza, and Ashkelon shall not be inhabited. And a bastard shall dwell in Ashdod, and I will cut off the pride of the Philistines. And I will take away his blood out of his mouth, and his abominations from between his teeth: but he that remaineth, even he, shall be for our God, and he shall be as a governor in Judah, and Ekron as a Jebusite. And I will encamp about mine house because of the army, because of him that passeth by, and because of him that returneth: and no oppressor shall pass through them any more; for now have I seen with mine eyes."
—ZECH. ix. 1-8.

WITH this ninth chapter begins the *second* part of the book, or, as some (reckoning chapters vii. and viii. as forming a separate prophecy) regard it, the *third* part. This differs so widely not only as respects subject-matter, but also in regard to language, style, and general contour and method from the earlier portion of the book, that to many it has appeared impossible to regard the two as productions of the same writer. Into this question, however, it is not necessary to enter here, as the interpretation of what is written does not depend on our ascertaining by whom it was written.

This latter part of the book, as it stands in the Canon, is divisible into four sections—the first containing ch. ix. and ch. x.; the second, ch. xi.; the third, ch. xii. and ch. xiii.; and the fourth, ch. xiv.

In the first eight verses of ch. ix. the overthrow of the nations and tribes hostile to Israel is threatened, while the people of God are assured of His protection and care. Zion and Jerusalem are then summoned to hail with exultation the advent of the Great King, who shall not only deliver His people from all hostile assault, but shall also raise them to the highest pitch of felicity, glory, and power, so that all their enemies shall fear before them (vers. 9–17). The general purport of the prophetic utterance is clear, though considerable obscurity attaches to some of the expressions used.

"The burden of the word of Jehovah in the land of Hadrach" (ver. 1). The phrase, "the burden of Jehovah," like the phrase the burden of or concerning some place or people which so frequently occurs as the title of the Divine utterances by the prophets, implies that the utterance is a weighty word, a word that is not empty and vain, but full of import, and that coming forth from the Lord, "shall not return unto Him void, but shall accomplish that whereto He hath sent it," and shall rest as a burden on those against whom it is directed. The word rendered by "burden" (מַשָּׂא, massa) is derived from a verb which signifies to lift up (נָשָׂא), and may be used of anything that is lifted up or carried. Thus it is used of the lifting up of the voice in song (1 Chron. xv. 22, 27);

and of instructions or counsels laid upon one to be borne by him (Prov. xxx. 1, xxxi. 1). Generally, however, it is used for load or burden laid on one, and so of a prophetic utterance of a minatory character; for as this comes forth as something sent upon those against whom it is directed, it is properly a burden which they have to bear. It has, indeed, been contended that the word is used of utterances which are not minatory, and from this it has been concluded that it means nothing more than "utterance" simply. But the only instances adduced of its being used of a favourable utterance are Zech. xii. 1 and Mal. i. 1, neither of which is conclusive. It is a mistake, indeed, to regard the utterance in Mal. i. as other than minatory, and that in Zech. xii. 1, though in its ultimate aspect favourable to Israel, nevertheless comes on Israel as a burden from the Lord, inasmuch as it represents Israel as itself suffering and in danger of being involved in the destruction of the people in its vicinity, and the house of David and inhabitants of Jerusalem as returning to the Lord from whom they had apostatised with deep mourning and bitter sorrow. The word *massa* is never used of those purely joyful messages which the prophets sometimes had to bring to the people of Israel.

The object of this burden is the land of Hadrach and Damascus, on (בְּ) the former of which the burden falls, and on the latter it rests. The term Hadrach occurs only here in Scripture, and many conjectural explanations have been offered of it. It has been suggested that it is a compound of חַד, *sharp*, and רַךְ, *tender, delicate*, and is descriptive of this prophetic utterance which is "severe to

the Gentiles and tender to Israel" (" R. Judah ben Elai,"*
cited by Pusey), or is a symbolical designation of an
object in which these two qualities are united, which in
one relation is "sharp" and in another "soft"—a symbol
according to some of the Persians, who were at once
fierce and voluptuous (Hengstenberg, "Christology," III.
379), and whose empire Alexander the Great was engaged
in subverting at the time to which this prophecy relates.
Some of the Jewish expositors understand it of the
Messiah, "who is to guide (להוריך) all who come into
the world by repentance before God" ("Midrash Shir
Hasshirim," cited by Pusey). Gesenius, Bleek, and others
regard it as the name of some Syrian king reigning at
Damascus; and others as the name of some idol deity
worshipped in that region. To all these explanations
serious objections have been urged, and they are now
universally renounced. The words of the text as they
stand naturally suggest that Hadrach is the name of a
place, and this, which Kimchi tells us was at an early
period asserted by R. Jose, "the son of a Damascus
woman," and has been reiterated by subsequent Jewish
expositors, and which some of the early Christian fathers
also maintained, has now been established as the true explanation. In the Assyrian inscriptions mention frequently
occurs of a city and region in the vicinity of Damascus
called Ha-ta-ri-ka, to which expeditions were sent (Smith,
"Assyrian Discoveries," p. 276; "Records of the Past,"
vol. v. pp. 46, 51; Pusey, "Min. Proph.," p. 550); and
this there can be no doubt is the Hadrach of this passage.

---

* A disciple of R. Akiba, Wolf, "Bibl. Heb." I. p. 411 (not II. 690, as given by Pusey).

The oldest explanation has thus in this case, as not infrequently in others, turned out to be the true one.

While the burden was to light upon Hadrach, its resting-place was to be Damascus. The meaning of this is that the Divine wrath, of which this oracle was the missive, should come down in heavy judgments on that city. Most commonly the term rest, or resting-place (מְנוּחָה), is used of quiet, peaceful resting, as that of "the ark of the covenant of the Lord" after its many removals (1 Chron. xxviii. 2), and that given by God to His people (cf. Deut. xii. 9; Ps. xxiii. 2, xcv. 11; Isa. xxviii. 12, xxxii. 18; Micah ii. 10, &c.); and so the Targumist takes it here: "And Damascus shall be turned so as to be of the land of the house of His majesty," *i.e.*, part of the land in which is the temple, the house of Jehovah. But with this the general tenor of the prophecy does not accord; it is not a message of blessing, but of judgment; and consequently the resting of the oracle on Damascus must indicate that as the place on which the judgment is to fall and abide. So in Ezek. v. 13 God says in reference to the judgment He was about to send on Jerusalem: "I will cause My fury to rest upon them." Not that on Damascus alone was the judgment to fall, but in that course of judgments which this prophecy announces Damascus and its surroundings should be the first to suffer.

In the words that follow a reason is assigned why on Damascus and the land of Hadrach the Divine judgment was to fall. Literally, the words are: "Because to Jehovah [is] the eye of man and all the tribes of Israel." This may mean either, as the A. V. has it, that the eyes of men generally, as well as of the tribes of Israel, are directed to Jehovah, or that Jehovah has an eye which is upon or over all men, as well as on or over the tribes of Israel. The former of these is what the words, as they stand, most readily suggest; but though grammatically justifiable, it seems to be excluded by the context, for the fact that all men look to the Lord can be no reason why judgment should come on any particular portion of mankind. The notion of some Jewish interpreter, that this refers to the conversion of the Gentiles and their union with the Jews in the worship of Jehovah, though apparently adopted by Pusey, is wholly foreign to the general strain of this context, and has had few supporters. The latter rendering is that generally adopted by interpreters. The Lord has an eye not only on the tribes of Israel, but also on men universally; He not only watches over Israel for good, but He watches the doings and the ways of the heathen that He may deal with them as is meet; He sees all their perversity, ungodliness, and wickedness; and consequently, when fitting occasion comes, sends His judgments upon them. So He had observed Damascus and the other places referred to in this oracle; and as the time of their visitation had come, His "burden" came forth and rested upon them.

With Damascus and the land of Hadrach is joined Hamath: "And Hamath also shall border thereby;" rather, "And Hamath also which borders thereon," *i.e.*, the burden rests not only on Damascus, but also on Hamath, which is conterminous with it. Hamath is a name of frequent occurrence in the Old Testament. It is the name of a city, the capital of a district lying to the north of Damascus. This city may be regarded as one of the oldest in the world; mention is made of it repeatedly as on the northern border of Canaan at the time the Israelites entered to take possession of that land (Num. xiii. 21, xxxiv. 8; Josh. xiii. 5, &c.); and from Gen. x. 18 it would appear it was founded by the youngest son of Canaan, the son of Noah. By the Greeks it was called Epiphaneia, in honour of Antiochus Epiphanes; but, like many other places in that country, it resumed its ancient appellation, and still subsists under the name of Hamah. Coupled with Damascus and the land of Hadrach, here it forms a group which may be regarded as representing Syria.

From Syria the oracle passes to Phœnicia, the two principal cities of which, Tyre and Sidon, are especially mentioned. Though Sidon was the older city of the two, it had become so entirely subordinate to Tyre that it is not only named after it, but appears as a mere appendage to it (cf. Ezek. xxvii. 8). This may account for the use of the singular pronoun here in the concluding clause, "Tyre and Sidon, though she be very wise." Tyre boasted her wisdom, *i.e.* her knowledge and skill—not the higher wisdom, the wisdom of moral goodness, but worldly wisdom, the wisdom to gather wealth and excel in material resources, to acquire power and surpass in fame. Such wisdom Tyre largely had. As the prophet goes on here to say, "Tyre did build herself a stronghold, and heaped up silver as dust, and fine gold as mire of the streets" (ver. 3). To the same effect Ezekiel says of Tyre (ch. xxviii. 4, 5)—" By thy wisdom and thine understanding thou hast acquired power, and filled thy treasures with gold and silver; by thy great wisdom in thy commerce hast thou obtained great power, and thy heart has exalted itself because of thy power" (comp. also ver. 12 and ver. 17).

Tyre had "built for herself a stronghold," or fortification. The word here used by the prophet is *mâtsôr* (מָצוֹר), which signifies a mound or bulwark, a fortress or fortification, but also distress, siege. It may have been with reference to this secondary meaning of the word that it was chosen here; but more probably it was only because of its assonance with Tyre that it was selected: "*Tsôr* built for herself *mâtsôr.*" This refers to the new walls with which the Tyrians had surrounded their city after the withdrawal of the Babylonians, by whom the former walls had been thrown down, and especially to the defences of the new city which they had built on an adjacent island, and which they had surrounded with a wall of extraordinary strength. These fortifications Tyre had constructed "for herself"; the לָהּ here is emphatic; it was solely for herself, for the protection of her inhabitants and the security of her treasures, that she erected these fortifications. And as it was by the skill and energy of her own people that these vast defences were constructed, she was proud of them, and boasted of them, and confided in them. Her internal resources also were immense: "She heaped up silver as dust, and fine gold as mire of the streets;" by her widely-extended commerce, which not only visited both shores of the Mediterranean, but sent her ships into the most distant seas, from India to Britain, she drew to herself the riches of the world.* Thus strong without and within, she thought herself secure, and proudly defied assault. But her ruin was already at hand; and here the prophet announces, as Isaiah, Amos, and Ezekiel had done before him (Isa. xxiii. 1 ff.; Amos i. 9; Ezek. xxvii. 26 ff.), her impending downfall. "Behold, the Lord shall cast her out," shall dispossess her—the word used is the same as is used in reference to the casting out of the Canaanites from before Israel (Ex. xxxiv. 24; Num. xxxii. 21; Deut. iv. 38, &c.); it conveys primarily the idea of ousting from a possession so as to make way for its passing to the occupancy of another; but it is also used in the sense of simply depriving, as in 1 Sam. ii. 5, where it means "impoverish," and some have so taken it here—"The Lord shall impoverish thee," as if it were said, Notwithstanding thine immense wealth thou shalt be made poor. "And He will smite her power in the sea;" that is, either will strike down her fortifications and cast them into the sea, or will, even in the sea to which she trusted for security, destroy her defences and scatter her wealth. The latter seems the preferable interpretation. Tyre thought herself safe because of her insular position, and scorned the attempt of the Macedonian conqueror to take her, asking "if he thought to prevail against Neptune"; but even in the sea God would smite her strength: 'The scene of her pride was to be that of her overthrow; the waves which girt her round should bury her ruins and wash over her site" (Pusey). Her fortress and her wealth should be cast into the sea, and she herself should "be devoured with fire."

* See Kenrick's "Phœnicia," chap. vi.; comp. Ezek. xxvii.

ENEMIES REBUKED.

Passing along the coast of the Mediterranean southwards, the prophet comes next to Philistia with its principal cities, Ashkelon, Gaza, Ekron, and Ashdod. So long as Tyre continued in strength and power the people of these cities thought themselves safe. Tyre was, as it were, a bulwark for them against the invader. But when Tyre fell they were at the mercy of the enemy. Then their confidence vanished and their hope was lost. Ashkelon should see and fear—*tayray, wetira'*, the seeing and the fear would be simultaneous; Gaza should see it and quake exceedingly, writhing like a woman in travail; Ekron also should see and be afraid, for her hope, her expectation of protection and security, shall be put to shame; from Gaza the king should perish, Gaza should no more have a king; Ashkelon should cease to be inhabited; a mongrel race (מַמְזֵר, one spurious, a bastard, the child of parents not lawfully connected, or of a mixed marriage, as of an Israelite with a heathen), a foreign and impure race, "a rabble" (Hengstenberg), should dwell in Ashdod; and the pride of the Philistines should be cut off; with the destruction of their power, the overthrow of their strong cities, and the rooting out of their nationality, all on which their pride as a nation was based, should be taken away, and their pride itself should be forever at an end. Their religion also should be abolished. Personifying the Philistian nation, God says of it by the prophet, "I will take away his blood out of his mouth, and his abominations from between his teeth," *i.e.*, will take away from them their idolatry and put an end to their idolatrous rites and usages. The "abominations" here referred to (שִׁקּוּצִים) are the sacrifices which they offered to their idols, and in connection with these the "blood" must be understood of the blood of the sacrifices which the heathen were wont to drink mingled with wine (cf. Ps. xvi. 4), or which they ate with the flesh of the sacrificial victim. The taking away of these implies the abolition of the religion of which they were the symbols and expression. Not utterly, however, should the Philistines be destroyed; of them as well as of Israel a remnant should be left, and that remnant should be turned to the Lord, should become His, and be incorporated with His people: "But he that remaineth, even he shall be for our God," rather, "And he also shall remain for our God,"—of the Philistines as well as of Israel there should be a remnant which should belong to the God of Israel; "and he," the people viewed as one man, "shall be as a governor," a chiliarch, a captain of a thousand, "in Judah, and Ekron shall be as a Jebusite." Philistia was the ancient and inveterate enemy of Israel, and the persistent upholder of idolatry in the immediate vicinity of the nation among whom Jehovah had set His name: and all the earlier prophets down to the time of the return from Babylon utter only denunciations of wrath and ruin against the Philistines. But God here declares that in Philistia also, though its people were to be subjugated and its cities destroyed, there should be a remnant which should be for God, should renounce idolatry, and become worshippers of the God of Israel. Thus turned to the Lord, the remnant of the Philistines should be merged in Judah, and become as one of the tribes of Israel (the chiliarch here being not the chief alone as an individual, but the chief with his tribe); and Ekron should be as a Jebusite, *i.e.* just as of old when Israel took possession of the promised land, the Jebusites were not extirpated with the rest of the Canaanitish peoples, but continued to "dwell with the children of Judah at Jerusalem," the very heart and centre of the Israelitish community, so should the Ekronites, as representing the Philistian remnant, dwell in the midst of Judah, incorporated with its people and united with them in the worship of Jehovah. The force, moreover, of the "also" here must not be overlooked; it implies that what is here affirmed of Philistia applies no less to Syria and Phœnicia, the lands and places previously mentioned; they too should be merged in Judæa, and the remnant of their peoples should be turned to the Lord.

That this prophecy, in the first instance, relates to the judgments which fell upon Syria, Phœnicia, and Philistia in the march of Alexander the Great from Asia Minor to Egypt hardly admits of a doubt. "The selection of the places, and of the whole line of country, corresponds very exactly to the march of Alexander after the battle of Issus, when the capture of Damascus, which Darius had chosen as the strong depository of his wealth, of Persian women of rank, confidential officers and envoys,* opened Cœle-Syria, Zidon surrendered; Tyre was taken with great effort after a seven months' siege;† Gaza, too, resisted for five months, was taken, and, it is said, plucked up. . . . History gives no other explanation of Zechariah's prophecy than this conquest by

---

* Grote's "History of Greece," xii. 173-4.
† Diod. Sic., xvii., 40-45.

Alexander; that conquest agrees minutely with the prophecy. No other event in history does."* Nor is it only in the general that this prophecy has been fulfilled; in several minute particulars the event corresponds to the prediction. Damascus was subjugated, but not destroyed; Tyre was utterly overthrown, its stronghold cast into the sea, and the city consumed by fire; Gaza was taken by storm, and left without a king; Ashkelon was thrown into ruins, and ceased to be inhabited; and in Ashdod a mongrel race grew up, and a rabble from different peoples occupied it (Neh. xiii. 24, 25). The historical fulfilment of the latter part of the prophecy is not so obvious; when, how, or to what extent the people of these districts became merged in the nation of the Jews we have no means of precisely determining. We know, however, (1) That many proselytes to Judaism were made from among these peoples, especially those of Philistia (Joseph. "Antiq.," xiii. 15. 4); (2) That after the return from Babylonia many of the Jews settled in Philistia, intermarriages took place between the Jews and the Philistines, and the two peoples gradually assimilated in manners and religion; (3) That in the time of our Lord the Philistines were no longer known as a separate nation, but what remained of them was mixed up with the Jews, or formed part of the undistinguishable population of the country; and (4) That the name Philistia, originally the designation only of the country of the Philistines, came to be accepted, under the form of Palestina, as the name of the whole land, which could not have been done had the district of Philistia remained

---

* Pusey, "Daniel the Prophet," p. 277-8.

the territory of a separate and heathen race hostile to the Jews. In this part of the prophecy, therefore, we have a prediction of what actually came to pass in later times as exact as (to use the words of Hengstenberg*) is consistent with the permanent distinction between prophecy and history.

But whilst calamity was thus impending on the cities of the heathen, the people of God are assured that under His protection they should be safe: " And I will encamp for My house from an army, from him that passeth through and him that returneth; and no oppressor shall pass over them any more; for now have I seen with My eyes" (ver. 8). By the house of Jehovah here is to be understood not the temple, but the people, the nation of Israel, the house of Israel, which was also the house of the Lord (cf. Num. xii. 7; Jer. xii. 7; Hos. viii. 1, ix. 15). For this, for its good and protection (*dat. commodi*), God would pitch a camp from an army (צבה the same as צבא), *i.e.*, either on account of, or, taking the verb in a pregnant sense, encamp so as to protect from an army. The phrase, "him that passeth through, and him that returneth," has reference to going to and fro in a country for any purpose whatever (Ezek. xxxv. 7; Zech. vii. 14); here it refers to the passing and repassing of an armed force. Not only should Israel be protected against this invasion, but no longer should an oppressor have dominion over them; Egypt, Assyria, Babylon, and now Persia had oppressed Israel, but henceforward they were to be free from such tyranny. "For now have I seen," says God,

---

* "Christology," iii. 369.

"with My eyes." The "now" here refers to the time when God should interpose for His people. "This may be explained from the general character of prophecy, in which the future is regarded as present; so that where definite announcements are made, it is not the actual, but the ideal, present which is intended." * God is said to see when He comes forth to act; His eyes are ever "in every place, beholding the evil and the good" (Prov. xv. 3); but it is only when He actively interferes in the affairs of men that His inspection of them is made manifest to men (cf. Jer. vii. 11).

The army against which God would protect His people is the army that should overrun and subjugate the provinces of Syria, Phœnicia, and Philistia—that of the Macedonian invader. In pursuing this route Alexander "passed by" Judea in the first instance without attacking it; but after the fall of Gaza he turned and advanced to Jerusalem, intending to inflict severe chastisement on it for the refusal of his demand of aid from the Jews against Tyre, and the transfer of their allegiance from the Persian monarch to him. From this purpose he was turned by the submission of the Jews, who, headed by their high priest, went forth in procession to meet and salute the conqueror. Alexander advanced alone to meet the procession, and respectfully saluted the high priest. The result was, that not only did he leave the city untouched, but he entered into relations of amity with the Jews, relieved them from the Persian oppressor, and took them under his protection. Thus remarkably was this

---

* Hengstenberg, "Christology," iii. 395.

prediction fulfilled—a prediction given by the prophet for the encouragement of the people to whom he delivered it, and the fulfilment of which affords one amongst the many evidences which the Old Testament prophecies supply of the Divine mission of the ancient prophets of Israel.

XII.

APPROACHING DELIVERANCE.

"Rejoice greatly, O daughter of Zion; shout, O daughter of Jerusalem: behold, thy King cometh unto thee: he is just, and having salvation; lowly, and riding upon an ass, and upon a colt the foal of an ass. And I will cut off the chariot from Ephraim, and the horse from Jerusalem, and the battle-bow shall be cut off: and he shall speak peace unto the heathen: and his dominion shall be from sea even to sea, and from the river even to the ends of the earth."
—ZECH. ix. 9, 10.

IT is not unusual in the utterances of the prophets to find predictions of calamity and woe followed by announcements of special triumph and felicity in connection with the people of God, and especially with the realisation of "the hope of Israel," the advent and kingdom of the Messiah. As it was in Him that all the blessings promised to Israel as a nation were secured; as all they had to expect of blessing rested on the fact that they were the people among whom the promised Deliverer was to appear, He was never far from the thoughts of the prophets when they had to speak of the future of Israel or of the world at large as the sphere of that kingdom which He as the King of Israel was to establish. "It was usual," as Calvin observes (Comment. in Jas. vii. 14–16), "with the prophets, in order to confirm special promises, to lay this as the foundation—that God would send a Redeemer. On this general prop God everywhere rests whatever He specially promises to His people.

Hence, as often as mention is made of famine, pestilence, or war, it is by placing the Messiah before their eyes that He seeks to inspire in them the hope of relief." So here. The prophet, after announcing the overthrow of the heathen cities and the turning of the remnant of the heathen to the Lord, conveys to the people of God the comforting assurance that He will protect His house against the advancing destroyer, and will deliver them from the oppressor; and then summons them to hail the advent of the Great King who is coming to Jerusalem, and who will establish His reign of peace and blessing all over the world.

Rapt into the future, the prophet sees the King whose advent he announces approaching, and he calls upon the daughter of Zion, the daughter of Jerusalem, to come forth with bounding exultation and shouts of triumph to behold and welcome her King. The daughter of Zion, the daughter of Jerusalem, are poetical expressions for the people of the covenant, the people of Jehovah, whose dwelling-place is Zion, and whose throne is in Jerusalem, the mother city of which the inhabitants, viewed collectively, are regarded as the child. Their joy on this occasion is to be expressed alike by gestures of delight (גִּיל, *to leap for joy*) and acclamations of triumph (הָרִיעַ, *to make a loud noise, to shout for joy*).

The person whose advent the daughter of Zion is summoned thus exultingly to hail is described as emphatically *her* King—" Behold *thy* King cometh unto thee " —He who alone stands to thee in that relation, whom alone thou art to reverence and obey, and from whom alone blessing can come to thee. The foreign prince whose assault she had dreaded had proved a friend, and had brought her deliverance; but he was not her king; he and his army had passed away; now her own proper King was coming and bringing with Him permanent deliverance and blessing. His character also is such as to command esteem and procure for Him welcome. He is described as "Just," that is, Righteous (צַדִּיק). This refers to His personal character as well as to His official conduct; nor, indeed, can the one be separated from the other, for when a ruler is not himself righteous, it is not to be expected that righteousness will characterise his administration. The King of Zion is first of all "the Righteous One." Righteousness is the primary attribute of His person, and righteousness characterises His administration, which is conducted on principles of the purest and most unbending rectitude. He is described further as "saved." This is the only legitimate rendering of the word which in the A. V. is rendered by "having salvation," a rendering which, though in accordance with that of the ancient versions (LXX, σώζων, Vulg. *salvator*, Chald. פָּרִיק, Syr. *poriqo*), is precluded alike by the form of the word (נוֹשָׁע, the niph'al participle) and the usage of the word elsewhere in the Old Testament. The participle only occurs in two other passages besides this; but the preterite and imperfect of the same form frequently occur, and always with the passive signification proper to that form. The two passages in which the participle is found are Deut. xxx. 29—"O people saved by the Lord," and Ps. xxxiii. 16—"There is no king saved by the multitude of an host." In both these passages the word is used in a modified sense, and this may guide to the explanation of it here. When it is said, "a king is not saved by the multitude of an host," the meaning can only be that he is not thereby delivered from defeat; in other words, it is not by this that he is secure of victory. So when it is said of Israel that it is "a people saved by the Lord," the saving predicated is that of deliverance from evil, protection against assault, sustenance in vigour and prosperity. In either of these modifications the word may be taken here: either we may read, "Thy King cometh unto thee righteous and victorious;" or we may read, "Thy King cometh unto thee righteous and protected, or sustained." In the former case the meaning is that the King here announced should not only be righteous in His claims and in the internal administration of His kingdom, but also victorious over all His adversaries, and so able to protect and save His people. In the latter case the meaning is, that being righteous in His claims and administration, He should be protected and sustained by God, so as to be fully able to hold His throne and to maintain order and peace among His subjects. The latter interpretation is on the whole to be preferred because in keeping with other prophetic representations in which the great King of Zion is represented as helped and sustained by Jehovah.*

Not, however, in pomp and with the apparatus of warlike force should He appear. When He came it would be as one humble and depressed, and riding upon

---

* It is, however, not to be overlooked that not only do the ancient versions take the verb as having an active signification, but many of the Jewish interpreters give it this meaning, and it is possible from the analogy of other words that it may have this meaning. Compare נכסף, Gen. xxxi 30; Ps. lxxxiv. 3, נשבע, *to swear*, lit. *to be sevened.*

an ass. "Lowly" in the A. V. hardly expresses the force of the original. The LXX, indeed, render by πραΰς, *meek, mild, gentle*, but the Hebrew word עָנִי has reference to condition rather than to character or disposition. It denotes lowliness in the sense of depression, poverty, or affliction. Elsewhere in the A. V. it is almost invariably rendered by "poor" or "afflicted." In keeping with this is the representation that He should come "riding on an ass even" (or, to wit; the ו here is not the mere copula, but is exegetical, as in Gen. xiii. 15; 1 Sam. xvii. 40), "on a colt the foal of an ass," *i.e.* not one carefully trained, but one as yet rough and unbroken. Time was when to ride on an ass was deemed not incompatible with the dignity of a chief (cf. Gen. xxii. 3; Judges v. 10, x. 4); and in the East at the present day the ass is held in much higher estimation than with us, and is, because of its sure-footedness and the ease of its paces, still used even by men of the highest rank. Not, however, on occasions of state is the ass used by persons of eminence; on such occasions the humblest pasha would consider himself degraded if he appeared otherwise than on horseback. The same feeling doubtless prevailed in Judæa in the time of Zechariah, for after Solomon had made the keeping of a stud of horses an appanage of royalty, the horse became in Judæa the animal not only of war, but of state and dignity (cf. Jer. xvii. 25); and it is worthy of note that in the account of those who returned from Babylon to Judæa with Zerubbabel and Joshua, it is mentioned that they had horses with them to the number of 736 (Ezra ii. 66; Neh. vii. 68). The coming of the King, then, to

Zion on an ass's colt betokened His humble condition, and the state of poverty in which He was to appear. There is, however, something more than this indicated. The horse was the animal of war, the ass was the animal of peace. In coming therefore on the latter rather than the former, it is indicated that the King would come to Zion as a peaceful one—one who should win, and keep, and administer His Kingdom, not by physical force or the power of the sword, but by means of a wholly different character. And that this is what the representation was designed most prominently to suggest appears probable from what follows: "And I will cut off the chariot from Ephraim, and the horse from Jerusalem, and the battle bow shall be cut off; and He shall speak peace unto the heathen, and His dominion shall be from sea even unto sea, and from the river to the ends of the earth" (ver. 10). By some the first part of this verse is regarded as a prediction of the downfall of the Jewish state through the overthrow of its warlike power. But this is not what the words in this connection naturally suggest. Rather do they intimate, in accordance with the symbolical character of the whole representation, the repudiation for the King here announced of all physical force for the maintenance and administration of His kingdom. The chariot, the horse, the battle bow are all implements of war or defence, and symbols of outward force (Ps. xx. 7, xxxiii. 17, xliv. 6; Hosea ii. 18; Micah v. 10); and the elimination of these from a kingdom indicates the entire absence from it of any such means and methods of defence or administration. God would remove from Ephraim and Jerusalem—that is, from the entire united

Israel, over which the King here announced was to reign —all emblems and instruments of outward force, so that by other means than these should the King maintain His authority and sustain His empire. Nor was it only within His kingdom that peace should reign: "to the heathen," to the nations at large, should the King "speak peace." This means not that He should authoritatively command the nations to be at peace, or practically enforce on them the peace of "the ideal theocratic king, as Hitzig and others suppose, but that He should *propose* to the nations peace, composing their mutual discords and reconciling them to His own dominion (cf. for the meaning of the phrase "to speak peace," Ps. xxviii. 2, xxxv. 20, lxxxv. 8; Esther x. 3). Thus should His empire be extended until it became world-wide; "His dominion should be from sea to sea," *i.e.* from the one sea to the other, from the sea on the east, the Dead Sea, to the sea on the west, the Mediterranean, "and from the river," *the* river by way of eminence, the Euphrates, "to the ends of the earth"—phrases which, originally limitedly definitive, as applicable to the land promised by God to Abraham and his seed (Gen. xv. 18; Deut. i. 7, 8), came latterly to have an indefinite significance, and were used to designate the world at large (cf. Ps. lxxii. 8; Amos viii. 12; Micah vii. 12). The meaning here, therefore, is that this King should reign over the whole world: "dominabitur quam late patet orbis terrarum" (Rosenmüller).

There is an almost unanimous consent among the Jewish expositors that this prophecy relates to the Messiah, and such seems to have been the belief of the

Jews generally from the earliest times.* In this the great majority of Christian interpreters concur. Nor is any other conclusion possible except on the assumption that no Messianic predictions are to be found in the Jewish Scriptures, and that the expectation of a Messiah by the Jewish people was a mere phantasy and delusion. What is here said of this king corresponds in every particular with what is said of the Messiah in other passages, and is applicable to no other of whom the sacred writers speak. Of the Messiah it was announced that He should be King in Zion (Ps. ii. 7 ff., xlv. 1, 6, 7, lxxii. 1 ff.; Isa. xxxii. 1; Jer. xxiii. 5); that He should be righteous both in His personal character and in His royal claims and administration (Ps. lxxii. 1, 2, 3, 4, 7; Isa. xi. 2-4, xxxii. 1; Jer. xxiii. 5, 6); that He should be protected and delivered by God (Ps. xviii. 50, xlv. 2, 6, cx. 1, 2, 5; Isa. xlii. 1, xlix. 1, 6, liii. 2, 12); that He should be depressed, poor, and afflicted (Ps. xxii. 6; Isa. liii. 3, 7); that He should be peaceful, and a peace-bringer to the nations (Ps. lxxii. 7; Isa. ii. 4, ix. 6, 7), and that His dominion should be world-wide and everlasting (Ps. ii. 8, lxxii. 8, 9, 17; Dan. vii. 13; 14). The King here, therefore, can be none other than that great Deliverer whom all the prophets announce, and whom the people of Israel expected as the promised Messiah.

The fulfilment of this prediction in Jesus Christ conclusively establishes this as the proper reference of this prophetic announcement. He came to get to Himself a kingdom, and He claimed to be a King; but His king-

---

* A copious collection of testimonies to this effect is given by Dr. Pusey in his note on this passage, "Minor Prophets," p. 557.

dom was not an earthly monarchy, to be upheld by force, and defended by the sword; it was a kingdom "not of this world," the rule of truth and equity over those who, being of the truth, should hear the voice of Him who came into the world to bear witness to the truth (Luke xvii. 21; John xviii. 27; Rom. xiv. 17). He was emphatically the Righteous One, the Holy One, and the Just (Acts iii. 14, xxii. 14; Rev. xix. 11). He appeared in a humble condition, and was the object of contempt and hostility to those to whom He came; but He was authorised by God, by Him sustained and protected (Mark i. 11; Rom. i. 4); and though allowed to fall under the power of His enemies, and to suffer death at the hands of His persecutors, He was eventually saved by "the working of God's mighty power, which He wrought in Him when He raised Him from the dead, and set Him at His own right hand in the heavenly places," &c. (Eph. i. 20, 21; cf. Acts ii. 24; Matt. xxviii. 18; Rev. xvii. 14, xix. 16). And being thus delivered from the power of the enemy, and highly exalted, He speaks peace to the nations, drawing men to Him by the attractive power of His Cross, reconciling men unto God, sending forth His servants to "preach the gospel of peace," and, "having by His Cross slain the enmity," uniting man to man and nation to nation in a holy and blessed harmony. As yet, indeed, " we see not all things put under Him," but we see Him on the throne, and already " a multitude which no man can number" has been gathered to Him; every day His reign is extending in the world; and His servants confidently anticipate that ere long His kingdom on earth shall be commensurate with the race, and all nations shall own His sway, and be blessed in Him. That our Lord Himself regarded this prophecy as predictive of Him is placed beyond doubt by what the Evangelists record regarding His triumphal entry into Jerusalem (Matt. xxi. 1 ff.; Luke xix. 29 ff.; John xii. 12 ff.). By the course which He adopted on that occasion, our Lord practically avowed His consciousness that this prophecy related to Him, and aimed at manifesting this to the people. There was no necessity for His riding on this occasion; He had often before traversed the road from Bethany to Jerusalem on foot, and He could have done so again had He seen meet. But His choice of an ass as the vehicle of transport; His special instruction that the animal on which He was to ride should be a colt on which never before had man sat, an untrained animal therefore, and should be accompanied by its dam; and His entry into Jerusalem in this fashion showed that He *meant* to apply this prophecy to Himself, and wished the people to see this, and accept Him as the Messiah in the condition symbolically indicated by the prophet, and exemplified by Him as He then appeared. By the Evangelists it is expressly declared that all " this was done that there might be fulfilled " what this prophecy had predicted; and we can account for the triumphant acclamations with which He was received by the multitude only by supposing that they, for the moment at least, recognised in Him who thus came to them the long-expected King of Israel, whose advent the prophet had described.

It is of the Messiah, then, that this prophetic oracle is to be understood. Indeed, if it do not refer to Him it is an utterance without meaning. After the time of Zechariah no king came to Jerusalem to whom any of the qualities here specified belonged, and certainly none of whom it could be said, even in a restricted sense, that his dominion was from sea to sea, and from the river to the ends of the earth. If this prophecy, then, does not refer to the Messiah, to the historical Christ, there is no one to whom it refers; it is a mere empty utterance, *vox et præterea nihil.*

Thus far in this chapter there is presented in striking contrast the advent of two mighty powers: the one proud, impetuous, destructive, the other humble, gentle, suffering, and beneficent; the one bringing war and desolation on the peoples, the other proclaiming peace to the nations, and diffusing its blessings far and wide; the one an instrument in the hand of God to punish the enemies of His people, the other sustained and supported by God that He might bless His people; the one victorious and powerful through his military prowess and resources, the other wholly renouncing all such methods, and proving successful through the might of truth and goodness; the one sweeping like a hurricane over the countries he invaded to establish only a limited and transient empire after all, the other quietly but surely carrying forward His enterprise until the world shall be subject to His sway and His dominion shall be everlasting. The primary purport of the representation was to assure the Jews that, while on the one hand God would preserve them from the ravages of the invader, encamping around that house which was His own, and delivering His people from foreign oppression, He would, on the other hand, fulfil to them the promise given to their race, and in due time would bring to them their proper King, the promised Messiah, who should sit on the throne of His father David, and sway the sceptre of a kingdom which should stretch to the very ends of the earth. How much of what this prophecy enfolds was perceived by those among whom it was first uttered it is impossible to say; but if we may form a conjecture as to this from the way in which later Jewish interpreters, whilst admitting that it refers to the Messiah, are puzzled to account for some parts of the description, and show their unwillingness to accept it in its plain and obvious meaning, we may believe it was to the Jews of the earlier times a "dark saying," of the meaning of which they had only a vague and misty conception. Even our Lord's own disciples and most devoted followers did not understand it fully until He had finished His work here, and passed from the humiliation and suffering of earth to the throne of His glory in Heaven (John xii. 16); and probably even to the prophet himself the prediction was obscure, and was one of the things regarding which he and the other prophets "who prophesied of the grace" that should come under the new dispensation "inquired and searched diligently, searching what or what manner of time the Spirit of Christ that was in them did signify, when it testified beforehand the sufferings of Christ and the glory that should follow" (1 Pet. i. 10, 11). To us who read this prophecy in the light of its fulfilment in the advent and work and glory of Christ, all is plain and clear. Not so much by our Lord's particular act in riding into Jerusalem on the occasion, and in the manner described by the evangelists, as by that which by this act was symbolised and indicated, namely, His advent to empire, His coming to get for Himself a kingdom, His appearing as the Saviour and King of His Church, and His gathering to Himself a people from among the nations, has this prediction been fulfilled. He came in poverty and humiliation to lay the foundation of His kingdom in obedience and sacrifice. It was from the field of sorrow and of suffering that He ascended to the throne. The crown came after the cross; the humiliation preceded the glory. All things have been put under His feet, all power and authority have been given Him in heaven and on earth, in the universe He reigns supreme. But it is because He was " obedient to death " that He has been thus " highly exalted." His kingdom rests on His propitiatory work; and it is in view of this, though then perhaps but dimly seen, that the prophet here calls upon Zion to behold and hail her King. And now that He hath ascended to the throne of His glory, the "glad tidings of the Kingdom" are to be proclaimed to all nations, and men of every tongue and clime are to be invited to behold their King, and submit to His righteous and benignant sway.

> "Joy to the world ! the Lord is come !
>   Let earth receive her King ;
> Let every heart prepare Him room,
>   And heaven and nature sing.
>
> He rules the world with truth and grace,
>   And makes the nations prove
> The glories of His righteousness,
>   The wonders of His love."

XIII.

PRIVILEGES OFFERED.

"As for thee also, by the blood of thy covenant I have sent forth thy prisoners out of the pit wherein is no water. Turn you to the strong hold, ye prisoners of hope: even to-day do I declare that I will render double unto thee; when I have bent Judah for me, filled the bow with Ephraim, and raised up thy sons, O Zion, against thy sons, O Greece, and made thee as the sword of a mighty man. And the Lord shall be seen over them, and his arrow shall go forth as the lightning: and the Lord God shall blow the trumpet, and shall go with whirlwinds of the south. The Lord of hosts shall defend them; and they shall devour, and subdue with sling stones; and they shall drink, and make a noise as through wine; and they shall be filled like bowls, and as the corners of the altar. And the Lord their God shall save them in that day as the flock of his people; for they shall be as the stones of a crown, lifted up as an ensign upon his land. For how great is his goodness, and how great is his beauty! corn shall make the young men cheerful, and new wine the maids."
—ZECH. ix. 11-17.

THE prophet having declared God's purpose to defend and protect His people, and celebrated the advent of the Great King whose throne in Zion should be established for ever, and whose dominion should be world-wide, turns now to address the people of the covenant, and invite them to avail themselves of the advantage and privilege thus secured. "As for thee also, by the blood of thy covenant I have sent forth thy prisoners out of the pit wherein is no water" (ver. 11). The words at the beginning of this verse are literally, "Also thou." The "thou" (אֵת) is the nominative absolute, and is properly resolved into "as for thee,"—"ad te quod attinet" (Rosenm.); the "also" presents a difficulty. To what does it refer? To what goes before or to what follows? Does the prophet say, "As for thee as well as the heathen (the *goyim*, the nations)," &c.? or does he say, "As for thee . . . also thy prisoners have I sent forth?" or is "also" here in the sense of "even," *q.d.*, "even for thee, apparently helpless and hopeless as thou art, a prisoner in a pit without water, there is deliverance; I have sent forth," &c.? All of these explanations have found favour with interpreters, but none of them is quite satisfactory. The first assumes a contrast or comparison between Israel and the heathen which does not lie in the passage, where "the heathen" have no prominent place, but are introduced merely incidentally to indicate the wide extent of the dominion of the advenient King; the second requires undue emphasis to be laid on the "thy," as if the prisoners of Zion were placed in contrast with the prisoners of some other nation; and the third proceeds on the assumption of a depressed and afflicted condition of Zion which is not in keeping with the assurance just given of protection by God to His house, and the summons to triumphant exultation, because of the advent to her of her own peace-bringing King, which the prophet has just addressed to the daughter of Zion. It may be suggested that as the concept of "also" runs very readily into that of "further" or "moreover," and as גַּם is rendered elsewhere by "moreover" (Gen. xxxii. 20; 1 Chron. xi. 2; cf. also Eccl. iv. 11; A. V., "again"), that rendering may be fitly adopted here: "Moreover, as for thee, by the blood of thy covenant, I have sent," &c. That it is "the daughter of Zion," the united people of Israel, that is here addressed seems indubitable. Some, indeed, have supposed that it is the King, the Messiah, who is the object of this address, and that the passage has reference to the spiritual deliverances which He is to accomplish for His people from spiritual evils. But as the pronoun here is in the feminine it obviously cannot be understood of the King; and the allusion in ver. 13 to Javan or Greece as the enemy to be overcome by Zion, shows that the utterance has a historical reference, and refers to events earlier than the time of the Messiah's advent. The feminine pronoun evidently points to the daughter of Zion as the party here addressed, and it is to her prisoners that deliverance is here promised. This was to be "by the blood of her covenant." The covenant here referred to is the Sinaitic covenant, the covenant which God made with Israel when He brought His people out of Egypt; and it is here called *their* covenant, because it was with them as a nation and for their behoof that the covenant was made. This covenant, like all ancient covenants, had been ratified and sealed by blood. When the covenant was established at Sinai, "Moses (we read) took the blood and sprinkled it on the people, and said, Behold the blood of the covenant which the Lord hath made with you" (Exod. xxiv. 8; cf. Ps. l. 5). Into this covenant the people were thus brought, and the blood which was sprinkled on them was the token of their reconciliation to God, and the pledge to them of God's protection. This covenant was still in force; the blood still rested on the covenant people; they still had the promise of deliver-

M

ance out of all trouble; and so they might rest assured that what yet remained for their entire deliverance from captivity and oppression should be accomplished. The verb here, שִׁלַּחְתִּי, being in the perfect, the passage is regarded by some as referring to the past, to God's interpositions on behalf of His people in earlier periods of their history, or to the deliverance from the Babylonish captivity of those who had already returned to their own land. But it is more probable that the verb is here to be taken as the prophetic perfect, and as consequently referring to the future, to something which God was yet to do for the covenant nation, and which, being in the purpose of Him whose counsel shall stand, was as certain as if it had been already done. By the words "thy prisoners" are not to be understood persons held by Zion in bondage, but those belonging to her, her own children who were still in captivity in Babylon; and they are described as "prisoners in a pit in which is no water," to indicate that they were, though really in bondage, yet not hopelessly doomed to destruction; they were in the pit, but it was a pit without water, so that they might be brought out of it alive, just as Joseph was out of the pit into which his brethren had cast him (Gen. xxxvii. 24; cf. Isa. li. 14). Or it may be that, without special reference to those still in Babylon and in captivity, the description applies to the people generally as at that time under restraint and difficulty because of their enemies; the being in a pit or dungeon being a formula expressive of distress and oppression (Ps. xxxv. 7, xl. 2, lxxxviii. 6; Isa. xxiv. 17; Lam. iv. 20). It was God's purpose that the covenant people, whether still in bondage in Babylon, or straitened and distressed by the enemy in their own land, should be wholly delivered, and this being in His purpose was already as good as done.

Their case was, therefore, not hopeless; on the contrary, being in the blood of the covenant, they had good ground for expecting deliverance. Hence they are here addressed as "prisoners of hope," and are invited to return and take refuge where they should be safe from all persecution of the enemy. "Prisoners of hope" the Targum explains as equivalent to "captives who hope for deliverance." The stronghold or fortress to which they are invited to return is by Kimchi said to be "God, for He is a stronghold and tower of strength;" and this explanation others adopt. To regard God as a tower or fortress to which men may betake themselves for refuge and protection is quite in accordance with scriptural representation; comp. Ps. xxvii. 1, xxxi. 3, 5, xxxvii. 39, xliii. 2, lii. 9, lxi. 3; Prov. xviii. 10; Joel iii. 16; Nah. i. 7. It is rather, however, to the place which God protects and defends, as contrasted with the pit in which the exiles were sunk, than to God Himself that they are here invited to return. In their own land, a place cut off from access, like an impregnable fortress, round which Jehovah should encamp,* they should find peace and security. In the language of prophecy, the exhortation to turn is equivalent to a declaration or assurance that they should turn; it is as if it were said, Though your condition may appear desperate, nevertheless you

* בְּצָרוֹן from בָּצַר to cut off, a place either by natural position or by circumvallation cut off from without, and so a place of safety. The word occurs only here.

shall surely return to a state of safety. Further, God by the prophet promises to give them prosperity greatly beyond the measure of the evils they had endured: " also (or even) to-day do I declare that I will render double unto thee "—a measure, that is, of blessing, the double of the sufferings to which they had been subjected; comp. Isa. lxi. 7.

And how was this to be accomplished? Not immediately by God, not by any miraculous or sudden effusion of Divine power, but by the raising up of agencies among themselves by which their deliverance should be achieved and their prosperity secured. "For I have bent Judah for myself, I have filled the bow with Ephraim, and raised up thy sons, O Zion, against thy sons, O Javan, and made thee as the sword of a mighty man" (ver. 13). By a bold figure the prophet represents God as a warrior who bends a mighty bow and fits to it a strong arrow wherewith to vanquish the adversary. The bow He wields is Judah, and the arrow with which He fills it is Ephraim. So far as the meaning is concerned, it matters not whether with the Massorites we join קֶשֶׁת with מִלֵּאתִי *I have filled*, or with דָּרַכְתִּי *I have bent* or *stretched*, as the LXX, Targum, and Vulgate have it; the latter is to be preferred only "because with the many meanings that דָּרַךְ possesses the expression דָּרַךְ יְהוּדָה needs a more precise definition; whereas there is no difficulty in supplying in thought the noun *qesheth*, which has been mentioned just before, to the verb מִלֵּאתִי" (*Keil*). The phrase to fill a bow with an arrow means to fit an arrow on the string of the bow when it is fully stretched, so as to discharge it against an object. What is intimated here is that the deliverance and recompense assured to Israel should be of God, but that Judah and Ephraim, the united people, should be themselves the instruments by which this should be achieved. They were to secure liberty with the attendant blessings of peace and prosperity, by fighting for it against those who sought to enslave and oppress them. As bows and arrows are effective only as a strong arm stretches the bow on which the arrow has been fixed, so should the people of Israel, the Jews, be successful only through God; they were the bow and the arrow in the hand of Him who alone is great in might. But being in His hand, the bow having been bent by Him, and the arrow fitted on it by Him, the result could not be uncertain; when He comes forth to act, that which He intends shall surely come to pass, however feeble in themselves, however unworthy, the instruments He employs may be.

The enemy against which God would raise up the sons of Zion and make them as a sword in the hand of a mighty man, is described as " the sons of Javan," that is, Ionia or Greece. By some this is supposed to refer to an insurrection of Jews, who had been sold as slaves to the Greeks, against their masters at a period much earlier than the time of Zechariah. That Jews were sold to the Greeks as slaves is testified by the prophet Joel (iii. 6); but that it is to an insurrection on the part of these against those who had purchased them that the prophet here refers is altogether improbable. Nothing is known of the condition of these enslaved Jews beyond the fact that they were sold to Greeks; there is no evidence that they were cruelly dealt with so as to provoke an insurrection, or to call forth the Divine vengeance upon their masters; no such insurrection, so far as is known, ever took place; and a mere uprising of a few captive Jews against their masters would never have been described as a raising up of the sons of Zion against the sons of Greece, terms which indicate nothing less than a general conflict of nation against nation. There can be no doubt that what is here referred to is the memorable uprising of the Jews against the tyranny of Antiochus Epiphanes in the time of the Maccabees, when they were brought into long and deadly conflict with the Greeks of the Syrian dynasty. Roused to cast off the yoke of their oppressor, and to resist his persistent efforts to subdue them, they proved under God "as a sword in the hand of a mighty man." Few in numbers as compared with the host of their enemy, and often in great straits and at the point of being utterly overthrown, they were nevertheless not only enabled to keep their ground through a series of conflicts, but ultimately to drive out their oppressor and secure their independence; "out of weakness they were made strong, waxed valiant in fight, turned to flight the armies of the aliens" (Heb. xi. 34).

It is impossible to regard this in any other light than as a real and very remarkable prediction. At the time it was uttered not only none of the things here intimated had any existence, but there was nothing that could suggest the probability of their happening. The Jews were still subject to the Persian rule, and many, perhaps the most, of them were still in exile. No Grecian force had been seen in Syria, nor had the invasion of Greece by Xerxes which led to the retaliatory invasion of the East by the Greeks been so much as purposed. No one could then form any conjecture as to what the prophet referred to when he spoke of the sons of Zion coming into conflict with the sons of Javan; certainly no one could then have dreamt of a Greek kingdom being set up in Syria which should be the cruel oppressor of the Jews; and as for the Maccabees and their gallant followers, who were the bow and arrow in the hand of God in effecting the destruction of the enemies of Israel and the deliverance of the sons of Zion from their oppressors, neither their family nor the place whence they sprung had as yet any historical existence. The only hypothesis on which such an utterance can be rationally accounted for is that which St. Peter supplies when he says that the ancient prophets, "holy men spake from God as they were moved by the Holy Ghost" (2 Pet. i. 21). What man could not have conjectured, what no human sagacity could have anticipated, the Omniscient clearly foresaw; and directed by Him the prophet foretold these things in language which could be fully understood only after the fulfilment had made His meaning clear.

Surrounded by powerful and hostile nations, Israel could hope for security only as it was protected and defended by God. To cheer and animate the people, therefore, the prophet goes on to convey assurance of the continued presence of God's power with the nation. This is the general drift of the verses that follow; but the thought is presented in varied details which are striking and full of interest. "The Lord shall be seen above them" (ver. 14); He should not only be with His people, but He should make His presence with them manifest by such tokens that they should, as it were, see

Him hovering over them to care for them and protect them. "And His arrow shall go forth as the lightning." The arrows of God are the judgments which He inflicts upon the wicked, or those whom He would chastise or destroy, such as famine, pestilence, fever, war, &c. (comp. Deut. xxxii. 23 ff., 43; Ps. vii. 13, xxxviii. 2, &c.). These come forth with sudden force like the lightning, which is also God's arrow (Ps. xviii. 14, lxxvii. 17, 18, cxliv. 6; Hab. iii. 11). "The Lord God will blow the trumpet and shall go with whirlwinds of the south," lit. "shall walk in storms of the south." The blowing of a trumpet was not only the signal of battle but also the note of impending calamity and destruction (comp. Num. x. 9; Ezek. vii. 14; Hosea v. 8, viii. 1; Joel ii. 1; Amos iii. 6; Zeph. i. 16). "Storms of the south" were the most violent known to the Hebrews; coming from the Arabian desert, lying to the south of Palestine, they swept with resistless fury over the Holy Land (Isa. xxi. 1; Joel i. 19, xxxvii. 9); even so suddenly and terribly should God come upon the enemy and sweep them to destruction (comp. Ps. xviii. 10, l. 3; Isa. xxviii. 2; Nahum i. 3; Ezek. xiii. 13). But whilst God should thus destroy the enemy, to His own people He would extend protection, and ultimately give them the victory over all that oppose them or would oppress them. "The Lord of hosts shall defend them [shall cover them over, shall protect them]; and they shall devour, and subdue with sling-stones" (ver. 15), or, as it is in the margin, "shall subdue the stones of the sling." In the former of these renderings the A. V. follows the LXX and the Vulgate; the latter is that of Kimchi, and is adopted by

Hengstenberg, Keil, Hitzig, and others. It is no valid objection to the rendering in the text that it introduces a preposition which is not in the Hebrew, for the noun here may be the adverbial accusative, and so describe the instrument by which the action of the verb is effected. But the meaning thus brought out is jejune and feeble; the mention of the instrument of subjugation adds nothing to the force of the statement that the enemy should be subdued, but rather detracts from it. The rendering in the margin of the A. V. takes the noun as the immediate object of the verb; the enemy should be subdued like stones from a sling which had missed their mark and were contemptuously trodden under foot; or without any figure, the stones which the enemy should in battle cast against the people of God, instead of injuring them, should fall innocuously to the ground and be trodden under foot. This last, which is the exegesis of Gesenius and Ewald, is to be preferred. The sling was an important implement of assault in the warfare with which the Jews were familiar; and to subdue or tread under foot the stones cast from a sling would convey to them a lively representation of the entire impotency of their assailants. But not only should they be unharmed by their enemies, they should utterly destroy them and triumph over them; they should "devour," "and should drink, and make a noise as through wine," like men exhilarated with wine, "and become full like bowls, and be as the corners of the altar." The object of their devouring and drinking is not stated; but as elsewhere this figure of eating or devouring, as a lion consumes his prey, is used to denote the destruction of an enemy (Num. xxiii. 24; Micah v.

8; comp. Deut. vii. 16; Ezek. xxxix. 17, 19), it is supposed there is an allusion to this here, and Israel is represented as, like a wild beast, eating the flesh and drinking the blood of their enemies. But as the lion is not mentioned here, and as the eating of flesh and drinking of blood "apart from the image of the wild beast would be intolerable to Israel, to whom the use of blood, even of animals, was so strictly forbidden" (*Pusey*), it is probable that nothing more is intended here than that Israel should slay and utterly destroy their enemies, just as elsewhere it is said of the sword that it shall "devour and be made drunk with blood" (Jer. xlvi. 10), where all that is meant is that the sword as the instrument of slaughter shall utterly destroy. In the words that follow it is supposed by some that there is intimated the consecration of Israel to God as the instrument in His hand of effecting His purpose; that they should "be hallowed like the bowls of the temple from which the sacrificial blood is sprinkled on His altar, or as the corners of the altar which receive it" (*Pusey*). But this is far-fetched; and it is more probable that the prophet here simply carries on the representation of the preceding words, and describes Israel as a body of warriors drunk with the blood of their enemies, and filled therewith as the sacrificial bowls were filled with the blood of the victims which was caught by the priests and sprinkled over the sides of the altar (Lev. i. 5, 11, &c.). It is the tumultuous joy of triumph that is here set forth.

Victorious over their enemies, Israel should also in that day be saved by the Lord "as a flock, as His people;" whilst the enemy should be trodden down and destroyed,

Israel should be rescued, and as the people of God whom He had chosen for Himself and the sheep of His pasture, should be enriched with blessing; the Lord would tend and care for them as a shepherd does for his flock (ver. 16). Precious in His sight, they should be exalted to honour; as stones in a diadem should they shine in His land. Great also should be their felicity and prosperity: "For how great is His goodness, and how great is His beauty! Corn shall make young men to grow, and new wine maidens" (ver. 17). It is a question whether the first part of this verse refers to Israel or to Jehovah. If to the latter, the meaning must be, How great is the goodness He bestows, and the beauty He confers! If the former, the meaning is, How great is the goodness, and how great the beauty which he [Israel] enjoys! Some, indeed, take the exclamation as referring to the personal attributes of Jehovah as supremely good and lovely. But though goodness is predicated of God in Scripture, nowhere is beauty (יֳפִי) ascribed to Him; and even if it were, "it would still be" (as Keil remarks) "unsuitable here." On the whole it seems best to understand this of Israel, whose goodness (not moral goodness, but temporal prosperity) and beauty (comp. Ezek. xvi. 14, xxvii. 3, &c.) are celebrated. "Corn and tirosh" (which is perhaps the freshly-expressed juice of the grape rather than must or new wine) are in Scripture the standing expression for that by which life is nourished and sustained; and where abundance of this is given there population naturally increases. So here the bestowal of abundance of this upon Israel is represented as marked by such an increase (comp. Ps. lxxvii. 16). The verb translated in the A. V.

"make cheerful" properly means *to cause to sprout, to produce*. In Ps. xcii. 15 [14] the Qal is used of the producing of fruit. "To thrive" is the rendering of Blayney and Henderson here.

From an early period a disposition has shown itself among Christian interpreters to allegorise or (to use St. Jerome's word) to tropologise this passage, and to use it as referring to deliverance from the tyranny and evil of sin, and the consequent enjoyment of spiritual blessings through the redemption which is in Christ.* To this use the passage readily lends itself, for there is an obvious and recognised analogy between the redemption of Israel from captivity, their deliverance from their oppressors, and their enjoyment of peace and plenty in their own land, and the redemption of men from the bondage of evil, their deliverance from spiritual tyranny, and their establishment in the peace and blessedness of the heavenly kingdom; and so long as the literal interpretation of the passage is not denied or ignored, this use of it cannot be denounced as illegitimate, while for homiletical purposes it may be very advantageous.†

---

* See Augustine, "De Civit. Dei," l. xviii. c. 35; Cyril. Alex., Theodoret, and Theophylact on the place; also the notes of Calovius and Thomas Scott.

† See the excellent homily on the passage in Wardlaw's "Lectures on the Prophecies of Zechariah," p. 209, ff.

XIV.

ISRAEL'S FULL SALVATION.

" Ask ye of the Lord rain in the time of the latter rain ; so the Lord shall make bright clouds, and give them showers of rain, to every one grass in the field. For the idols have spoken vanity, and the diviners have seen a lie, and have told false dreams; they comfort in vain: therefore they went their way as a flock, they were troubled, because there was no shepherd. Mine anger was kindled against the shepherds, and I punished the goats: for the Lord of hosts hath visited his flock the house of Judah, and hath made them as his goodly horse in the battle. Out of him came forth the corner, out of him the nail, out of him the battle-bow, out of him every oppressor together. And they shall be as mighty men, which tread down their enemies in the mire of the streets in the battle: and they shall fight, because the Lord is with them, and the riders on horses shall be confounded. And I will strengthen the house of Judah, and I will save the house of Joseph, and I will bring them again to place them; for I have mercy upon them: and they shall be as though I had not cast them off: for I am the Lord their God, and will hear them. And they of Ephraim shall be like a mighty man, and their hearts shall rejoice as through wine: yea, their children shall see it, and be glad; their hearts shall rejoice in the Lord. I will hiss for them, and gather them; for I have redeemed them: and they shall increase as they have increased. And I will show them among the people: and they shall remember me in far countries; and they shall live with their children, and turn again. I will bring them again also out of the land of Egypt, and gather them out of Assyria; and I will bring them into the land of Gilead and Lebanon, and place shall not be found for them. And he shall pass through the sea with affliction, and shall smite the waves in the sea, and all the deeps of the river shall dry up: and the pride of Assyria shall be brought down, and the sceptre of Egypt shall depart away. And I will strengthen them in the Lord; and they shall walk up and down in his name, saith the Lord."—ZECH. X. 1-12.

IN this chapter there is no new oracle, but only a continuance of the prophetic utterance in the preceding section. The prophet here sets forth an expansion of the blessing promised to restored Israel, ending in the announcement of the final and full salvation of the people of God. The first two verses are neither to be connected with what precedes as a conclusion, nor with what follows as the commencement of a new turn in the address; they form rather the connecting link of the two sections—the channel through which the stream of continuous thought flows. The promise of abundance of the fruits of the field (ix. 17) suggests the supply of the moisture necessary for the growth of the herbage (x. 1), and the abundance of grass in the field suggests the flocks that are to be sustained by it, and the shepherds by whom these may be tended (verse 2).

The prophet calls on those whom he addresses to "ask of the Lord rain in the time of the latter rain." The rainfall in Palestine is normally periodical; occasional showers and even storms of rain may occur at any season, but as a rule it is at the time of the autumnal and that of the vernal equinox that the rain for the year falls. These two periodic seasons of rain the Hebrews spoke of as the early and the latter rain; and on the occurrence of them the fruitfulness of the field and the return of harvest depended. In other passages, both the former and the latter rain are referred to as indispensable to this. At an early period God promised to Israel that He would "give the rain of their land in due season, the first rain and the latter rain, that they might gather in their corn and their wine (*tirosh*) and their oil" (Deut. xi. 14); and by the prophets the sending of rain, the former and the latter rain in their season, is represented as the manifestation of special regard for His people by Jehovah (comp. Hos. vi. 3; Joel ii. 23; Isa. xxx. 23; Jer. v. 24). The latter rain only is mentioned here, probably because this was the more important for the fructification of the grain; and possibly also, because, being this, it might be regarded as including or representing temporal blessing generally. This the prophet here exhorts the people to ask of the Lord "at the time of the latter rain," *i.e.*, at the season when it was due; though God had promised it to His people, it was fitting and needful that they should pray to Him for it at the time when it was required. This "direction to ask" does not "simply express the readiness of God to grant their request" (Hengstenberg); it does this, for when God enjoins on men the asking for blessing, He implicitly engages to give the blessing asked for; but besides this, and even more than this, there is intimated here that the obtaining of promised blessing is conditioned, by its being specially asked of God in the season of need. God's promises are given not to supersede prayer, but rather to encourage and stimulate to prayer.

The latter part of this first verse does not, as in the A. V., express a consequence that will result from the asking, but rather assigns a reason why they should ask. Let them ask for rain from the Lord, *for* "it is the Lord who maketh lightnings, and showers of rain will He give them, to every one grass in the field;" as God alone can so move and combine the atmospheric influences as to cause rain to descend on the earth, as it is to Him that prayer for rain is to be directed, and as it is He who gives the showers that come with fructifying efficacy on the field, so is each one who desires to see his field covered with herbage to ask of God the rain without which vegetation will not advance. The word rendered by "grass" includes here, as in other passages (comp. Gen. i. 29; Ex. x. 15; Ps. civ. 14; Am. vii. 2), all vegetable products that are for food to man and cattle. Lightnings are introduced as frequent harbingers of rain * (comp. Ps. cxxxv. 7; Jer. x. 13; Job xxviii. 26); the rendering in the A. V., "bright clouds," is singularly infelicitous here, there being no connection between bright clouds and rain, but rather the opposite.†

The heathen were accustomed to apply to their idol gods for the supply of what was needed for sustenance and prosperity, and Israel had been too much tempted to look to the same source for help and aid. But this was vain as well as impious: "The Teraphim have spoken vanity, and the diviners have seen a lie, and dreams of deceit have they spoken; they comfort in vain; therefore they wandered about as a flock, they are distressed because there is no shepherd" (verse 2). The Teraphim were domestic idols, household gods, corresponding to the Penates of the Romans; they were supposed to have the power of giving responses in respect of things hidden or uncertain, and were regarded with veneration as the givers or procurers of temporal blessings (Gen. xxxi. 19, 30; Judges xvii. 5, xviii. 24; Ez. xxi. 21; Hos. iii. 4).

---

* " . . . . . Grato a i caldi giorni è il tuono che speranza di pioggia al mondo apporte."—Tasso, *Ger. Lib.* I., 71.

† The rendering, "bright clouds," is retained from the Bishops' Bible. Coverdale has, "So shall the Lorde make clouds and give you rayne enough." The Geneva Bible has "white clouds." The word in the Hebrew is not the proper word for lightning ($baraq$), but a word signifying primarily *darts* or *arrows* (*Hazizim*, pl. of *Haziz*, from a verb signifying *to pierce*); but the use of the word, Job xxviii. 26, xxxviii. 25, determines it to mean lightning.

Their oracles are here declared to be mere vanity; and the diviners, or soothsayers, who also were sought to as capable of divulging the unknown and predicting the future, are denounced as deceivers and misleaders of the people, who utter to them delusive dreams and comfort them in vain. Unhappily, Israel had confided in these idols and diviners, and the consequence was that they had wandered into exile, and were as sheep without a shepherd; the prospect of peace and prosperity that had been held out to them had proved but an idle and deceitful dream, and in its stead dispersion, oppression, and distress had come upon them. The verb rendered in the A. V. by "they went their way" (נָסְעוּ), means primarily *to pull up*, thence *to break up a camp* or *settlement* by pulling up the tent-pegs, and so *to remove, to journey, to migrate;* in Jer. xxxi. 24, it is used of the wanderings of nomades with their flocks, and here of the wanderings of the flock itself. Israel was as a flock without a shepherd, having, in the overthrow of their state, lost their proper rulers, whose it was, as shepherds, to go out and in before them, to lead them, guard and provide for them (Num. xxvii. 17; Jer. xxiii. 4, 1. 6; Ez. xxxiv. 2 ff.).

In the third clause of the verse it is doubtful whether the word rendered by "dreams" is to be taken as the subject or as the object of the verb "speak,"—whether the clause should be translated "they (the diviners) speak dreams of deceit," or "dreams speak deceit." The latter is the construction approved of by the LXX, and by Hengstenberg, Ewald, and others, and it is that which the accentuation slightly favours. The former is adopted by the Vulgate, and is followed by Keil, Henderson,

Lange, and others. It is, on the whole, to be preferred, because (1) in the three parallel clauses it is more probable that the subject should be the same throughout, than that in the middle clause a different subject should be introduced; (2) soothsayers may speak dreams of deceit, but it is strange to say that dreams speak deceit; (3) if "dreams" were the subject it should have the article "*the* dreams," the same as "*the* diviners," for it is not all dreams that are pronounced false, but only those declared by these diviners.

When Israel lost their own proper shepherds, they came under the power of foreign and evil shepherds, the heathen rulers who oppressed them (comp. Jer. vi. 3, 4, xlix. 19; Isa. xliv. 28). Against these, though the instruments of inflicting on the people of God the chastisement which He saw meet they should receive, His wrath was kindled because of the cruelty and oppression to which, in the carrying out of their own evil designs, they had subjected Israel. "My wrath is kindled against the shepherds, and the he-goats will I punish" (ver. 3). There is no material difference between the shepherds and the he-goats, both words designate the heathen rulers who oppressed Israel; or, if there be a distinction, it may be that the former designates the supreme, and the latter the subordinate governors; comp. Isa. xiv. 9, where the word rendered by "he-goats" here (*attûdîm*) is rendered by "chief ones of the earth." These evil shepherds God would punish, for, says He, "Jehovah of hosts visiteth His flock, the house of Judah, and maketh it as the horse of His state in the battle." The house of Judah is mentioned here, not as exclusive of Ephraim, but "as the stem and kernel of the covenant nation, with which Ephraim is to be united once more" (Keil), and which is to give its name to the whole united people. This, His flock, God "visits;" the verb is in the perfect, but it is the prophetic perfect, which indicates not so much what has been done as what God purposes to do and ever will do for His people. He visits them; the verb here is the same as in the preceding clause, but with a different preposition; the shepherds He will *visit upon* (פָּקַד עַל), *i.e.*, will punish, but His flock He will *visit* (פָּקַד אֶת), *i.e.*, will assume the care of and provide for. (Comp. Jer. ix. 25, xliv. 13, with Gen. l. 24; Exod. iii. 16; 1 Sam. xvii. 18; see both constructions in Jeremiah xxiii. 2.) Not only would God visit His people to care for them and deliver them from the oppressor, He would also use them to tread down the enemy; they should be as His stately war-horse in the day of battle; just as before He had said that He would make Judah His bow and Ephraim His arrow against the sons of Javan (ix. 13). Israel should not only be delivered; Judah and Ephraim, reunited as one people, should triumph over those who had enslaved and cruelly treated them.

The representation of warlike reprisal to be made by Israel on their heathen oppressors is continued in the following verses. "From him corner, from him nail, from him battle-bow, from him goeth forth every oppressor together" (ver. 4). The figurative expressions in the beginning of the verse are taken from the construction and furnishings of a house. The "corner" is the corner-stone, as in Isa. xxviii. 16, on which the whole building rests; the "nail," or "peg" (יָתֵד), is the pin let into the wall on which household utensils may be suspended (Isa. xxii. 23, 24; see Lowth's note on this passage; Ez. xv. 3); the "battle-bow" stands synecdochically for implements of war in general, as in ix. 10. By the first of these figures is indicated the firmness with which the restored state should be established under some strong ruler; by the second the upholding or sustaining of the power and wealth of the state by the constituted authorities; and by the third the warlike powers by which the state should be defended and protected against foreign assailants. The last expression, "every oppression," is less easy of explanation. It must be considered in connection with the "from him," for its meaning will depend on whether the reference of this is to Israel or to Jehovah. If to Israel, the meaning will be that from him comes the ruler or taskmaster of the subjected peoples; over them Israel shall rule. If to Jehovah, the meaning will be that from Him, as the supreme disposer of all, comes the oppressor whom He permits to tyrannise over those whom He sees meet to chastise. Between these two constructions interpreters are much divided. On the whole, the former seems the one to be preferred. The prophet is describing the change that is to take place in the relation of Israel to the heathen nations by whom they had been oppressed; from being subjected to oppression they should become conquerors, and by warlike prowess subjugate those who had ruled over them. With such a theme it is more in keeping that he should introduce a representation of Israel as sustained by its own chiefs and heroes (cf. Jer. xxx. 21), and as sending forth rulers to dominate the nations, than that he should introduce a new subject, viz., the agency of Jehovah, alike as the source of blessing to His people, and the appointer of instruments by which they may be afflicted when He sees meet that chastisement for their sins should come upon them. Further, though God may choose and appoint wicked men and nations to be the instruments of punishing His people, it is not in accordance with Scripture phraseology or representation to describe these as *going forth* from Him; such language implies that before being sent these were *with* God, which is a representation wholly foreign to the Bible. Besides, how can *every* oppressor be said to come forth from God, even in the sense of being chosen and used by Him as instruments? There are rulers so utterly wicked, cruel and diabolical, that though their actings may be overruled by God for His own ends, they themselves can only be regarded as proceeding from Satan, not from God; as saith the proverb of the ancients, " Wickedness proceedeth from the wicked" (1 Sam. xxiv. 13). All rulers, however, are not of this sort, even though set to exercise rule over subjugated nations. Such a ruler is of necessity regarded by those over whom he is set as *noges*, a taskmaster, an exactor, and so an oppressor; but he may nevertheless be both righteous and clement in his administration. It is in this sense that a *noges* is here said to come forth from Israel. Delivered from foreign rule, so that "no noges should pass through them any more" (ix. 13), Israel should send forth those who should subjugate and govern foreign nations.

Thus furnished and endowed, Israel should be mighty in conflict and should overcome all their enemies: "And they shall be as mighty men [heroes, *gibbôrim*] treading down *their enemies* in the mire of the streets in the battle; and they shall fight, for Jehovah is with them, and the riders on horses shall be ashamed" (5). The participle in the first clause (בּוֹסִים) may be taken intransitively, and the clause be rendered "as heroes treading upon the mire of the streets;" in which case "the mire of the streets" is to be regarded "as a figurative expression for the enemy, and the phrase 'treading upon street-mire,' as a bold figure denoting the trampling down of the enemy in the mire of the streets, analogous to their treading down sling-stones" (ix. 15), (Keil). But the verb בּוּס is properly transitive, and is followed by its object in the accusative, and there is no reason why it should not be so taken here, for though the accusative is not actually given, it can be readily supplied from the context, as in the A. V., "their enemies," or "the enemy." The rendering of the Vulgate, "conculcantes lutum viarum in praelio," overlooks the preposition בּ before טִיט (mire); and is, besides, objectionable, as it makes the treading of mire a special characteristic of a hero. Fitted for this conflict and helped of Jehovah, Israel should vanquish the enemy, though he should come against them with a heavy force of cavalry; before the infantry of Israel the proud cavalry of the enemy should be put to shame. "The scene is a vivid picture of the Maccabean times, in which the Jews met with remarkable success, 'turning to flight the armies of the aliens,' though they were strong in cavalry, which formed the most powerful portion of the armies of the Greeks." (See 1 Macc. iii. 39; iv. 7, 31; vi. 30, 35; ix. 4, 11; x. 73, 77; xv. 13, etc.) (*Wright.*)

In this conflict not Judah alone should be engaged and prove victorious; Ephraim also should share alike in the struggle and the victory: "And I will strengthen the house of Judah, and will save the house of Joseph, and shall place them (or shall bring them back); for I have compassion on them; and they shall be as if I had not cast them off; for I am Jehovah their God, and will hear them" (verse 6). The house of Joseph, Ephraim, should receive the same salvation as the house of Judah; both should be delivered and restored. The verb in the third clause הוֹשְׁבוֹתִים is abnormal in form, and it is disputed whether it is to be referred to the root שׁוּב *to turn, to return*; hiphil, *to cause to return, to bring back*, or to יָשַׁב, *to sit down, to dwell*; hiphil, *to cause to dwell, to place*. The latter is to be preferred because—1, "to bring back" affirms too little here, it does not furnish a sufficient counterpoise to the "cast off" in the appended clause; and 2, this is the less comprehensive phrase, for whilst their being placed necessarily involved their being first brought back, their being brought back did not necessarily imply their being replaced in their former estate. The A. V. makes a compromise by giving both renderings, "will bring them again to place them;" but this cannot be justified. Thus restored and replaced Ephraim should, no less than Judah, be heard of God when he cried to Him for blessing, for Jehovah was their God also; and Ephraim as well as Judah should become as a mighty man, and their hearts should rejoice as through wine, *i.e.*, should exultingly hasten to the battle "like a mighty man that shouteth by reason of wine" (Ps. lxxviii. 65, 66); and this their children should see and rejoice with them, so that the exultations should be universal and continuous. "Their joy should be joy in the Lord;" He would be with them and be their God; and "because He had been their help, therefore in the shadow of His wings should they rejoice" (Ps. lxiii. 7).

Still further to assure them of protection and blessing, the deliverance of Ephraim is more fully dwelt upon: "I will hiss to them and gather them; for I have redeemed them; and they shall increase as they have increased" (verse 8). The allusion in the beginning of the verse is either to the practice of those who, to entice bees to settle in a desired locality, make a hissing or tinkling noise,* or to the use of the pipe in summoning people to congregate; more probably the former (comp. Isa. vii. 18, v. 26). God would allure Ephraim and draw him to his resting-place and home; and then the nation should multiply and increase even as it had increased in former times, even during the exile. Though many were still in captivity, the nation was already virtually redeemed, for God's purpose could not fail of effect; and by a succession of startling events, such as the disasters which had come upon Babylon, and subsequently the overthrow of the Persian empire, He had been effectually calling and would still call His people out of captivity to return to their own land. Meanwhile they should spread and prosper even in the countries whither they had been carried. "And I

---

* Comp. Virgil, *Georg.* iv. 64: "Tinnitusque cie, et Matris quate cymbala circum: Ipsae consident," etc.

will sow them among the peoples: and they shall remember me in the far-off lands; and they shall live with their sons and shall return" (verse 9). By some the verb in the beginning of this verse is understood, in a bad sense, as describing banishment or dispersion by way of punishment. The word, however, is always elsewhere used in a good sense, and in reference to persons, express their increase. (Comp. Hos. ii. 25; Jer. xxxi. 27; Ezek. xxxvi. 9, 10.) Even in the land of their exile God would multiply them; and as there, when far away from their own land, they should remember and turn unto the Lord, He would give life to them and their sons, and cause them ultimately to return to their former habitations. They should be brought back from every place whither they had been scattered: "And I will bring them back out of the land of Egypt, and gather them out of Asshur, and bring them into the land of Gilead and of Lebanon; and room shall not be found for them" (verse 10). Egypt and Assyria are specified as the places whence the Israelites should be gathered so as to be restored to their own land. There is a difficulty connected with the mention of both these places here. Why should Assyria be named as the country from which they were to be delivered, seeing it was from Babylonia that they had to be brought? And why should Egypt be mentioned, seeing it was not thither that the people of Ephraim had been carried captive? To the former of these questions it seems a sufficient answer to say that as it was by the Assyrians, under Tiglath-pileser, that the territory of Ephraim was invaded, and into Assyria that the captives of the northern tribes were carried (2 Kings xv. 29, xvii. 6, 23), it was fitting that their return should be spoken of as from that country and nation rather than from Babylonia, though Assyria no longer existed as an independent kingdom. It is also to be observed that as Assyria had been subjected to Babylon and formed an important part of the kingdom of Babylonia, the king of Babylon is, in the latter books of the Jews, sometimes called the king of Assyria (Ezra vi. 22; 2 Kings xxiii. 29; Judith i. 7, ii. 1; comp. 3 Ezra vii. 15, where the Persian monarch is called "king of Assyria").

The other question is not so easy to answer satisfactorily. It is probable, however, that at the time of the Assyrian invasion numbers from among the northern tribes had fled into Egypt, where they remained while their brethren were carried into Assyria, and that it is to their return, or rather that of their descendants, that reference is here made. It is certain that a large number fled from Judea into Egypt at the time of Nebuchadnezzar's invasion; and it may be supposed that a similar secession took place from the northern kingdom at an earlier period. Some, indeed, have supposed that Egypt and Assyria, as the two countries in which the Israelites, as a nation, had been in bondage at different periods of their history, are here introduced typically as representing places of bondage generally; but as Assyria was really the place whence the tribes were to return, only Egypt would be used here with a typical significance, and there would thus be such a combination of the real and the typical as is wholly unexampled and inadmissible. But though not types of lands of bondage in the general, Assyria and Egypt, as the two extremes, may be specified as including all the places whither the people of Israel had been exiled. From all they were to be brought back; and they would return to the land of Gilead and Lebanon, to the territory their nation had formerly occupied, here described by its south-eastern and north-western extremities. And as during their exile they had not been diminished, but had been sown among the nations so as greatly to increase, they should return in such numbers that their former place should be too strait for them, room should not be found for them.

When Israel of old escaped from the land of bondage in Egypt, the Lord "led them through the deep as a horse in the wilderness, and brought them up out of the sea with the shepherd of His flock;" even so would He deliver them from the Assyrian bondage and bring them through that sea of affliction in which they were then immersed, so as to settle them again in their own land: " And He will pass through the sea of affliction, and will smite the sea of waves, and dried up shall be all the depths of the river; and the pride of Asshur shall be brought down, and the staff of Egypt shall depart " (ver. 11). The subject here is Jehovah, the " Saviour of Israel in the time of trouble " (Jer. xiv. 8). The words " sea " and " affliction " are in apposition (יָם צָרָה, *sea, affliction*). They have been variously interpreted. The LXX take צרה as an adjective, and render by ἐν θαλάσσῃ, στενῇ; Kimchi supposes that דבר is to be understood before צרה, as if it were " a thing of adversity (=adversity) shall pass over them like a sea." Ibn Ezra supplies רוח before צרה, *q.d.*, " there shall pass through the sea a wind of affliction or adversity." But צרה, which is feminine, cannot qualify as an adjective יָם, which is masculine; nor, for the same reason, can it be construed with the verb עָבַר. There is no need, however, for supplying or understanding anything here. Of two substantives in apposition the latter may indicate the material of which the former is composed, or that by which it is characterised; so that *yâm tsârâh* here means not "the strait or narrow sea," as the LXX give it, but the sea of which affliction is the characteristic (like מַיִם לָחַץ *waters, affliction*, Isa. xxx. 20; דְּבָרִים נִחֻמִים *words, comforts*, Zech. i. 13), equivalent to Shakespeare's phrase, "a sea of troubles." The "river" here (יְאוֹר) is the Nile, the drying up of which is expressive of the casting down of the hostile power by which Israel had been enslaved. The pride of Asshur and the staff or rod of Egypt are specified because pride was specially characteristic of the Assyrian oppressor (Is. x. 7, cf.), and the rod of the taskmaster was specially the instrument of Egyptian tyranny. Whilst the enemy and oppressor should be brought low, Israel should be exalted and fortified: "I will strengthen them in Jehovah, and in His Name shall they walk, saith Jehovah" (ver. 13). The Name of Jehovah is God Himself as revealed, and to walk therein is to live and act in constant dependence on Him, and trusting to Him for needed help and sustenance. Thus walking Israel should be strengthened of the Lord. He, "the Father of mercies and the God of all comfort," would build them up, endow them with might, and give them help according to their need. "Strong in the Lord, and by the power of His might," the house of Joseph, no less than Judah, should be saved (ver. 6) and walk on in the light of the Lord (Isa. ii. 5).

The opinion of Kimchi that this prophecy relates to events still in the future, and specially to the restoration of Israel from their present dispersion among the nations, has found favour with many Christian expositors. There is nothing, however, in the prophecy itself that points decidedly to such an interpretation, and Kimchi admits that by the ancient Jews, "the commentators of the second temple," it was not so interpreted. It is the final restoration of Israel from the Babylonish captivity that is here immediately set forth, and what is specially announced is the salvation of entire Israel by the reunion of the tribes, and the prosperity and increase of the nation thus restored to its original integrity. At the same time it may be that, as Keil observes, "the principal fulfilment is of a spiritual kind, and was effected through the gathering of the Jews into the kingdom of Christ, which commenced in the times of the Apostles, and will continue till the remnant of Israel is converted to Christ its Saviour." Comp. Rom. xi. 26 ff.

XV.

THE FALLEN CEDAR.

"Open thy doors, O Lebanon, that the fire may devour thy cedars. Howl, fir-tree; for the cedar is fallen; because the mighty are spoiled: howl, O ye oaks of Bashan; for the forest of the vintage is come down."—ZECH. xi. 1, 2.

IN this chapter there is an announcement of the judgment that was to come on the Jewish state and nation because of their ungodliness, and specially their contemptuous rejection of Him whom God sent to be their Shepherd. The prophecy here is not in any way connected with that in the preceding chapters, except as it may be regarded as continuing the account of God's dealings with Israel, and their behaviour towards Him consequent on the events predicted in these chapters. Hitherto the prophet has been the bearer of good tidings to Zion, tidings of deliverance from oppressors, and restoration to former privilege and felicity. But there was a dark side to the picture as well as a bright one. All trouble and conflict had not ceased with their restoration to their own land; nor was their tendency to rebellion and apostasy from Jehovah, their Shepherd and King, finally subdued. Treating Him with contempt, His favour should be withdrawn from them, and the bonds that united them as a people should be broken. The iron hand of foreign oppression should again be laid heavily upon them, and the ruin of their state and desolation of their land should mark the greatness of their sin by the severity of the penalty it had entailed.

The prophecy begins with a picture of ruin and desolation overspreading the land, and then the process is detailed by which this was brought about, and the cause of it indicated. The chapter thus divides itself into three parts, viz., the judgment that should come upon the land (verses 1–3); the action of the good Shepherd and the sin of the people in their contemptuous treatment of Him (verses 4–14); and the action of the evil shepherd in destroying the flock after the good Shepherd had been rejected with his doom (verses 15–17).

The description of the judgment commences dramatically. Lebanon is summoned to open her doors, that the fire may enter to consume her cedars; the cypress is admonished to howl or wail because the cedar is fallen, because the noble and glorious trees are destroyed; the oaks of Bashan are called upon to join in the wail, for the inaccessible forest is laid low. Of the trees of Palestine the noblest and most valuable were the cedar, which grew to its greatest height and strength on Lebanon; and the oak, which had its principal site to the east of the Jordan, on the fertile steppes of Bashan; comp. Isaiah ii. 13, "The cedars of Lebanon that are high and lifted up, and the oaks of Bashan." Next to them in importance was the *berosh*, a species of the cypress (the *Cupressus sempervirens*), the wood of which being close-grained and durable, and also fragrant, was much used by the Hebrews for a variety of purposes, especially for rafters and floors of buildings. The cypress is here called to lament for the fall of the cedar of Lebanon, the glory of the forest, not as deploring that calamity so much as anticipating for itself a like fate. "The mighty" (rather the noble, splendid, or glorious ones, *addirim*) are the cedars, the noblest of the trees; and over their destruction the oaks of Bashan are called to wail because the forest, here described as difficult of access (בָּצוּר, part. pass. of בָּצַר *to cut off, to render difficult of access*, comp. the use of the word, Deut. i. 28, iii. 5; Isaiah ii. 15), is laid low (literally, hath descended). For בצור the Keri reads בציר, a noun signifying the act of cutting off, especially the cutting off of grapes, and this the A. V. has followed; hence the rendering there, "forest of vintage." But this gives no good sense here, gives a sense, indeed, wholly inappropriate, for the forests of Lebanon and Bashan had nothing to do with vines; and the correction, made probably for reasons of grammar, is not at all required, for though in general the article is not prefixed to an adjective when the substantive with which it agrees is anarthrous, this rule is not invariably observed, and is transgressed especially where the adjective is a participle (Ges. *Gr.*, § 111, 2, a). The Vulgate rendering is "saltus munitus," which is followed by the A. V. in the margin, "defenced forest;" but it is not the fortified or defended condition of the forest, but rather its inaccessibility or imperviousness that is here indicated. "The mighty" or "excellent" are not heroes or eminent persons, but the noblest among the trees, the cedars and cypresses here referred to; comp. Ezek. xvii. 8, 23, where the cognate *addareth* is used of the vine and the cedar; and Isa. xxxiii. 21, where *addir* is used of a ship. The same is the application in verse 3 of the expression "their glory" (*addartam*), which is not, as Keil interprets, the pasture where the shepherds fed their flocks, but the trees under whose glorious shadow the flocks found shelter. The destruction of these was a calamity to the shepherds, and hence they are represented as bewailing it: "a voice of the howling of the shepherds, for their glory is spoiled," or, as it might be rendered, "Hark! a howling of the shepherds," &c. (קול has sometimes the effect of "hark;" thus Gen. iv. 10,—"Hark! thy brother's bloods are crying to me;" Jer. x. 22,—"Hark! a rumour! lo, it cometh," &c.; xxv. 36, &c.) As the trees were to the flocks so was "the pride of Jordan," that is, the thickets and brushwood that clothed the banks of the Jordan, to the wild beasts to which it furnished a covert; comp. Jer. xii. 5, where the land of peace is contrasted with the pride of Jordan, because of the dangers to which the wild beasts that frequented the banks of the Jordan exposed the passer-by; and xlix. 19, where the invader of Edom is represented as coming up like a lion from the pride of Jordan; comp. also the use of the phrase the pride [A. V., excellency] of Jacob (Ps. xlvii. 5; Amos vi. 8) for the Holy Land. This too should be destroyed, and over it the young lions, driven from their lair, should lament and howl (verse 3).

That this description is to be taken literally cannot be supposed; the language is too forcible and the picture too vivid to be understood merely of the destruction by fire of a few trees, even though these were the finest of their kind. On the other hand, there seems no sufficient reason for regarding this description as symbolical and wholly figurative. This is the view most commonly given by commentators; but the diversity of opinion which prevails among them as to the meaning and application of these supposed symbols suggests grave doubts as to the soundness of this view. Among the Jews some understand by the trees here mentioned the kings and princes of the nations inimical to the Hebrews; while others contend that by the cedar of Lebanon is meant the temple at Jerusalem, in the construction of which this wood was so largely employed. Of more recent interpreters some understand by the trees the later kings of Israel, and others the rulers of the Jews in still later times; while some have even specified the Pharisees and the Sadducees as the powers here prefigured. All this seems to be mere conjecture. Instances, indeed, may be adduced in which individuals are compared to cedars (see Ezek. xvii. 22 ff.; xxxi. 3); but this does not prove that the cedar of Lebanon or the oak of Bashan was a recognised symbol of a ruler, whether heathen or Hebrew. Besides, if the cedars and oaks are here to be taken as symbols, how is "the pride of Jordan" to be taken? Is that also a symbol? and if so, of what? And what of the lions which had their lair in the thicket that constituted the pride of Jordan, and which are represented as howling over the spoiling of it? If they also are rulers and tyrants, the bushes and underwood which supplied them with covert must be something else; but what else who shall say? Then, as to the shepherds and the lions, if these are symbols, and the former be understood of the princes of Israel, as is most natural, of what are the latter symbols? Not also of great men of Israel, for the lion is of necessity not the guardian or defender, but the enemy and destroyer of the flock; not of foreign hostile powers, for such had not their native abode by the Jordan, nor would such bewail the destruction of the pride of Jordan, of which they themselves were probably the instruments. In short, the allegory cannot be carried out consistently; and for this as well as because of the diversity of opinions as to the meaning of the symbols among those who adopt the view that the passage is symbolical, this view must be rejected. The more simple and tenable view is that which Calvin has advocated, viz.: that by the places here mentioned is intended " per synecdochen " the whole land of Judea, the desolation of which is predicted by the prophet by this graphic description of the destruction of its "loca insigniora." " Summa est," Calvin concludes, " neque Judæam neque terram decem Tribuum immunem fore a Dei vindicta." This view is adopted by Rosenmüller, Keil, Chambers, and Wright. It is that also of Bleek (Einleit, s. 558) and Pressel, who, in accordance with their opinion as to the date of the second part of Zechariah, regard this passage as relating to the devastation of the land by the Assyrians under Tiglath-Pileser. In other passages the devastation of the land is described by the destroying of the cedars and cypresses and forests of the country; comp. 2 Kings xix. 23; Isa. xxxvii. 24, xiv. 7, 8; Hab. ii. 16, 17.

The catastrophe thus depicted was brought about by the misconduct of the people, and especially their shepherds or rulers, towards the Great Shepherd of Israel, whom God sent forth to feed and tend the flock. This is described in what follows, where the prophet is represented as acting as the representative of another, and as such is addressed. It cannot be supposed that the person addressed is the Angel of Jehovah or the Messiah, as some have suggested, for the person addressed in ver. 4 is evidently the same as the person addressed in ver. 15, and what is there said does not in any way apply to the Angel of Jehovah or the Messiah. Nor can it be supposed that the prophet is here addressed in his own person, for as it was no part of the prophetic office to act as a shepherd of Israel, it could not be to the prophet as such that the command here given was addressed. The only supposition that can be tenably made is that what is here narrated passed as a vision before the inner sense of the prophet, in which he saw himself as the representative of another, first of the good shepherd who is sent to feed the flock, and then of the evil shepherd by whom the flock was neglected, and who should be destroyed for his iniquity.

XVI.

THE UNFAITHFUL SHEPHERD.

"There is a voice of the howling of the shepherds: for their glory is spoiled: a voice of the roaring of young lions; for the pride of Jordan is spoiled. Thus saith the Lord my God; Feed the flock of the slaughter; whose possessors slay them, and hold themselves not guilty: and they that sell them, say, Blessed be the Lord; for I am rich: and their own shepherds pity them not. For I will no more pity the inhabitants of the land, saith the Lord: but, lo, I will deliver the men every one into his neighbour's hand, and into the hand of his king: and they shall smite the land, and out of their hand I will not deliver them. And I will feed the flock of slaughter, even you, O poor of the flock. And I took unto me two staves; the one I called Beauty, and the other I called Bands; and I fed the flock. Three shepherds also I cut off in one month; and my soul loathed them, and their soul also abhorred me. Then said I, I will not feed you: that that dieth, let it die; and that that is to be cut off, let it be cut off; and let the rest eat every one the flesh of another."—ZECH. xi. 3-9.

THE prophet, as representing the good shepherd, is commanded by God to feed the flock: " Thus said Jehovah, my God, Feed the flock of the slaughter, whose buyers slay them and are not held guilty, and their sellers say, Blessed be Jehovah! I am becoming rich; and their shepherds spare them not" (verses 4, 5). The flock here is the flock of God, the chosen people, the flock of His pasture (Ezek. xxxiv. 31), the flock of His heritage (Micah vii. 14), the flock of His people (Zech. ix. 16), His flock, the house of Judah (x. 3). They are described as "the flock of the slaughter," because under the tyranny of their

foreign masters they were given over to destruction.*
This flock the prophet is commanded to feed. He who
feeds Israel is Jehovah Himself, and He here commissions
the prophet, in His name and as His representative, to do
this. That the prophet does not appear here as acting
in his own name, or as representing the prophetic office,
is evident from verses 8, 12 and 13, where actions are
ascribed to him which no prophet ever did or could do;
and from verse 10, where he is identified with God, who
alone can make a covenant with all peoples. God visits
and provides for His people in the person of the prophet
His representative. "The distinction between the prophet and Jehovah cannot be adduced as an argument
against this; for it really belongs to the symbolical representation of the matter, according to which God commissions the prophet to do what He Himself intends to
do, and will surely accomplish." (Keil.) The flock was
given over to slaughter by those who claimed to be its
owners by purchase, and who did this with impunity, not
being held guilty or condemned to any penalty because of
their cruelty. The rendering in the A. V., "hold themselves not guilty," though pleaded for by some, is not in
accordance with the usage of the Hebrew. The verb
אָשַׁם signifies *to be guilty*, or *to bear guilt*, *i.e.*, to suffer
the penalty of transgression; so that לֹא יֶאְשָׁמוּ here can

---

* Keil renders by "flock of strangling," alleging that "*hárag* does not
mean to slay, but to strangle." A rash statement. *Harag* occurs many
times in Scripture, but never in the sense of strangling. Where the mode
of slaying is specified, it is by the sword or by stoning that the deed is done.
The word is even used of the destruction of life by the bite of a viper (Job
xx. 16), and of vines by hail (Psalm lxxviii. 47). For the most part the
word is used quite generally of killing. For the phrase "flock of slaughter,"
comp. Psalm xliv. 23.

only mean "are not guilty" or "do not bear guilt,"—are not condemned and made to expiate their offence by enduring the penalty. On the contrary, they continue in prosperity and power, and regarding the flock as their absolute property, they use it for their own advantage, slaughtering or buying and selling the sheep as they please; and, as if they were making lawful gain, blessing the Lord because they were becoming rich. Meanwhile the shepherds of the flock, those who should have cared for and protected it, looked on with indifference, not pitying or sparing the flock. These shepherds, as distinguished from the buyers or possessors of the flock, can only mean the native rulers, civil and ecclesiastical, of the nation, who instead of protecting those of whom they had charge, left them to the mercy of their foreign oppressors. The verbs here are in the imperfect, by which is indicated that the treatment of the flock here described was what was customary and usual at the time.

To this state of things an end must be put; Jehovah will feed and protect His flock, and deliver it from those who were thus harassing and destroying it: "For I will no longer spare the dwellers on the earth, saith Jehovah" (ver. 6). "The dwellers" here are not the people of the land of Israel, but the people of the earth generally, or specially the world-powers by which the people of God were oppressed. The people of Israel cannot be here intended, for they were the flock of slaughter, and as distinguished from this the inhabitants of the earth can only be other nations or powers. The words, indeed, יֹשְׁבֵי הָאָרֶץ may mean "inhabitants of the land," and might be used to designate the people of Israel; and so they are taken by some. But the flock was to be fed, which can only mean that they were to be tended, protected and cared for, whereas these inhabitants were not to be spared, but to be destroyed. The "for" at the beginning of ver. 6 thus connects this with ver. 4: Jehovah would now feed the flock, *for* at length He would unsparingly punish their oppressors. "Israel was given up by Jehovah into the hands of the nations of the world, or the imperial powers, to punish it for its sin. But as these nations abused the power, the Lord takes charge of His people as their shepherd, because He will no longer spare the nations of the world, *i.e.*, will not any longer let them deal with His people at pleasure without being punished." (Keil.) These enemies of Israel God would punish by giving them up to civil dissension and to the tyranny of their own kings: "And behold, I am causing the men to fall each into the hand of his neighbour, and into the hand of his king, and they shall smite the earth, and out of their hand I will not deliver." By "the men" here (הָאָרֶם) are intended the people of the world collectively—the inhabitants of the earth before mentioned. Them God would cause to fall into the hand of each other, *i.e.*, would give up to mutual dissension, oppression and conflict, and into the hand each of his own king, to be dealt with as he should please in the exercise of absolute power. By the simultaneous action of the people against each other, and of the kings against the people, the earth should be smitten; intestine conflict and tyrannical oppression would bring ruin on the nations; nor would God interpose to save them from this deplorable issue of their own misconduct.

As commissioned of God and representing Him, the prophet fed the flock: "And I fed the flock of slaughter, verily the wretched ones of the flock, and I took to me two staves, the one I called Grace, the other I called Bands, and so I fed the flock" (ver. 7). The second clause of this verse has been variously rendered and interpreted. The phrase עֲנִיֵּי הַצֹּאן cannot be taken as directly equivalent to "wretched" or "miserable sheep," as the construction requires the rendering "the wretched of the sheep," *i.e.*, however, not the most wretched of sheep, but the wretched among the sheep, like צְעִירֵי הַצֹּאן, "the least of the sheep" (Jer. xlix. 20), and this comes to much the same as "the wretched sheep." The principal difficulty is with the לָכֵן. This some regard as the second personal pronoun feminine (with Tsere in place of Segol under the כ), and render by "you, O miserable (or poor) of the flock" (A.V.); others take *lachen* as an adverb, in the sense of "therefore" or "therewith;" others give it the meaning of "truly," "yea, truly," or "actually;" and others take it as a preposition, "on account of." The word occurs very frequently in the prophets, and has generally the causal sense of "therefore," introducing something as the consequence of what is mentioned before. The peculiarity here lies in its being used in the middle of the sentence, and not, as elsewhere, at the beginning (as *e. g.* in Isa. v. 24). Thus placed it must be held as indicating that what follows in the clause is consequent on or involved in what precedes. It may therefore be fitly translated by "therewith," which is Keil's rendering, or "at the same time." The whole clause may be thus rendered:—"And

I fed the flock of slaughter therewith the wretched among the sheep." In order to feed the flock the prophet takes two staves or shepherds' crooks; the one of which he names Favour or Grace, נֹעַם pleasantness, or loveliness, but also favour, Ps. xc. 17; the other Bands or Binders, חֹבְלִים, part. of חָבַל to bind = binding ones. Two staves are taken, not because the flock consists of two portions, but in order to indicate that a double benefit is to be conferred on the flock, or that two distinct effects of the shepherd's care are to come to it. What these are the names given to the staves are designed to express; the one, Grace, as the symbol of that covenant of peace under which favour was showed by God to His people; the other, Bands, to indicate the uniting of the sheep in one body, more especially the union of the house of Judah and the house of Ephraim as one nation. Other interpretations of these symbols have been suggested, but the above seems that which the prophet's own words in the subsequent context plainly instruct us to adopt; see verse 10 and verse 14. The staff of the covenant was Grace because it was a covenant of favour, and God was now about to show favour to His people; the staff of the union was Bands, because the shepherd who bore it was to gather into one body and bind with firm ties the dispersed of Israel.

Israel, the flock of God, had been in the hands and under the tyranny of the heathen, who had assumed the place of shepherds over them only to distress and make gain of the sheep. Against these evil shepherds the wrath of God, the true Shepherd of Israel, was directed, and He would punish them for their cruelty: "And

I cut off [destroyed] three shepherds in one month" (ver. 8). As no three shepherds in particular have been mentioned, the A. V. has rendered the clause indefinitely "three shepherds," that is, any three. Others render "three of the shepherds," which comes to much the same thing. These renderings are allowable; but properly the phrase is definite, "*the* three shepherds," and must be understood as pointing to some three shepherds in particular, presumed to be well known.* These three shepherds the prophet, representing Jehovah in the vision, destroyed. What is intended here is very uncertain. How obscure the passage is may be inferred from the multitude of conflicting interpretations which have been offered of it; not fewer, it has been said, than forty. Of these, however, the greater part are purely conjectural, and need not to be noticed.

It may be presumed that in a symbolical vision it is symbols rather than persons or natural objects that are represented. We may therefore start by assuming that by the shepherds here are not intended certain historical individuals; it may be that powers or dynasties or offices are thus represented, but not persons. On the same grounds a month cannot be taken literally as a calendar month of thirty days or thereabouts, but must be understood indefinitely as the sign of a period neither very short nor very long; just as in iii. 9 the phrase "one

---

* As a rule when a numeral is combined with a substantive, having the article (as is the case here), it is the numeral that is thereby made definite; but this rule does not hold invariably, as may be seen from Exod. xxvi. 3, 9; 1 Sam. xx. 20, and other passages, where the article appears as qualifying the substantive—"five of the curtains," "three of the arrows." (Gesen. *Gr.*, § 111, note.)

day" is the sign of a brief period. It is evident also that the cutting off of the shepherds represents not their natural decease but their judicial excision, and that by violent means; comp. the use of the verb in Exod. xxiii. 23; 2 Chron. xxxii. 21; 1 Kings xiii. 34, and in verse 9 of this chapter. It is evident also that it was for the deliverance of the flock from external (foreign) oppression that these shepherds were to be cut off, so that it is not in any powers or offices within the Jewish state that we are to seek for that which the shepherds symbolise. These considerations enable us to set aside at once such suggestions as that the three shepherds are the three kings of Israel,—Zechariah, Shallum, and Menahem (which is the hypothesis of those who ascribe the second part of the book of Zechariah to a pre-exilian prophet); for though these three kings were cut off within a comparatively short time, it was not literally within a month that they were cut off, and though as kings they might be regarded as shepherds of Israel, their being cut off was in no respect a deliverance of Israel from foreign oppression, to say nothing of the incongruity of representing the cutting off of kings of Israel, when it was separate from and hostile to Judah, as a benefit to the conjoined body of Judah and Ephraim at a far later period. We may also discount the opinion that by the three shepherds are intended the three orders by which the nation was ruled, the civil authorities, the priests and the prophets (or in later times, when the order of prophets had ceased, the scribes), for of these the first alone were regarded as pastors or shepherds (comp. Jer. ii. 8; Ez. xxxvii. 24), nor could the cutting off of these from the midst of the nation be a deliverance of it from foreign oppression; and besides, it was not till after the good shepherd had relinquished his work that these were in any sense cut off, so that it could not be by him that they were destroyed. More probable is the suggestion that by the three shepherds are intended the three kings of the Syro-Macedonian dynasty, Antiochus Epiphanes, Antiochus Eupator, and Demetrius I., who successively invaded Judea and were in turn cut off; and that the one month within which they were cut off is a symbolical month, in which each day stands for a year, and so a period of thirty years or thereabouts, a period which would synchronise with that "from 172 B.C., when Antiochus Epiphanes made his terrible attack on the holy city, and desecrated the sacred temple, up to the year 141 B.C., when the three evil alien shepherds of the Jewish nation were cut off, and the last trace of Syrian supremacy was removed by the expulsion of the Syrian garrison from its fortress in Jerusalem."[*] But plausible as this appears, it rests upon too dubious a basis to be accepted as satisfactory. There is no evidence that Zechariah used designations of time symbolically; nor does it appear that "day" or "month" was used by the Hebrews as the symbol of a year. On one occasion, indeed, Ezekiel was commanded to observe a certain posture for so many days, each day being appointed to represent a year (iv. 4–6); but this is no proof that a day was a commonly received symbol of a year; on the contrary, the care which is taken to explain the usage in that particular instance shows plainly that the usage was not common, and required to be explained

[*] Wright, "Zechariah and his Prophecies," p. 317.

before it could be understood. Then, how could the three princes named be designated shepherds of Israel? Antiochus Epiphanes, indeed, held for a time supreme power over Judea, and so might be entitled to this appellation; but his successors never attained to this, and instead of being in any sense shepherds, can only be regarded as thieves and robbers, who sought to enter the fold not by the door, but by climbing up some other way. Besides, as it is probable that dynasties and not individuals are represented by the symbol of shepherds, these three princes belonging to one and the same dynasty would constitute only one shepherd, not three. That dynasties are here represented may be regarded as accepted by the majority of recent interpreters; and no opinion seems better supported than that of Ebrard, Kliefoth, Köhler, Keil, von Hoffmann, and others, that the three dynasties which successively held Israel in possession, the Babylonian, the Medo-Persian, and the Macedonian, are here adumbrated. These were emphatically *the* three shepherds from whose tyrannical despotism God delivered His people when He came forth to feed His flock of slaughter, and these were all cut off, were made to disappear (as the word literally means) in a comparatively short time. It was not in one *day*, not immediately, simultaneously and by one fell swoop that they were cut off; one after the other they were made to disappear, and that within a period comparatively short, yet long enough to admit of successive dynastic catastrophes. A more special explanation of the phrase "in one month" is given by Keil, following Köhler and Kliefoth. Assuming a month as consisting of thirty days, they divide the month into three parts of ten days each, and taking each ten days as the time employed in the destruction of a shepherd, they conclude that by this is indicated, " On the one hand, that the destruction of each of these shepherds followed directly upon that of the other; and on the other hand, that this took place after the full time allotted for his rule had passed away, ten being the number of the completion or the perfection of any earthly act or occurrence." It is no valid objection to this that it is fanciful, for in interpreting symbols fancy has its legitimate place. But it seems unnecessary. It is enough if the phrase be understood as an indefinite expression of a period neither short nor long, as compared with the whole period of the nation's existence.

The latter part of verse 8 is connected with what follows and begins a new paragraph, in which the activity of the shepherd, with the conduct towards him of the flock, is described.

XVII.

THE GOOD SHEPHERD REJECTED.

"And I took my staff, even Beauty, and cut it asunder, that I might break my covenant which I had made with all the people. And it was broken in that day: and so the poor of the flock that waited upon me knew that it was the word of the Lord. And I said unto them, If ye think good, give me my price; and if not, forbear. So they weighed for my price thirty pieces of silver. And the Lord said unto me, Cast it unto the potter: a goodly price that I was prized at of them. And I took the thirty pieces of silver, and cast them to the potter in the house of the Lord. Then I cut asunder mine other staff, even Bands, that I might break the brotherhood between Judah and Israel."—ZECH. xi. 10-14.

THE cutting off of the three shepherds or world-powers by which Israel had been oppressed and harassed was for the benefit of the flock, thereby delivered from those who were wrongfully misusing it. But unhappily the flock was not sensible of the kindness which had thus been shown to it by God; on the contrary, it resented His interference and refused His guidance; and so there came to be alienation and discord between them: "And my soul loathed them [rather—became weary of them, lost patience with them], and their soul also abhorred me" (ver. 8). The phrase "my soul," "their soul," is often used as a substitute for the personal pronoun, equivalent to "I myself," "they themselves;" but here it is used properly to express the intensity of the emotion felt.

The verb in the first clause means primarily to be shortened or cut short, and with "soul" (נַפְשִׁי) it expresses the idea of weariness, impatience, or vexation, the cutting short of one's power of endurance; comp. Judges xvi. 16; Job xxi. 4; Micah ii. 7. The verb in the latter clause occurs only here and in Prov. xx. 21; in the latter passage it conveys the idea of greedy eagerness (נַהֲלָה בְחָלַת): "An inheritance greedily acquired;" here it is used in the sense of loathing or abhorrence.* By some this latter part of the verse is understood of the three shepherds mentioned in the earlier part, and it is supposed that God here declares the reason of His cutting them off; it was because mutual loathing and abhorrence had arisen between them and Him. But though at first sight the pronoun "them" may seem naturally to refer to the shepherds in the immediately preceding clause, the construction of the larger context points to "the flock" in verse 7 as that here referred to. The verbs are all in the imperfect with vaw conversive, and must be translated in the same tense, the perfect; but if the latter part of the verse is understood of the shepherds, the verbs there must be taken as pluperfects (for God's impatience with the shepherds, and their abhorring of Him, must have preceded their being cut off, which would be incongruous, even if legitimate.†

---

* It may be doubted if the verb occurs anywhere but here; in Prov. xx. 21 the K'ri has מבהלת (*mbhlth*) "hastily gotten," and as all the ancient versions follow this reading, it may be regarded as the true one. בחל (*bchl*) is thus *hapaxlegomenon*, and is best explained from the Syriac *bhilo*, "to have nausea." The meaning "to be greedy" is derived from the verb from the Arabaic *bahala* "avarus fuit."

† "It is a moot and delicate question how far the imperfect with ן denotes

P

Further, from verse 9 it is evident that it was with the flock, and not with the shepherds, that God by the prophet became impatient, so that He relinquished the care of it, and left it to its fate. It is best, therefore, to regard the first part of verse 8 as a parenthetical clause, or as ampliative of the assertion "and I fed the flock," in verse 7 (the cutting off of the shepherds being part of what He did for the tending of the flock); and to understand the latter part of verse 8 as indicative of what led to the catastrophe described in the following verses.

The good shepherd had come to tend and protect the flock, but utter alienation and antagonism had arisen between them and him. Refusing to acknowledge him or to receive his care, they even returned abhorrence for his kindness; and he, despised and rejected by them, could no longer bear with them, his patience was exhausted, and so, after long effort, he was constrained to turn from them and leave them to their fate: "Then said I, I will not feed you; let that which dieth die, and let that which is cut off be cut off; and let those that remain eat each the flesh of another" (ver. 9). The flock was to be left, some to perish, and the rest to devour and destroy one another; the shepherd would no longer interpose to succour or protect them. The verbs

---

a *pluperfect*. There is, of course, no doubt that it may express the *continuance* of a pluperfect, . . . but can the imperfect with ן *introduce* it? Can it, instead of conducting us as usual to a *succeeding* act, *lead us back* to one which is chronologically anterior? . . . The imperfect with ן is, in the first place, certainly not the usual idiom chosen by the Hebrew writers for the purpose of expressing a pluperfect. . . . And, in the second place, the instances in which ן is even supposed to introduce a pluperfect are extremely rare; and the supposition rests upon a most precarious basis."
—Driver, *Use of the Tenses in Hebrew*, p. 92.

here are not jussive, but simply permissive or concessive, as the form תָּמוּת shows; the participles הַמֵּתָה and הַנִּכְחָדֶת are used here as presents; the feminine forms in this verse are to be accounted for from the words being collectives and neuters. (Ges. § 107, 3, d; Müller, pp. 46, 47.) The language in verse 9 "is most affecting. It is the language of one whose patience was exhausted; who was weary of repenting; who heaves the sigh of mingled pity and indignation, and throws up his charge in hopelessness" (Wardlaw). Hengstenberg remarks that "There are three kinds of destruction referred to here, as a comparison of the parallel passages will show: *plague*, such as usually breaks out in besieged cities; *violent death* from foreign foes; and *a terrible strife* among the citizens themselves, in consequence of existing distress." Comp. Jer. xv. 1, 2, xxxiv. 17; Ezek. vi. 12; Isa. ix. 19.

In the verses that follow there is a symbolical action described with its meaning. "And I took my staff Grace and cut it asunder, to frustrate (or abrogate) my covenant which I made with all peoples" (ver. 10). The covenant here referred to is not, as has been suggested, God's covenant with Noah as the father of the nations after the flood (Kliefoth), nor a covenant made by God with the nations, under which "they received good, in that the shepherd appointed by Jehovah ever and anon removed the shepherds that successively arose and destroyed the flock" (Hofmann, *Schriftbeweis* II., 2, p. 607); but an engagement in virtue of which the Lord put a restraint on the nations, so as to prevent their disturbing the peace of Israel. The restraining of any power from violence is elsewhere in Scripture described as a making of a covenant with that power; comp. Job v. 2, "With the stones of the field shall be thy covenant;" Hosea ii. 20 [18], "In that day will I make a covenant for them with the beast of the field," etc.; Ezek. xxxiv. 25, "I will make for them a covenant of peace, and will cause the evil beasts to cease out of the land," etc.; Isa. xxviii. 18, "We have made a covenant with death," etc.* As a covenant was made with the beast of the field, with the stones and with death, so as to restrain them from doing hurt to those for whose benefit the covenant was made, so God had covenanted with the nations, thereby to restrain them from doing injury to His flock. This was a covenant of grace for Israel; but no longer would the good shepherd thus care for the safety of the flock. His patience was exhausted by their obduracy, and the covenant He had made for their behoof should be dissolved. In token of this the shepherd cut in pieces his crook Grace. The covenant was abrogated just as the staff was destroyed; the thing signified was simultaneous with the symbol. The consequence was that Israel was harassed by violence from without, the nations being no longer restrained from attacking it; and so there was a fulfilment of the doom announced in the preceding verse. From this the pious part of the nation learned that this was indeed the word of the Lord: "And it [the covenant] was broken in that day; and so the wretched of the flock that observed me

---

* In Ecclus. xiv. 12 the phrase "covenant of Hades," διαθήκη ᾅδου, occurs, but there in a different sense. "Hades is personified. The covenant of Hades, that which Hades has made with thee, and which naturally includes the determining of thy death."—O. F. Fritzsche, *Ex. Hdb. dεn Apocr.* p. 70.

knew that it was the word of Jehovah" (ver. 11). Though rejected by the flock as a whole, there were some who had regard to the shepherd, and heard his voice and followed him. These are described as the wretched or miserable among the flock, *i.e.* without a figure, the poor and humble and suffering among the people. By them he was *observed*, regarded, that is, with respect and esteem, and heed was given to his words; comp. for this use of שָׁמַר Ps. xxxi. 7 [6 "regard"]; Prov. xxvii. 18; Hosea iv. 10; 2 Chron. vi. 16. Hence, when the restraint which had been put upon the nations was removed, and the covenant people were exposed to the assault of their enemies, these right-minded people, though the poor and despised of the community, recognised in the message which the shepherd had brought the word of Jehovah. When the prophet says, "They that regarded or gave heed to me," he speaks as the representative of the Lord, the good shepherd who came to feed the flock. "In that day," the day when he broke his staff and withdrew his protection from the flock. "So" (כֵּן), from this fact, "the prophet speaks of the event as past, because in the vision which passed before his mind the things described had actually occurred" (Hengstenberg).

The breaking of the staff Grace intimated the withdrawal of the shepherd's care from the flock. But before finally leaving them he demanded of them a return for his service to them: "And I said unto them, If it be good in your eyes, give me my wage; but if not, let it alone. And they weighed as my wage thirty silverlings" (verse 12). The speaker here is still the prophet, as representing the good shepherd. Those from whom he demands his wage are not, as some suppose, the shepherds of the flock (that is, the rulers of Israel), nor are they the poor of the flock, but the flock itself viewed as a whole; the apparent incongruity of the shepherd demanding his wage from the flock being obviated by the consideration that the flock, in this case, are rational beings—men. The shepherds, as the leaders of the nation, are, of course, included among those of whom the demand is made; but as it was not specially as *their* servant that the shepherd had acted, it was not from them that he could seek his wage. It was the flock that he came to minister to and to help, and it was, therefore, from them properly that he asked a return for his service. But what return could the flock give to him? The only return that a flock can render to its shepherd is that they should, as a whole, or in part, become his for his use. This was probably the way in which shepherds were paid for their work. "Who feedeth a flock and eateth not of the milk of the flock?" asks the Apostle, regarding this apparently as a matter of course (1 Cor. ix. 7). The wage which Jacob required for keeping the flock of Laban was that a portion of the flock should be allotted to him as his property; and had Jacob been the proper owner of the flock, he might have justly required that the whole should ultimately have been recovered by him. So here, the return which God, as the shepherd and proprietor of Israel, demanded of them as His flock was *themselves*. He sought nothing else, and with nothing else would He be satisfied. His reward for the care He had bestowed upon them was that they should return from all their wanderings and apostacy, and, with a true repentance and a sincere devotion, yield themselves unto Him, to be wholly and for ever His. Repentance, faith, obedience, loving trust and grateful piety, these are the only return which man can render to God for His beneficence, and these alone are such as He will accept. To secure these was the end of His coming, and these He demanded of the flock as His right. He left it, however, with themselves whether they would give or refuse what He claimed. He is no hireling, who *needs* to have His wage made over to Him, or will *enforce* the payment of it. It was not for His own sake that the demand was made, but for the sake of the sheep themselves, that an opportunity might be given them to acknowledge His goodness and submit anew to His guidance and care. Instead of this, however, what they actually displayed was their alienation from Him, and their contempt of His services; in lieu of what was His due, they weighed to Him as His "wage thirty pieces of silver," a paltry and contemptible sum, the price at which a female slave might be obtained (Hosea iii. 2), the compensation which the law appointed for the killing of a slave (Ex. xxi. 33). This was not only a foul insult, but also suggested an intention to compass His death. They despised His goodness, they would none of His service, they sought to cut Him off, and they were ready to pay the penalty which the law prescribed for the murder of one of so mean a condition.

Hitherto the prophet, as representing Jehovah, has been the speaker, but now the Lord Himself appears and speaks. Recognising the insult offered to His representative as an insult to Himself, He says to the prophet,

"Cast it unto the potter—the splendid price at which I have been valued by them!" (verse 13). This is the language of bitter irony and contempt. A blank refusal would have been less offensive than the offering of such a wage. God, therefore, commands His representative to cast it away in scorn, to fling it out as carrion might be flung to dogs, or as a dead body might be cast away unburied (compare Ex. xxii. 30 [31]; Jer. xxvi. 23, xxxvi. 30, where the same verb is used as here). The phrase "cast to the potter" is probably "a proverbial expression for contemptuous treatment, although we have no means of tracing the origin of the phrase satisfactorily" (Keil). Such modes of expression are in all languages; as the Greeks said ἐς κόρακας, and the Latins *in malam rem*, so we say "to the dogs," and the Germans *zum Schinder*, "to the Flayer" or "Knacker."* The origin of these phrases we may be able to trace, but our inability to do this in the case of the Hebrew phrase does not preclude our recognising it as analogous to them. Other interpretations of the phrase as here used have been given. Some of the ancient versions for "potter" have *treasury* (Syr.) or *treasurer* (Targ.); and this Ewald, Hitzig, Gesenius, and others among recent interpreters approve, some regarding יוֹצֵר as an Aramaism for אוֹצָר, *storehouse* or *treasury*, or as another form of that word, or of אוֹצֵר, *treasurer*. This is possible; but the supposition that the sacred treasury, or so high an officer as the Temple

---

* Βάλλ ἐς κόρακας, Arist. *Nub.* 133. I hinc in malam rem cum ista magnificentia. Ter. *Phorm.* V. 7, 37.{

> Had Colepepper's whole wealth been hops and hogs,
> Could he himself have sent it to the dogs?
> —Pope, *Mor. Ess.* III., 65.

treasurer, is here intended, is irreconcilable with the contemptuous form in which the command is conveyed. Grotius suggests that "potter" is here equivalent to "pottery," and that as there was a place near the Temple where the fragments of broken vessels that had been used in the Temple were thrown out, and where was probably a receptacle for rubbish of all sorts, the casting of anything to the potter means the treating it as a thing of no value, not more to be esteemed than the fragments of a potter's vessel. But there is no evidence that there was any such place near the Temple into which rubbish was thrown, and if there was it would hardly be known as the pottery, for a pottery is a place where vessels are made, not a place where the fragments of vessels are cast out. Hengstenberg endeavours to show that the Temple potter,—whom he supposes to be here indicated by the prefixing of the definite article, "for we cannot imagine there was only one potter in Jerusalem,"—had his workplace in the valley of Hinnom, and as this was regarded with disgust and abhorrence as an unclean place, the phrase "cast it to the potter" is equivalent to "Throw it into an unclean place." But the article here is simply generic; it indicates not an individual, but a class; nor is there any evidence that the potter who made vessels for the Temple had his workplace in the valley of Hinnom; on the contrary, not only is it in itself improbable that one whose business it was to prepare vessels for the Temple should have his manufactory in a place proverbially unclean, but in one of the passages cited by Hengstenberg to prove his point, the very opposite seems to be clearly taught, viz.: Jer. xix. 2, where we read, "Go forth into the valley of the son of Hinnom, which is at the entrance of the pottery gate," etc., from which it would appear that the pottery was not out in the valley, but inside the gate of the city by which that valley was approached; besides, if "the potter" is here an actual person, it appears from the following clause that it was in the Temple itself, and not outside the city, that he was to be found.

Another explanation is, that the sum being just enough to pay for a set of pots, purchased from the potter, the command to cast it to the potter is equivalent to "expend it on what is worthless:" just as we are accustomed to say of one who spends his money foolishly, that he throws it away; but earthenware pots are not altogether worthless, and if the purchaser got pots, the exchangeable value of which was equal to what he paid for them, he could not be said to have thrown away his money; not to mention that when money is paid to an artificer for his goods it is not flung to him contemptuously, but is put into his hand, or is told out before him deliberately. On the whole, no explanation seems so tenable as that above given from Keil.

In obedience to the Divine command, the prophet in vision cast away the thirty silverlings in the Temple: "And so I took the thirty pieces of silver and cast it in the house of Jehovah to the potter" (ver. 13*b*). This does not mean as Hengstenberg, to bring it into accordance with his explanation of the potter, has it, "I cast it into the house of Jehovah that it might be carried to the potter;" this is to put a meaning on the passage, not to interpret it; the meaning is simply what the words express, that the casting of the money, the wage (אתו *it*), to the potter was done in the Temple. The significance of this is that as the Temple was the place where God met with the people, and as this money was what they offered to Him as a return for His care of them as their shepherd, it was fitting that His indignant rejection of it should be shown in the place where it was customary for them to present their offerings, and where, when they gave to Him the return He required, He accepted their offering and gave them blessing in return.

The rejection by the shepherd of the offered wage was virtually the rejection of the flock by which it was offered, as, on the other hand, the offering of such a wage was virtually the rejection on their part of him as their shepherd. The relation between them was thus at an end; and in token of this the shepherd broke his other staff, and so left them to their fate: "And I broke asunder my second staff Bands, to annul the brotherhood between Judah and Israel." The union of Judah and Israel after the captivity was the restoration of the nation to its original integrity; the dissolving of this was the giving up of the nation to internal discord and strife. To this fate the nation was left when no longer guarded and tended by the good shepherd; and the breaking up of the nation into parties bitterly opposed to each other, hastened its ruin by making it an easy prey to the invader.

Thus by this symbolical vision the prophet intimated to his contemporaries the ultimate rejection of Israel by God, and the overthrow of their state in consequence of their wicked rejection of Him as their shepherd, in the person of His commissioned representative. Beyond this, however, there lies in this prophecy a prediction, the purport of which can be discovered only from its fulfilment. From the New Testament we learn that it is to the conduct of the Jews towards Jesus, the circumstances connected with their final rejection of Him, and the consequences to them as a nation of this, that the prophecy relates. Our Lord Himself claimed to be "the good shepherd," One with the Father, who had come to care for the sheep, and who was recognised as such by those who were truly His (John x. 14). For this the Jews sought to stone Him, accusing Him of blasphemy because He thus made Himself equal with God (verse 31 ff.), a charge which they persistently urged against Him, and on which He was ultimately adjudged to death. They thus requited Christ's fidelity as a shepherd with base ingratitude and cruel hatred, rejecting His pretensions, despising His person, condemning His services, and subjecting Him to shameful and barbarous treatment. The value at which they esteemed Him was measured by the price they were willing to pay for His capture, thirty pieces of silver, the value of a slave's life. This was paid to His betrayer, but was by Him afterwards offered back to those from whom he received it, and being refused by them, was flung down in the Temple, whence it was taken and expended on the purchase of a piece of ground know as "the potter's field" (Matt. xxvii. 3–8). There is thus a close correspondence between the prophet's description and the facts in our Lord's history in relation to the Jews, their treatment of Him and the circumstances attendant on His death; and in these the Evangelist finds the fulfilment of what is here spoken by the prophet (Matt. xxvii. 9, 10).

That it is this prophecy which the Evangelist says was thus fulfilled appears unquestionable; not only in the general, but in the main details, the narrative of the Evangelist corresponds so closely to the description of the prophet, that it cannot be doubted that it is to this he refers when he says, "Then was fulfilled that which was spoken by the prophet." There are, however, some difficulties in the way of this conclusion. The chief of these arises from the fact that the Evangelist ascribes the words he cites to Jeremiah and not to Zechariah. That this is a mistake appears certain. There was only one Jeremiah, the prophet known to the Jews, the prophet whose writings are extant in the Old Testament Canon; and among these there is no passage which corresponds to that cited by the Evangelist. How the mistake occurred it is impossible to say. That it is to be traced to the Evangelist himself can hardly be credited; for even supposing that in the haste of composition he had made the mistake, is it conceivable that he should have neglected to correct it before sending forth his writing to the world? More probable is it that it originated with the first or an early transcriber of the Evangelist's manuscript; and there is great probability in the suggestion that as St. Matthew, in citing from the prophets, usually does so without naming the prophet from whom he cites, he wrote here simply, "thus was fulfilled that which was spoken by the prophet," and the name Jeremiah was interpolated by the transcriber. At the same time it is not easy to see what motive any copyist could have had to make such an addition to the text; or if he made it by mistake, why it was not immediately corrected. It has, indeed, been suggested that St. Matthew, writing his Gospel in Hebrew, wrote ביד הנביא and that the translator reading ביר instead of ביד took this as a contraction for בירמיהו, and so boldly wrote it, in full, in Greek διὰ Ἰερεμίου; but this, besides assuming what is not certain —that the first Gospel was originally written in Hebrew —is only too ingenious to be accepted as probable. It has also been suggested that as the name of Jeremiah stood in the beginning of the volume which was in the transcriber's hands, and that as when references were made to a collection of writings it was usual to quote the name given in the general inscription; the name of Jeremiah was inserted here, not as that of the author of the prophecy, but as the title of the book in which the prophecy is found. Of this all that can be said is that it is possible; but as no other instance can be produced in which the prophecies are cited by the New Testament writers in this way, it is not probable that in this solitary case this has been done. It is best to confess that we cannot account for the copyist making such a mistake; but nevertheless it may yet remain probable that it is by him that the mistake has been made.

Between the passage as cited by the Evangelist, and as it appears in the language of the prophet there are some marked discrepancies, and this occasions a difficulty in the way of regarding this as the prediction said to be fulfilled by the facts narrated by the Evangelist. The difficulty, however, is not insurmountable. The Evangelist, it is evident, does not cite the prophecy directly either from the Hebrew or from the LXX, and may be therefore regarded as not having intended to do more than simply to note generally the purport of the prophet's representation, without exactly translating his words. Accordingly the clause, "the price of Him that was valued whom they of the children of Israel did value," may be viewed as a free rendering, or an exposition, from the Evangelist's point of view, of the exclamation in the prophecy, "a splendid price at which I was valued by them!" So in respect of the payment of the money and the ultimate appropriation of it, the difference between the two statements is merely a difference in point of form, not of substance; the price is the same in both; in both that price measures the value set upon the services of Him who was thus prized, and indicates the contempt with which He was regarded by those whom He came to serve; in both the money is represented as flung down in the Temple and appropriated ultimately to the potter; and in both this is represented as done in obedience to the Divine appointment, the words, "as the Lord appointed me," in the Gospel being parallel to the words, "and the Lord said to me," of the prophecy. That it was Judas and not Christ Himself to whom the thirty pieces of silver were given; that they were paid by the high priests and elders as the representatives of the nation, and not by the people themselves; that the money was cast away, not in scorn of the vileness of the price, but from remorse and horror on the part of him who had accepted it as the price of betraying innocent blood; and that it was expended on the purchase of the potter's field instead of being cast away to the potter,—what are these but simply the forms by means of which the vague and dim symbols of the prophecy came to be translated into actual historical fact? Therefore " however indirect and obscure the prefiguration might be, we are not to regard the reference by Matthew as a mere *accommodation*. There was in what befell the prophet a designed foreshadowing of what in the future should befall the prophet's Lord " (Wardlaw).

XVIII.

THE EVIL SHEPHERD'S DOOM.

" And the Lord said unto me, Take unto thee yet the instruments of a foolish shepherd. For, lo, I will raise up a shepherd in the land, which shall not visit those that be cut off, neither shall seek the young one, nor heal that that is broken, nor feed that that standeth still: but he shall eat the flesh of the fat, and tear their claws in pieces. Woe to the idol shepherd that leaveth the flock! the sword shall be upon his arm, and upon his right eye: his arm shall be clean dried up, and his right eye shall be utterly darkened."
—ZECH. xi. 15–17.

THE flock having contemptuously rejected the shepherd who had come to feed them, and he on his part having indignantly repudiated them and left them to their fate, his place was taken by a shepherd of another kind, by whom the flock was neglected or harassed. As the prophet had represented the good shepherd in the former vision, he is summoned to personate the evil shepherd in this: "And Jehovah said to me, Take unto thee yet again the implements of a foolish shepherd" (ver. 15). The "yet again" (עוֹד) connects this new symbolical action with the preceding one, for it implies that previously the prophet had taken the implements of a shepherd in his hand. The implements of a shepherd are the things he uses in the feeding and tending of his flock, especially the staff, or crook, and the taking of these is emblematical of his actually engaging in the work of a shepherd. In this case it was a foolish shepherd that the prophet was to represent; one, that is, not only unwise, imprudent, and unskilled, but also ill-disposed; one whose action towards the flock would be to the injury and destruction of that which he professed to tend and keep. That by the shepherd here is intended not a succession of native rulers of the Jewish nation (as Hengstenberg supposes), but some one dominant power by which the nation was to be subdued and oppressed, appears evident from the contrast of this evil shepherd with the good shepherd, who was Jehovah Himself, the King and Shepherd of Israel. It is doubtless, as Keil remarks, "the possessor of the imperial power into whose hand the nation was given up after the rejection of the good shepherd sent to it in Christ, *i.e.*, the Roman empire which destroyed the Jewish state," that is here represented.

Whilst the good shepherd tended the flock carefully and kindly, the evil shepherd had no regard to it except as he might violently rend it for his own uses: "For lo, I raise up a shepherd in the land; those that be cut off he will not visit, the dispersed he will not seek, the wounded he will not heal, neither will he sustain that which is strong; but the flesh of the fat he will eat, and their claws (hoofs) he will tear off" (ver. 16).

The "for" introduces the reason why the prophet was to act symbolically the part of the evil shepherd; it was because God had determined to let Israel fall under the power of a shepherd who should not merely neglect the flock, but harass and destroy it. "The cut off" (cf. verse

9) are not those actually destroyed (for such there could be no possibility of visiting), but such as are cut off or separated from the flock, so that they cease to belong to it or disappear from it (LXX, τὸ ἐκλεῖπον ἐκλιμπάνον, Vulg. *derelicta;* in Job xv. 21, the verb is used of cities forsaken or deserted). Rosenmüller explains it by "gravissime aegrotantes," and the reference probably is to such as were separated from the flock because of some disease, and which were, therefore, proper objects for the shepherd to visit. For "the dispersed" the A. V. has "the young," taking נַעַר here in the sense in which it commonly appears, that of "young man," and so of the young of animals generally, in this case of sheep. But *na'ar* is nowhere else used of the young of the lower animals, and it seems incongruous to think of lambs in this connection, for, as Bochart remarks, "A lamb seldom needs to be *sought,* for it hardly ever strays from the flock, but is wont to abide by its dam" (*Hierozoic.* p. 489). It is better to regard the word as a formation from נָעַר *to shake,* in Piel, *to shake out, to scatter* or *disperse.* Hence *a casting out, a dispersion,* and, the abstract for the concr., *cast out, scattered, dispersed;* so the LXX here τὸ ἐσκορπισμένον, the Vulg. *dispersum,* Targ. *d'ittaltalu,* "who have been dispersed," or "have wandered." "The wounded," lit. "the broken," those injured through the fracture of a limb; opposed to which are "they that stand" (הַנִּצָּבָה) that is, are firm on their limbs, whole and strong (LXX ὁλόκληρον).

Besides thus neglecting the flock, the evil shepherd should devour and destroy it, not only consuming the flesh of the fat ones, but even tearing asunder the cloven hoof of the animal, that nothing might escape his devouring greed. Thus Israel should be destroyed of the destroyer. God had, before this, punished His people for their apostacy, by delivering them up to harsh and rapacious rulers (comp. Jer. xxiii. 1, 2; Ez. xxxiv. 2-4); but as their rebellion against Him had now culminated in their rejection and maltreatment of the shepherd He had sent to them, the penalty had at length come upon them to the uttermost, and they should be wholly consumed of the enemy.

But whilst the evil shepherd should thus be the instrument of punishing Israel for their apostacy, he himself should be in turn the object of the Divine vengeance, because of his iniquity: "Woe to the worthless shepherd who leaveth the flock! The sword shall be upon his arm and upon his right eye; his arm shall wither away, and his right eye shall become utterly dim" (verse 17). The shepherd who neglects his flock is of nought as a shepherd; he is worthless, and being such deserves to be punished. And as he neglected to use his arm and his eye, the organs properly required for the tending and watching of the flock, his fitting punishment is the depriving him of the use of these. "The sword" is here simply the emblem of a destructive power. There is no reference here to the sword as that which is to hew off the arm and pierce out the eye, as is evident from the addition that the arm is to wither and the eye to become dim; the two descriptions simply express strongly the certainty and severity of the punishment that should come upon the worthless shepherd; he should be utterly deprived of that power which he had so badly used. In the A. V. the shepherd is described as the "idol shepherd;" but though, from the fact that idols were counted as things of nought (οὐδὲν εἴδωλον ἐν κόσμῳ, 1 Cor. viii. 4), the epithet, "the nought, the worthless," is applied to them in Scripture, there is no reason for introducing the word "idol" here. "With this threat, the threatening word concerning the imperial power of the world (chapters ix.–xi.) is very appropriately brought to a close, inasmuch as the prophecy thereby returns to its starting-point." (Keil.)

XIX.

ISRAEL'S CONFLICT AND VICTORY.

"The burden of the word of the Lord for Israel, saith the Lord, which stretcheth forth the heavens, and layeth the foundation of the earth, and formeth the spirit of man within him. Behold, I will make Jerusalem a cup of trembling unto all the people round about, when they shall be in the siege both against Judah and against Jerusalem. And in that day will I make Jerusalem a burdensome stone for all people: all that burden themselves with it shall be cut in pieces, though all the people of the earth be gathered together against it. In that day, saith the Lord, I will smite every horse with astonishment, and his rider with madness; and I will open mine eyes upon the house of Judah, and will smite every horse of the people with blindness. And the governors of Judah shall say in their heart, the inhabitants of Jerusalem shall be my strength in the Lord of hosts their God. In that day will I make the governors of Judah like an hearth of fire among the wood, and like a torch of fire in a sheaf; and they shall devour all the people round about, on the right hand and on the left: and Jerusalem shall be inhabited again in her own place, even in Jerusalem. The Lord also shall save the tents of Judah first, that the glory of the house of David, and the glory of the inhabitants of Jerusalem, do not magnify themselves against Judah. In that day shall the Lord defend the inhabitants of Jerusalem; and he that is feeble among them at that day shall be as David; and the house of David shall be as God, as the angel of the Lord before them."—ZECH. xii. 1-8.

WITH this chapter commences a new section of the prophetic utterances concerning Israel, extending to the end of chapter xiv. It comprises two distinct but closely allied prophecies; the one relating to the conflict of Israel with the nations—the victory and ultimate sanctification of the covenant people (xii. 1–xiii. 6); the other setting forth the judgment by which Israel should be wholly refined, and with that the final glory of Jerusalem (xiii. 7, xiv. 21). In the former of these there are four sections, viz., xii. 1–4, the conflict with the nations and their destruction; 5–9, the endowment of the princes of Judah and inhabitants of Jerusalem with strength to overcome all their foes; 10–14, the pouring out on them of the spirit of grace, so that they shall bitterly repent their maltreatment of the Divine Shepherd; and xiii. 1–6, the cleansing of Israel and their entire restoration from all apostacy. The inscription, "The burden of the Word of Jehovah," is the title of the entire prophecy.

"The burden of the Word of Jehovah over (or concerning) Israel." This title corresponds to that inscribed on the preceding prophecy, chapter ix. 1. *Massa* has here, as there, its proper meaning of *burden;* but as the prophecy is not directed immediately against Israel, but rather against the enemies of Israel, though, at the same time, intimating that it was through affliction and trial that Israel was to pass to victory and blessing, the burden is not said to be *on* (בְּ), but rather *over* or *concerning* (עַל) Israel. There is a difference also in the reason by which the oracle is enforced; in the former it is the omniscience of God, whose eye is upon all men, that is referred to; here it is the Divine omnipotence to which appeal is implicitly made. This oracle is the saying of Him "who stretcheth out the heavens and layeth the foundation of the earth, and formeth the spirit of man within him" (ver. 1). As God upholds and directs all the material universe by the word of His power, and as

He moulds and regulates each man's inner nature as He sees meet, there can be no uncertainty as to the accomplishment of all that He predicts. It is not so much to the original creation of all things material and spiritual by God that reference is here made, as to the continual agency of God in maintaining and ordering the universe He has formed in all its parts. He implanted in man a spirit, an intelligent nature, at first, and He fashions (יצר, moulds as a potter) each man's spirit not only in its original constitution, but also in its dispositions, tendencies and actings (cf. Prov. xxi. 1; Jer. xix. 1 ff.; Rom. ix. 21; Phil. ii. 13). He who stretched forth the heavens like a curtain and settled the earth on its basis, has power over that which He has thus framed, to order it as He wills (cf. Ps. civ. 2 ff.). The resources of the universe are at His disposal; "He doth according to His will in the army of heaven and among the inhabitants of the earth; and none can stay His hand or say unto Him, What doest Thou?" (Dan. iv. 35.) With perfect confidence, then, may His people rest assured that what He has promised He will perform, what He has said He will bring to pass.

The enemy hovering over Jerusalem should make an attack upon it, but only to be himself thrown back and made to stagger to ruin like a drunken man: "Lo, I will make Jerusalem a bowl of reeling to all the peoples around, and also upon Judah shall it be in the siege against Jerusalem" (ver. 2). "The bowl of reeling" is a goblet filled with intoxicating drink, of which those who partake are maddened and destroyed. The figure is often employed in Scripture to denote the judgment which God inflicts upon transgressors for their punishment (cf. Isa. li. 17; Jer. xxv. 15 ff., xlix. 12; Ezek. xxiii. 31 ff.; Hab. ii. 16). As those who drain the intoxicating cup are sickened or frenzied thereby, lose all power of self-direction and ultimately fall helplessly to the ground, so are those upon whom the judgment of God falls paralysed, cast down and destroyed. Such a source of misery and ruin should Jerusalem be to those hostile powers by which it was assailed; "Ita enim eos inebriabit ut vertigine correpti ruant, atque ad mortem soporentur" (Rosenm.). The latter part of this verse is obscure, and has been variously explained. According to the Authorised Version, the statement is as to the *time* or *occasion* when Jerusalem shall prove a bowl of reeling to the nations around it; but this interpretation is obtained at the expense of an entire misrendering of the words of the passage. St. Jerome's explanation is that "Judah, during the siege of Jerusalem, being captured by the nations, and passing into alliance with them, is compelled to join in the siege of its own metropolis," which is substantially the explanation of the Targum and Jewish interpreters, as well as of Rosenmüller, Ewald, and others, among those of more recent times. In support of this it is urged that the phrase יִהְיֶה עַל involves the idea of obligation resting upon the party who is the object of it, so that to be upon Judah here means that obligation is laid on Judah. But, thus construed, the sentence is incomplete, for, to make sense, we must supply some such phrase as "to be" or "to act," and read the clause thus: "And on Judah it shall be laid to be in the siege," etc. But this is to *make* a meaning for the passage, not to bring out the meaning of the passage as it stands. Besides, "There is not the slightest indication in what follows of any participation on the part of Judah in the siege of Jerusalem; on the contrary, Judah is represented as the ally of Jerusalem, by whose victories, obtained through the help of the Lord, Jerusalem is to be delivered" (Hengstenberg). The statement in xiv. 14 that "Judah shall fight also against Jerusalem," relates to a later epoch and a different condition of affairs from this. In the Geneva Version the clause is rendered, "And also with Judah will she be in the siege against Jerusalem," with the explanatory note "Jerusalem shall be defended against all her enemies; so shall God defend all Judah also;" and this rendering is retained in the margin of the Authorised Version. To the rendering, as such, no objection can be taken; but as the Lord is the speaker here, it is obviously improper to regard Him as the subject of the clause. It is better, therefore, to render "also against Judah shall it be in the siege against Jerusalem." This, however, leaves the subject of the clause undetermined. Various suggestions have been offered as to this. Hengstenberg says, "The subject to יִהְיֶה is to be obtained in part from מַשָּׂא, *burden*, in part also from the previous clause." Pusey adopts this in the main, affirming that *massa* "is the only natural subject," and explaining the purport of the clause to be, that "the burden of the word of the Lord which was on Jerusalem should be also on Judah, *i.e.*, upon all, small and great;" and with this Keil also is substantially in accordance. "The best course," he says, "is probably to take it [the subject] from the previous clause, 'that which passes over Jerusalem.'" Adopting this, the purport of the clause is, that the country at large should be involved in the same kind of calamity as the capital; as Jerusalem should be besieged, Judah should be at the same time invaded by the peoples round about.

To those who assailed Jerusalem she should be a bowl of reeling; to those who sought to remove and carry her away she should prove a burden that would only injure those who attempted to bear it: "And it shall be in that day that I will make Jerusalem a burdensome stone to all the peoples; all who lift it shall surely be lacerated, and all the nations of the earth shall be gathered against her" (ver. 3). Jerome supposes that allusion is here made to a custom in the towns of Palestine, which prevailed even in his day, of placing large round stones of great weight, with which the youths exercised themselves by attempting to lift them; and he gives the sense of the passage as, "I will place Jerusalem to all nations as a heavy stone to be lifted; lift it indeed they will, and according to their power will devastate it; but of necessity through the effort to raise so heavy a weight the stone will inflict a certain rent or wound on those who lift it." But as the case supposed here is not that of exercise for amusement or for display of strength, but that of hostile attack and capture, it is better to understand the figure of the raising of a stone for the purpose of carrying it away, or of using it in building or otherwise. The stone would be found not only heavy and burdensome, but would positively injure the bearer by lacerating his hands or dislocating his sinews; even so Jerusalem would prove, to those who sought to take her and use her for their own ends, not only a heavy burden, but a cause of injury and distress. As the statement is quite general, there is no need for inquiring what special end it is to which those who lift up Jerusalem may intend to adapt her—such, for instance, as that suggested by Dr. Wright, the "fitting of the stone of Jerusalem into any of the political structures which they might seek to erect;" it is enough to accept the general declaration that they who would seize on Jerusalem and make her subserve their own ends shall find her a burden, which, too heavy for them, will overtask their strength, and recoil with disastrous effect upon themselves. And this shall happen not once only, or with one nation only; time after time, and with the world powers generally, will this take place: "All the nations of the earth shall be gathered against her;" "The prophet marshals them all against Jerusalem only to say how they should perish before it" (Pusey) (cf. Joel iii. 2 [Heb. iv. 2]).

In what follows, the entire overthrow of those who would oppress and suppress Israel is announced: "In that day, saith the Lord, I will smite every horse with consternation, and its rider with madness; but upon the house of Judah will I open my eyes, and every horse of the peoples will I smite with blindness" (ver. 4). The three plagues, *consternation, madness*, and *blindness*, are those which God threatened to send upon the Israelites in case of their disobedience (Deut. xxviii. 28); these He now declares He would inflict on the enemies of Israel. In Scripture, "the horse and his rider" is a phrase characteristic of warlike strength and power, and is specially used of the power of the heathen (cf. Ex. xv. 1, 21; Job xxxix. 18; Jer. li. 21; Hag. ii. 22); and the smiting of these here indicates that God would utterly paralyse the enemies of Jerusalem, so that though the whole world conspired against her, He would thwart all their efforts, repel their assault, frustrate their designs, and ultimately destroy them. Struck with consternation, utterly infatuated and blinded with terror, they should rush on their own ruin; confusion would reign through their ranks; and they should "come down every one by the sword of his brother" (Hag. ii. 22; cf. Judges vii. 22; 1 Sam. xiv. 20; Zech. xiv.). But whilst destruction thus awaited the assailants of Jerusalem, the Lord would open His eyes on Judah. The eyes of the Lord are upon the righteous (Ps. xxxiv. 15); and of the land of Israel it was said by Moses, ages before this, "It is a land which Jehovah thy God careth for; the eyes of Jehovah thy God are always upon it, from the beginning of the year even unto the end thereof" (Deut. xi. 12). This secures for Israel the protection and care of the Almighty (cf. 1 Kings viii. 29; Neh. i. 6; Jer. xxiv. 6). "The house of Judah" is here the covenant nation as a whole.

In the next verse the governors or chiefs of Judah are represented as reposing with confidence in the strength of the capital and the valour of its inhabitants under God: "And the princes of Judah will say in their hearts, 'Strength to me are the dwellers in Jerusalem, by Jehovah of hosts their God'" (ver. 5). "The princes of Judah" are the leaders of the people in war, and the confidence which they feel is that with which the entire nation is inspired. To " say in their hearts " is to have a firm, settled conviction—not a loud, boastful profession, but a quiet, serene, heartfelt assurance. The singular " to *me* " expresses the individuality of the conviction; each individual in the host had it as for himself. This assurance which they had in the inhabitants of Jerusalem rested not on anything in them, but because Jehovah of hosts was with them and would help them. From Him would come united counsels, wise plans, ready co-operation, as well as courage and might, to both rulers and people; and so they would be made strong against all their adversaries (cf. i. 17, ii. 12, iii. 2, x. 12). The effect of this would be that they should overcome and destroy their enemies: " In that day will I make the princes of Judah as a pan of fire among sticks, and as a flaming torch in a sheaf; and they shall consume on the right hand and on the left all the people round about; and Jerusalem shall dwell in her place, in Jerusalem, continuously " (ver. 6). Strengthened and sustained by God, the princes of Judah should as readily vanquish their enemies as a pan of fire cast among dry faggots would consume them, or a torch placed under a sheaf of corn would reduce it to ashes. As a consequence, Jerusalem, personified here as a female, should continue to sit in her own place, in Jerusalem her city. And not only should the capital, the strong city, abide in safety; the country at large, even the outlying villages and the dwellers in huts, should share in the security: " The Lord also will succour the tents of Judah first (or, according to another reading, supported by the LXX, Syriac and Vulgate, as in former days), in order that the splendour of the house of David and the splendour of the inhabitants of Jerusalem may not exalt itself over Judah" (ver. 7). By "the tents of Judah" are designated the inhabitants of the land generally; not, as has been suggested, those dwelling in "huts which cannot afford any protection to their inhabitants" (Calvin), but the country at large, with its inhabitants, as distinguished from Jerusalem, with its princes and people. It is not of much moment which of the two readings above noted is followed, as in either case it is the deliverance of Judah as preceding that of Jerusalem that is intimated. This should be in order to preclude any exaltation of itself by the capital or its princes over the nation at large. "The splendour (תִּפְאֶרֶת, beauty, magnificence, glory, not boasting here) of the house of David," is the glory and honour which God should put upon Zerubbabel, in whom the royal line was continued (cf. Hag. ii. 20–23; Zech. iv. 6–10, 14); and "the splendour of the inhabitants of Jerusalem" is the dignity and honour which rested on that city because of God's habitation there, and the glory that should come upon it from this (cf. i. 16, ii. 8–13). The general purport of this announcement is that the whole covenant nation should participate in the salvation of the Lord alike, and that this should be brought about by the country at large being delivered sooner than the metropolis, so that the latter should have no vocation to lift itself up above the former, but both should rejoice together in that salvation which the Lord had brought.

Through the assault of the heathen powers Jerusalem was plunged in conflict; but, endowed with marvellous strength, she should be able to resist all their efforts and ultimately to overcome and destroy them. "In that day shall the Lord protect the inhabitants of Jerusalem; and he that is feeble among them in that day shall be as David; and the house of David shall be as God, as the angel of Jehovah before them" (ver. 8). Jerusalem was the city of God, the place of His habitation, and over it He would watch with constant care to protect it from all harm (cf. 2 Kings xix. 34, xx. 6; Isa. xxxi. 5, xxxvii. 35, &c.). In it there were some who were weak; some who through weakness could not stand steady on their feet, but stumbled (*hannikshal*) (1 Sam. ii. 4). These, when God came to protect the inhabitants of Jerusalem, should be as David, strong and brave and potent as was He, the great hero of their nation (cf. 1 Sam. xvi. 18; 2 Sam. xvii. 18; 1 Chron. xiv. 17). And whilst the weak should thus be made strong, they that were already strong and powerful, "the house of David," the chiefs and leaders of the people, should be endowed with supernatural might; they should be as God, mighty as the angel of Jehovah who went up with Israel out of Egypt, discomfited their enemies and led them through the wilderness to the promised land (Ex. xxiii. 20 ff.; Josh. v. 13 ff.; Ps. cvi. 9, 10). "The general meaning is that the Lord God will strengthen the weakest and give additional elevation, honour, and influence to the highest, and add divinely to the might of the mightiest, so that no opposing power shall ever stand before them, any more than when that Divine angel of the covenant was commissioned to be their conductor and guardian, of whom Jehovah said, MY NAME IS IN HIM" (Wardlaw). And whilst God thus endows His people with strength, He will come forth against their enemies and seek to destroy them (ver. 9). God here speaks after the manner of men. He says that He will *seek* to destroy the enemies of Jerusalem, to indicate that this was His determined purpose, that on which He was bent and which He certainly would effect.

XX.

PENITENCE AND GRACE.

"And it shall come to pass in that day, that I will seek to destroy all the nations that come against Jerusalem. And I will pour upon the house of David, and upon the inhabitants of Jerusalem, the spirit of grace and of supplications: and they shall look upon me whom they have pierced, and they shall mourn for him, as one mourneth for his only son, and shall be in bitterness for him, as one that is in bitterness for his firstborn. In that day shall there be a great mourning in Jerusalem, as the mourning of Hadadrimmon in the valley of Megiddon. And the land shall mourn, every family apart; the family of the house of David apart, and their wives apart; the family of the house of Nathan apart, and their wives apart; the family of the house of Levi apart, and their wives apart; the family of Shimei apart, and their wives apart; all the families that remain, every family apart, and their wives apart."—ZECH. xii. 9–14.

STILL more than all previous kindnesses would God do for His people; not only should their enemies be discomfited and destroyed, they themselves should be resuscitated and restored. This should be effected by the pouring out upon them of the spirit of grace and supplication, so that they should come to a knowledge of their sin and a sincere and genuine repentance: "And I will pour out upon the house of David, and upon the inhabitants of Jerusalem, the spirit of grace and of supplications: and they will look upon me whom they have pierced, and will mourn over Him like the mourning for an only son, and will bitterly lament like the bitter lamenting for a firstborn" (ver. 10). Though in the preceding context the house of David and the inhabitants of Jerusalem are distinguished from the people of Judea, they seem here to stand synecdochically for the people as a whole, since the effect of the outpouring is described as extending to every family of the nation (12-14): on the nation at large God would pour forth the spirit of grace and supplications. This is often explained as meaning the spirit which is gracious, whose working is of grace, which is also the spirit of prayer, as that which produces, leads to, and directs prayer. But there is a manifest incongruity in this interpretation; the two genitives, which are evidently analogous, being treated as different; the one the genitive of subject, the other of object. It is better to take both as *objective*; the spirit of grace as that which produces or bestows grace, the spirit of supplications as that which leads to prayer and teaches to pray. Properly, indeed, *grace* is the favour felt and shown by a benefactor to the object of his regard; but in Scripture, according to a figure of speech frequently used, grace often means, not the favour which produces certain effects in men, but the effects themselves thereby produced (cf. Ps. xlv. 2 [3], lxxxiv. 11 [12]; Prov. iii. 34; Zech. iv. 7; Rom. i. 5, v. 2; 1 Cor. xv. 10; 2 Cor. iv. 15, viii. 6, 7; Eph. iv. 29; Phil. i. 7; 2 Pet. iii. 18). Here accordingly "grace" may be taken as equivalent to "grace-gift," and as signifying that disposition or condition of mind, or that state of privilege and blessing which comes from God's favour, and makes the recipient of it gracious and blessed. Of this the Holy Spirit, the Spirit of God is the author, and hence He is here called "The Spirit of Grace," not, as some have suggested, because He draws forth the Divine grace to men (which is not a biblical representation), but because He is Himself the author of grace and blessing to men (cf. Heb. x. 29). Some would render here by "a spirit," but though רוּחַ is without the article, yet being in the construct state it may be regarded as definite (Müller, *Heb. Syn.*, § 66). He is also "The Spirit of Supplications," because it is by Him that men are prompted and taught to pray. The word here used, תַּחֲנוּנִים, is derived from the verb חָנַן, which, in the hithpahel from which the noun is formed, signifies to implore favour, to ask for grace (Deut. iii. 23; Esth. iv. 8; Job xix. 16; Ps. xxx. 8 [9]; Hos. xii. 4 [5]); it is used for the most part where a cry to God for favour or blessing is intended; here probably also with allusion to חֵן "grace" in the conjoined clause. This spirit God would pour out on all classes, great and small, rich and poor, governor and subject (cf. Joel ii. 28, 29 [iii. 1, 2]); and consequent on this should be a general penitential mourning and bitter sorrow throughout the nation. "They shall look" (*habîtu*), shall look earnestly, look with interest and feeling (cf. Num. xxi. 9; Isa. lxiii. 5), "upon me whom they have pierced." The speaker here is Jehovah; and here lies the difficulty of the passage. How, it may be asked, can it in any sense be said that God is pierced? The difficulty has been felt from the earliest times, and various expedients have been resorted to in order to surmount or evade it. In several MSS. the reading אֵלָיו *on Him* is substituted in place of אֵלַי *on me;* but this is evidently an arbitrary correction suggested by the עָלָיו in the following clause; the textual reading is that of the majority of MSS., including the best, and is supported by all the ancient versions. The other reading derives no support from John xix. 37, for the Evangelist is not there quoting the passage in the words of the prophet, but rather giving the purport of it as from his own point of view; nor is there any force in the objection that the textual reading is at variance with the עָלָיו of the next clause, for in the poetical and prophetical books a change of one person for another in the same context is not uncommon. It is probable that here the introduction of the clause אֵת אֲשֶׁר may have had the effect of inducing the change. These words Kimchi takes as equivalent to בַּעֲבוּר שׁ in the sense of "because of Him whom," and this interpretation other Jews adopt; but it cannot be shown that *'eth 'asher* can have this meaning. The rendering in the LXX is ἀνθ' ὧν κατωρχήσαντο *pro eo quod insultaverunt,* because 'that they insulted or derided. This rendering Jerome suggests that they adopted from reading רקדו in place of דקרו, but more probably they designedly adopted this in order to soften the expression, understanding "pierce" metaphorically as equivalent to piercing with words, assailing with cutting reproaches, just as נקב *to bore* is used in the sense of *blaspheme, curse.* All the other ancient Greek versions, however, have ἐξεκέντησαν; and though Calvin, Rosenmüller, Gesenius, and other interpreters of eminence take the verb metaphorically (" confixio pro continua irritatione," Calv.; " probris lacessiverunt," Ros.), it is undoubtedly to be taken here in its proper sense. For (1) this verb which occurs in ten other places is nowhere used except in the literal acceptation of piercing or stabbing, and generally to the effect of slaying (cf. Num.

xxv. 8; Judges ix. 54; 1 Sam. xxxi. 4; 1 Chron. x. 4; Isa. xiii. 15; Jer. xxxvii. 10, li. 4; Lam. iv. 9); and (2), as Hitzig remarks, the connection requires the verb to be understood literally, otherwise how could the lamenting be described by the verb סָפַד, which, followed by עַל of the person, properly expresses mourning for the dead? Keil proposes to get over the difficulty by regarding the Maleach Jehovah, the Angel of Jehovah, as the object of the piercing; but this leaves the difficulty as great as ever, for as the angel of Jehovah is identified with Jehovah Himself, so that (as Keil himself remarks) "the slaying of the Maleach" might be described "as the slaying of Jehovah," the one representation is as hard to conceive as the other. Not a few interpreters think the difficulty solved by a reference to the two natures, the Divine and the human, united in the Person of the Messiah; but even if we regard this as a direct Messianic prediction, the twofold constitution of Christ's person will not help to account for the language here used, inasmuch as it was only the human body of our Lord, and not His Divine nature, that was pierced. The explanation suggested by Hitzig is by much the best: "The passage is explained simply from the identification of the Sender with the Sent (comp. Barachoth, v. 5, כָּמוֹהוּ שְׁלוּחוֹ שֶׁל אָדָם; Mark ix. 37; Luke x. 16), Jehovah with the prophet. By this, as we have seen, the words *which I had made*, &c., in the mouth of the prophet—xi. 10—are to be explained; and as there the paying off of him is that of Jehovah, ver. 13, so here the slaying of the prophet is viewed as if it had been that of Jehovah." The Good Shepherd is still present in the prophet's vision; and in the piercing of him, as Jehovah's representative, there is symbolically shadowed forth what took place in fact when the real representative of Jehovah, the Good Shepherd Himself, after being contumeliously treated, was pierced and put to death by those He had come to feed. Beholding Him whom they had pierced, and, as they beheld, awakened to a sense of the greatness of their sin, they should be filled with penitential sorrow, and would bitterly deplore their misconduct; they should mourn for Him (not as Iarchi proposes *for it*, i.e., the crime of which they had been guilty; the comparison of this mourning to that over an only son and a firstborn shows that it is a *person* and not a *deed* that is here referred to). Keil thinks that "the transition from the first person (אֵלַי) to the third (עָלָיו) points to the fact that the person slain, though essentially one with Jehovah, is personally distinct from the Supreme God;" but for this there seems no good ground; the change is purely arbitrary, and is merely one of phraseology. The mourning should be like that for an only son or a firstborn, proverbially the deepest and bitterest lamentation (cf. Jer. vi. 26; Amos viii. 10). The rendering in the Authorised Version "be in bitterness" is not an exact rendering, but it gives excellently well the meaning of the Hebrew; the verb being taken intransitively, and the inf. abs. being construed as the finite verb (Ges., § 131, 4 a; Müller, § 106). As the firstborn son was especially esteemed (Gen. xlix. 3; Exod. iv. 22; Deut. xxi. 17; Micah vi. 7), the death of such was most bitterly deplored.

The mourning was to be not only deep and poignant,

but also *universal*. The prophet compares it to "the mourning of Hadad-rimmon in the valley of Megiddo" (ver. 11), that is, the mourning occasioned by what took place there. The mourning referred to is that of the nation over King Josiah, who was slain in battle with Pharaohnecho at Megiddo, and whose death was deeply and widely lamented throughout the nation (2 Kings xxiii. 29, 30; 2 Chron. xxxv. 20–24). Hadad-rimmon was a place, Jerome tells us, in the plain of Megiddo, near to Jezreel, and known in his day by the name of Maximianopolis; it has recently been identified with a place called Rummâneh, where there are the remains of a town or village at the south-western part of the plain of el-But-tauf, not far from Lejjun, the supposed site of Megiddo.* The death of King Josiah was a signal calamity to the Jewish nation; with it "the last gleam of the sunset of Judah faded into night" (Pusey); and the shadow of that calamity rested on the nation for generations afterwards. For him Jeremiah wrote a lamentation. Dirges for him were preserved in the national archives, and were periodically recited by the minstrels of the nation; and thus to lament for him in dirges became an ordinance in Israel which survived the captivity (2 Chron. xxxv. 25). No lamentation in Judah equalled this for King Josiah; and so it came to be associated in the minds of the people with the highest degree of sorrow and mourning. Hence the allusion to it here; even to the height of this hitherto unequalled sorrow, should the mourning of Israel over their great sin

---

* This identification, however, is called in question by some eminent explorers and critics. See "Survey of Western Palestine," Vol. II., p. 90.

rise. The notion of Hitzig that the mourning of Hadad-rimmon is to be understood of the mourning for Adonis is simply preposterous. There is no evidence that Adonis ever was known by the name of Hadad-rimmon, or that this was the name of any idol in Phœnicia or elsewhere; the mourning referred to by the prophet is a mourning for the lost dead; but the "weeping for Thammuz" (Adonis) was only the prelude to a burst of joyous exultation over his resuscitation;* and especially how can it be believed that the mourning of Israel over their sins would be compared by a prophet of Israel to the "cultus abominabilis" of a heathen idol? The word Hadad-rimmon, it is true, contains the name of one Syrian idol—Rimmon (see 2 Kings v. 18), and probably that of another—Hadad (comp. Ben-hadad, Hadad-Ezer, like Ben-hanan, Eliezer); but this name was probably given to the place because both idols had their worship specially celebrated there; though Hadad may be only an appellation appended to the proper name.†

Not in Jerusalem alone, but throughout the land should this mourning extend: " And the land shall mourn, every family apart; the family of the house of David apart, and their wives apart; the family of the house of Nathan apart, and their wives apart; the family of the house of Levi apart, and their wives apart; the family of

---

* "Mulieres gemitus et lamenta ob amissum Adonim et jam denuo repertum in sacra commutabant gaudia, miraque laetitia quod reliquum erat festi, Deum excipientes, peragebant." Selden, *De Dis Syris*, c. 11.

† In two inscriptions of Shalmaneser the name Rimmon-hidri occurs as that of the Ben-hadad of the Bible, whose personal name Professor Sayce concludes was Rimmon-adar ("Records of the Past," iii. 99; v. 34). Hadad should probably be read Hadar, both when alone and when joined with another word.

the Shimeite apart, and their wives apart; all the rest of the families, every family apart, and their wives apart" (ver. 12-14). The mourning was to be universal; the whole land should mourn; through all the families of the nation should the lamentation extend. And the sorrow should be individual; not only should each family mourn apart, but each person should mourn as for his or her own particular grief, the husband apart from the wife, the wife from the husband. Four families are specially mentioned. Two of these, the house of David and the house of Levi, are easily discernible; the former the descendants of David the King of Israel, the latter the posterity of the patriarch Levi. As to the other two, there is less certainty. By the Jewish interpreters, Nathan is taken to be the well-known prophet of that name; and the family of the Shimeites is understood of the tribe of Simeon, which they say furnished teachers to the nation. Thus, according to them, there are represented here the regal, the prophetical, the priestly, and the didactic orders of the nation. But this view is open to serious objections: (1) Nathan, though a prophet, was not the head of any order, and therefore could not stand as the representative of the order of prophets; (2) there is no evidence that from the tribe of Simeon teachers were especially supplied to the nation; and (3) the patronymic of Simeon is Shimeoni (Num. xxv. 14; Josh. xxi. 4; 1 Chron. xxvii. 16), not Shimei, which is the word here used. The more probable view is that the Nathan of this passage is Nathan the son of David, from whom Zerubbabel was descended, and that the family of the Shimeite is that descended from Shimei, the son of

Gershon, the son of Levi (Num. iii. 17), of whom it is recorded, "came the family of the Shimeite" (ver. 21). According to this view the prophet here "of two tribes mentions one leading family and one subordinate branch, to show that not only are all the families of Israel in general seized with the same grief, but all the separate branches of those families" (Keil). This is the view now generally entertained. "The rest of the families," or the remaining families (hammishpâchoth hannish'-âroth), are not the survivors of some that had become extinct (Henderson), nor the less renowned as compared with those mentioned (Köhler), but simply the family remaining after these. The mourning was to be universal; all classes and conditions, families and individuals, men and women alike, were to be the subjects of this deep penitential sorrow and bitter lamentation.

We have now to inquire to what this prophecy refers, and to what we are to look for its fulfilment.

We may dismiss at once the opinion that it is to the time of the Maccabees and to the restoration of the Jewish state at that crisis in its history that this prophecy refers. Not only is there no traceable correspondence between the description of the prophet and the facts or events of the Maccabean struggle, but the whole cast and tenor of the prophet's utterances point to something far more solemn and spiritual than is involved in the circumstances and issue of a nation's struggle for independence. The penitential and believing look which is here described as turned by the people to Him, the representative of the Shepherd of Israel, whom they had rejected, maltreated, and pierced to death, points to the

Messianic age as the time when this prophecy finds its fulfilment. From the connection of this prophecy with that in the preceding chapter, where the rejection of the Messiah by the Jews, and what came consequent on that, are described, we seem shut up to the conclusion that it is to the death of the Christ and the effect of that on the people that this prophecy refers.

This prophecy began to be fulfilled when our Lord was crucified. The Evangelist saw an express fulfilment of the prediction that the Messiah should be pierced, in the piercing of the side of Christ by the spear of a soldier, as He was hanging on the cross (John xix. 37). It is not meant by this that the solitary act of the infliction of such a wound is all that is intended by the prophet, or all that the Evangelist regarded as fulfilled on that occasion, but that by this act was conspicuously consummated that career of obloquy and suffering which the Messiah was to endure, and through which Jesus the Christ actually passed. "The, so to speak, literal fulfilment in the outward circumstances only served to make the internal concatenation of the prophecy, with its historical realisation, so clear that even unbelievers could not successfully deny it" (Keil). A literal fulfilment, also, of the looking with penitential lamentation on the pierced one, was seen when "all the people that came together to this sight, when they saw the things that were done, returned smiting their breasts" (Luke xxiii. 48); thus giving expression to their mourning and sorrow. "The crowds who but a short time before had cried out, 'Crucify Him,' now smite their breasts, overpowered by the proofs of the superhuman dignity of Jesus, and mourn for the deceased and their own sin" (Hengstenberg). In this, however, there was but the commencement of the fulfilling of this prophecy. With this began "a powerful movement, which brought large bodies of penitent Jews to the Christian Church." On the day of Pentecost this movement came to a height. When St. Peter, in his address to the multitude that had come together of "Jews, devout men out of every nation under heaven," charged upon them the guilt of killing "the Prince of life," they "were pricked in their hearts," and cried out to Peter and the other Apostles of Christ, "Men and brethren, what shall we do?" and when, in answer to this appeal, they were summoned to repentance, multitudes obeyed the call; and as the work went on, "believers were the more added to the Lord, multitudes both of men and women;" so that ere long there were many thousands of believing Jews numbered among the Christians (Acts ii. 36, 37, 38, iii. 14, 19, v. 14, xxi. 20). Among these were some doubtless of the family of David; at least we may safely conclude that the brethren of our Lord, who before His crucifixion did not believe on Him, but were afterwards devoted adherents to His cause, were among those whom His death awakened to repentance, contrition, and faith; and they were, as He was, "of the house and lineage of David." Nor was the family of Levi without its representatives in this great national mourning, for among those who at the beginning of the gospel were obedient to the faith of the Crucified, was "a great company of the priests" (Acts vi. 7). This, however, was still but the beginning of the fulfilment. We err when we assume that prophecy is fulfilled all at once, or by any one act, or at any precise time. The interpretation of prophecies must (as Bacon, with his wonted sagacity, teaches) "allow that latitude which is agreeable and familiar unto Divine prophecy, being of the nature of the Author, with whom a thousand years are as one day, and therefore are not fulfilled punctually and at once, but have springing and germinant accomplishments throughout many ages, though the height or fulness thereof may refer to some one age." * For the complete fulfilment of the prophecy here announced we have to look on through the whole period of the Messiah's reign. The converts on the day of Pentecost formed but the nucleus of a larger body, which all through the ages shall be ever expanding, "until the fulness of the Gentiles shall be come in, and so all Israel shall be saved" (Rom. xi. 25, 26).

* "Advancement of Learning," Book II., chap. 11.

XXI.

PURIFICATION AND ENLIGHTENMENT.

"In that day there shall be a fountain opened to the house of David, and to the inhabitants of Jerusalem, for sin and for uncleanness. And it shall come to pass in that day, saith the Lord of hosts, that I will cut off the names of the idols out of the land, and they shall no more be remembered; and also I will cause the prophets and the unclean spirit to pass out of the land. And it shall come to pass, that when any shall yet prophesy, then his father and his mother that begat him shall say unto him, Thou shalt not live; for thou speakest lies in the name of the Lord: and his father and his mother that begat him shall thrust him through when he prophesieth. And it shall come to pass in that day, that the prophets shall be ashamed every one of his vision, when he hath prophesied; neither shall they wear a rough garment to deceive: But he shall say, I am no prophet, I am an husbandman; for man taught me to keep cattle from my youth. And one shall say unto him, What are these wounds in thine hands? Then he shall answer, Those with which I was wounded in the house of my friends."
—ZECH. xiii. 1-6.

THIS passage is closely connected with what goes before in the preceding chapter. There the prophet represents Israel as overwhelmed with penitential sorrow for the sin they had committed in their rejection and maltreatment of the good shepherd, the emissary and representative of Jehovah. Shall this penitence be in vain? By no means. God, who Himself had brought about this state of mind in the people, by pouring out on them the spirit of grace and supplication, the spirit that awakens to a sense of the evil of sin and leads to a sincere contrition and penitence because of it, would meet them in their deep sorrow with His redeeming grace, and would supply to them that absolution and cleansing for which He had taught them to cry. "In that day shall a fountain be opened to the house of David and to the inhabitants of Jerusalem for sin and for uncleanness" (verse 1). The expression "in that day" carries us back to the same expression as used in the preceding chapter, where it indicates the time when the great mourning of the people, because of their sin in rejecting and putting to death the Messiah, should break forth; the provision for their absolution and cleansing should be contemporaneous with their mourning. A fountain or water-source should then be opened; a passage should be made for the waters so long hidden to burst forth and come to manifestation so as to be for use (cf. Isaiah xli. 18). The fountain should be for cleansing; the water that flowed from it should be for "the sprinkling of the unclean" that they might be freed from their impurity. In the words "for sin and for uncleanness" there is apparently an allusion in the former to the water used in the purification of the Levites at their consecration, which is called מֵי הַשָּׂאת, water of sin, *i.e.*, water of purification from sin (Num. viii. 7), and in the latter to the water for the purifying of the congregation of Israel, prepared from mixing the ashes of the red heifer slain as a sacrifice with water, and which was, from the use to which it was applied, called מֵי נִדָּה, water of cleansing (Num. xix. 9, "water of separation," Authorised Version). As water applied to the person removes outward defilement, it becomes a fitting emblem of that which removes from the inner man moral defilement (cf. Ps. li. 2,

7; Is. i. 16; Ez. xxxvi. 25). Here the reference is to the cleansing energy which He who pours on men the spirit of grace and supplication bestows on all who truly repent, and which comes to men through the sacrificial death of Christ, whose " blood cleanseth from all sin " (1 John i. 7). Under the Law, "without shedding of blood there was no remission" of sin or cleansing from moral defilement (Heb. ix. 22). Hence a Jew's entire conception of salvation from sin was folded up in these two —remission of guilt through sacrifice, and moral purification through Divine grace, consequent on remission. Accordingly here the removal of moral defilement is connected with the removal of guilt, and both fall back on what is said in the preceding chapter regarding the piercing of the Shepherd, and the looking of the penitent people to Him whom they had pierced.

The fountain opened, its cleansing waters are free to all, to the inhabitants of Jerusalem as well as to the house of David. As the sin was universal and as the spirit of grace was poured on the people promiscuously, so should the cleansing be for all alike. The grace of salvation is free to all without respect of persons.

True repentance will show itself on the part of those who are subjects of it, in the relinquishment of all former objects of evil attachment, and the entering upon a new life of godliness and holy service. So should it be with the covenant people after the great mourning and the attendant cleansing: "And it shall come to pass in that day, saith Jehovah of hosts, that I will cut off the names of the idols out of the land, and they shall not be remembered any more; and the prophets also and the spirit of uncleanness will I remove out of the land" (verse 2). As the sins to which Israel was most prone, and which brought on the nation the Divine judgments, were idolatry and false prophecy, so the restoration of the people to a new life of godliness and righteousness is depicted by the extermination of idols and false prophets from the land. The names of the idols should be cut off; they should so utterly be abolished that their very names should perish and be forgotten (cf. Hosea ii. 19). That by "the prophets" here are intended the false prophets, that is, those who pretended to speak in the name of God but had not been sent by Him, and who, consequently, uttered as from God what was only their own thought or device, is evident from their being associated with idols, of which "lying vanities" the false prophets were the principal advocates; and with the "spirit of uncleanness," that is, the evil spirit, the diabolic spirit, the seducing spirit, the Satan, adversary and antagonist of the spirit of grace, to whose malign influence and working "all deceivableness of unrighteousness," and all lying divinations are to be traced (comp. 2 Thess. ii. 9, 10; 1 Tim. iv. 1, 2; Rev. xvi. 14; Ez. xiii. 6; 2 Kings xxii. 22, 23). That the restoration to a state of genuine godliness, and the prevalence of true spiritual religion in the Messianic age should be represented by the extermination of idols and false prophets, at a time when idolatry and false prophesying were no longer known in Israel, is to be accounted for by the fact that the ancient prophets were in the habit of using the forms of the past in predicting the future. In the earlier ages of the nation, idolatry, with its accompaniment false prophecy, was the form in which ungodliness most manifested itself, and even in the time of Zechariah tendencies to this among the people were not wanting (see Neh. vi. 10–14, xiii. 23 ; Ezra ix. 2 ff.). How, then, could the prophet more vividly present the conception of a return to sincere godliness than by announcing the utter abolition of idolatry and the extermination of its advocates and promoters? In the days of our Lord, moreover, when He came to His own heritage, and they that were His own received Him not, there were false teachers among the people who were now leading them away from God; and though idolatry in its grosser forms was unknown among them, in the more subtle form of ritualism and self-righteousness it predominated throughout the community. All evil of this sort God should make to pass away (אַעֲבִיר *transire faciam*) from His people. A reign of righteousness and truth should be inaugurated, into which "the righteous nation that keepeth the truth" should enter, and where only "they that are of the truth" should find a place.

So entire should be the deliverance of the people from idolatry and the influence of false prophets, that not only would there be no toleration of these in the land, but, should any such appear, their nearest and dearest friends, even their parents themselves, should rise up against them and destroy them: " And it shall come to pass, that should a man yet prophesy, his father and his mother, his parents, will say unto him, Thou shalt not live; for thou hast spoken falsehood in the name of Jehovah: and his father and his mother, his parents, shall pierce him through because of his prophesying" (verse 3). According to the law of Moses any one who sought to persuade to idolatry, or who presumed to speak in the name of God what God had not commanded him to speak, or should speak in the name of other gods, was to be put to death (Deut. xiii. 6–11, xviii. 20). It does not appear that this law was ever put in force during the continuance of the Israelitish state, for though false prophets who instigated the people to idolatry were not wanting, no instance is recorded of their being put to death by those whom they sought to seduce. In the case supposed by the prophet, however, this law would be revived in all its stringency, and not only so, but, in their newly awakened zeal, the people should go beyond the law and inflict the penalty without using those precautions which the law prescribed. For the law evidently enacts that it is only by a judicial procedure after due investigation, and in the presence of the people, that the penalty of death by stoning is to be inflicted on the false prophet; whereas in the case described by the prophet, it is instantly, and by a vengeful stroke, that the offender is to be punished. The representation is intended to depict vividly the utter recoil of the nation from idolatry and false prophets, and their determination to put down and extirpate all who by false teaching would seduce and mislead the people. *His parents* (יֹלְדָיו *qui eum pepercerunt*), even they, the authors of his being, instead of protecting him, or seeking to conceal or palliate his offence, should be the first to denounce him and inflict on him the penalty of death (דָּקַר *to thrust through, to pierce, to put to death,* cf. xii. 10). This should be simply " because of his prophesying." This rests on the assumption that God, ere this, had ceased to speak to His people by His prophets; consequently, should any one still (עוֹד) after this pretend to speak as a prophet, he would, *ipso facto*, be convicted of having spoken falsehood in the name of Jehovah. So entirely discredited should be the prophetic function, and so strong the reaction in the public mind against it, that the false prophets, though not wholly silenced, should be ashamed to come forth openly to utter their pretended oracles, should anxiously seek to obliterate the remembrance of their former pretensions, and should use all means to avoid the imputation to them of a profession so repugnant to popular feeling and conviction: "And it shall come to pass in that day, that the prophets shall be ashamed every one of his vision, when he hath prophesied; neither shall he wear a garment of hair to deceive" (ver. 4). The "garment of hair," the *Addereth se'ir*, was a large mantle or cloak made of goat's or camel's hair, much like the 'Abba now commonly worn by the peasantry in Palestine; it was the usual costume of the prophets, and was distinctive of them (1 Kings xix. 13, 19; 2 Kings i. 8; Matt. iii. 1); so that to assume it was *pro tanto* to pretend to be a prophet. This the false prophets used to do; but, ashamed of the pretensions they had made, and fearing to encounter the popular abhorrence of such pretensions, they would divest themselves of every outward mark of this. They would now assume a less offensive appearance, and give themselves out for farm labourers, who from their youth had been the bond-servants of others: "And he shall say, I am no prophet, I am a tiller of the ground; for a man had possession of me from my youth" (ver. 5). The "he" here is the "every one" (אִישׁ) of verse 4; אֲדָמָה

עָבַד one who labours the soil, cultivates land, a tiller of the ground (as in Gen. iv. 2); הִקְנָה hiph. of קָנָה, *to get, to possess,* appears here with the same signification as the kal (perhaps *to cause oneself to get, to possess*), or it may be a denominative from מִקְנֶה, *a possession,* signifying to make a possession, to cause to become a possession, and so to have in possession; the rendering in the Authorised Version "man taught me to keep cattle" is that of Kimchi, but it is not easy to see how this can be got out of the words in the Hebrew. The false prophet thus pleads the impossibility of his having been a prophet at all, seeing he had from his youth been engaged in servile pursuits in the fields; just as Amos confirms the assertion that he was no prophet by declaring that he was "a herdsman and a gatherer of sycamore fruit" (vii. 14). In bar of this plea those who are taking him to task demand an explanation of certain marks of freshly inflicted wounds which are seen on his person: "Then shall one say to him, What are these wounds in thine hands?" (ver. 6). The word used here for "wounds" primarily means a blow or stroke (Prov. xx. 30, Authorised Version, "stripes"; Isa. xiv. 6), then the effect of a stroke, a wound; it cannot be understood here of the cicatrices of old wounds which had been healed, but had left their mark. These wounds were "between (בֵּין) the hands," which may mean that they were upon the breast or arms (cf. "between his arms," 2 Kings ix. 24); but more probably בֵּין is used here for בְּ as in Prov. xxvi. 13, "in the streets"), and the hands must be regarded as the site of the wounds. Seeing these wounds still fresh on the hands of the accused, his examiner implicitly suggests that they are such as idolaters were wont to inflict upon themselves in the worship of their false gods, or when waiting for the afflatus by which they were supposed to be enabled to utter oracles from the Deity; and the accused is asked to say how, if he had been a simple farm-servant from his youth, he came to have these marks of idolatrous rites in his hands. To this his reply is that these wounds are not self-inflicted wounds, such as the prophets of Baal inflicted on themselves, but wounds which were received by him in private society: "Then he shall answer, Those with which I was wounded in the house of those who love me" (ver. 6). Kimchi understands by this, wounds which the false prophet says he received in the Beth Hammid-rash (house of study) when his relations (parents or guardians) beat him because he neglected his work in the fields that he might pursue learning. In this case, however, it could only have been the mark of stripes or blows received long before that were seen, not fresh wounds such as the word here used denotes. That the wounds were not self-inflicted is rendered evident by the form of the verb, which is passive (*hukkeythi*, I was wounded); and this sets aside the suggestion that the wounds were such as persons inflicted on themselves in mourning for the dead, as well as the supposition that the accused here confesses his guilt in that he had followed those idolatrous rites in which persons wounded themselves when invoking the Deity. It seems certain that the man intends, by what he says, to obviate the suspicions of his accuser by assigning another cause of the wounds than that which his accuser had insinuated; and as his words are quite indefinite it seems needless to attempt to assign to them a special and precise meaning. "It may be possible that he meant simply to suggest that the fresh wounds which were so suspicious had been accidentally inflicted when with his friends, or he may have suggested that these wounds were received by him on the occasion of some carousal with boon companions" (Wright).

The recovery of the Israel of God from apostacy, and the banishment from it of all forms of ungodliness and all false teaching, is what this prophecy is intended to set forth. It is not to be restricted to any particular period or historical standpoint; "the day" is not any point in time, but is that "day of the Lord," that day which He "makes," and which, beginning at a point in time, stretches through the ages to the end of time, and during the lapse of which the prediction of the prophet is often fulfilled, and in many different ways. It is not merely or even specially idolatry and false divinations that are to be extirpated; these are here but typical instances, introduced to represent all forms of ungodliness and falsehood by which true religion may be corrupted, and men be led astray from the truth and from God. The opening of the fountain for sin and for uncleanness was the unveiling of "the mystery which had been hid from ages and from generations, but was at length made manifest to those to whom God would make known what is the riches of the glory of this mystery among the Gentiles; which is Christ in you, the hope of glory" (Col. i. 26, 27). It is not to the advent of a person or to the occurrence of any historical event that the prophecy in the beginning of this section refers; what is announced is the establishment of the economy of grace, the bringing in of the kingdom of God, free access to which should be given to all, small and great, the revelation and manifestation of the "mystery which had been before made known by the scriptures of the prophets, according to the commandment of the everlasting God" (Rom. xvi. 26). Then was provision made for the cleansing from sin and uncleanness of all without respect of persons; the Jew first, but also the Greek. The manifestation of this was by the appearing of our Saviour Jesus Christ, who came to take away sin by the sacrifice of Himself; but it is the thing done rather than the doer of it that is here announced.

It is for the house of David and the inhabitants of Jerusalem that this fountain is said to be opened. They seem to err grievously, however, who infer from this that this prophecy refers to the final conversion of the Jewish people. The prophets are wont to describe the new dispensation in language borrowed from the condition and usages of the old; and we interpret them aright when, keeping this in view, we understand their descriptions, not as representations of simple historical facts, but as serving as the copy and shadow of the heavenly things, and as finding their fulfilment in crises and conditions of the kingdom of heaven on earth. They go upon the presumption that the Israel of God was never to be abolished, that its continuity was never to be interrupted, that though the outward national Israel might be cast off because of their rejection of the Good Shepherd, the true Israel, the reality of which the other was but the symbol, the Israel that was really Israel ("for they are not all Israel that are of Israel"), should continue for ever. This idea our Lord and His Apostles adopted, and in their teaching and administrations carried out. With them there was no such thing as the termination and abolition of the ancient church, and the formation in its place of a new one. Their thought was that the one church which had been from the beginning should continue on—that Judaism should expand into evangelism; the church of a nation into the church of the world; and that this should come to pass by Jews first embracing Christ, and then receiving into their society Gentiles, by whom also He had been embraced. So it was in point of fact. The kingdom of the Christ at first included only Jews or proselytes to Judaism. The church had become a comparatively large body before a single convert from among the Gentiles was made, or the Gospel was preached to the Gentiles. The commission which our Lord gave to His Apostles bound them to preach the glad tidings to the nations, but it no less bound them to "begin at Jerusalem." When their commission was opened on the Day of Pentecost, it was to Jews only that their message was addressed; and the order in which they proceeded in fulfilling their ministry was the order of the promise itself they were sent forth to announce. "The promise," said St. Peter, in his opening address, "is to you and your children, and to all that are afar off, as many as the Lord shall call" (Acts ii. 39). In accordance with this St. Paul teaches that the new dispensation was not the planting of another tree; the one olive-tree remained with its roots fixed ineradicably in the soil; the only change made was that decayed and worthless branches were cut off, and fresh branches were grafted in. Addressing Gentile converts, St. Paul tells them that though in their former state they were "aliens from the commonwealth of Israel, and strangers from the covenant of promise," they, by receiving Christ, by becoming Christians, had ceased to be strangers and foreigners, and had become "fellow-citizens with the saints ('Israelis,' ver. 12, Bengel*) and of the household of God" (Eph. ii. 12, 19). In accordance with this, the Church of which believers in Christ are members, is described as "the Jerusalem which is above" (Gal. iv. 26); and Christians are said to have "come to Mount Sion, and unto the city of the living God, the heavenly Jerusalem ... to the general assembly and church of the firstborn" (Heb. xii. 22, 23). That in this building up of the church, by the bringing into it of Gentile converts to Christ, the Apostles saw the fulfilment of the promises in the prophetic writings concerning the perpetuity of Israel and the establishment of the house and throne of David, appears most distinctly from the utterance of St. James in the assembly at Jerusalem, in reference to the conversion of the Gentiles. "To this," said he, "agree the words of the prophets; as it is written, After this will I return, and will build again the tabernacle of David, which is fallen down; and will build again the ruins thereof, and I will set it up; that the residue of men might seek after the Lord, and all the Gentiles, upon whom my name is called, saith the Lord,

---

* "*Fellow-citizens with the saints, i.e.,* with Christians as citizens of the Theocracy begun under the Old Testament, completed under the New Testament (comp. Rom. xi. 16, &c.); or with the true Israel (Gal. vi. 16); not, however, with Jews [as such], nor with Jews and Gentile Christians, for the antithesis with verse 12 must be maintained." De Wette, on the place.

who maketh these things known from the beginning of the world" (Acts xv. 15-18, Revised Version). Here it is explicitly stated that the opening of the church, previously composed only of Jews, freely to the Gentiles, is what the prophet intended when he announced that in "the day of the Lord" God would raise up the tabernacle of David, which had fallen down, and raise up the ruins thereof, and build it as in the days of old (Amos ix. 11). As St. James spoke on this occasion by the Holy Ghost, his words not only convey to us a just explanation of the prophecy cited by him, but also furnish us with a canon of interpretation for the Old Testament declarations concerning the restoration and final establishment of Israel.

"Christianity is Judaism continued under an expanded form. It is the polity of the New Jerusalem, the 'city which hath foundations, whose builder and maker is God.' There still exists a body of men, insulated from the world by peculiar institutions, and dedicated to God,—though no longer conspicuous as a temporal state, or outwardly eminent above the nations of the world,—but a spiritual community—the citizens and freemen of heaven. When the Lord called Abraham and promised to make him a great nation with the particular promise, He joined the evangelical declaration that all families of the earth should be blessed in the Patriarch. Into the temporal and partial character of the religion subsequently instituted a perpetuity and an universality were also introduced. It was declared that the institution of providential government then begun should never cease. Judaism, accordingly, has both ceased and not ceased. It has evidently ceased in certain respects. 'The sceptre' is departed 'from Judah,' and 'the lawgiver from between his feet.' The Temple has scattered its ruins in the dust. The Holy Land is desecrated with the steps of strangers; and the posterity of Abraham are themselves strangers in the land which the Lord gave them for a possession. But there are living possessors of the evangelical promise—the heirs of the faith of Abraham—a spiritual Israel—a people who date their origin as a chosen race from one of the seed of Abraham, and who are the actual depositaries of the Divine blessing, announced at his call. 'For ye are all,' says the Apostle to the Galatians (iii. 26 ff.), 'the children of God, by faith in Christ Jesus. . . . And if ye be Christ's, then are ye Abraham's seed, and heirs according to the promise.' In Christianity, therefore, we behold the perpetual duration of Judaism. In Christianity all the promises of everlasting continuance attached to the religion of the Law find their completion. 'Jerusalem' that was 'is in bondage with her children;' but 'Jerusalem which is above is free, which is the mother of us all' (Gal. iv. 25, 26). Judaism, therefore, *as Judaism*, is dead; but *as Christianity* it lives and will live for ever."* Exception may be taken to one or two of the expressions in this extract, but as a whole it must be commended as exhibiting in clear and precise statement the proper method of interpreting the prophecies to which it relates.

* Bishop Hampden, "Parochial Sermons," pp. 281-3. Second edition.

XXII.

THE FLOCK SCATTERED.

"Awake, O sword, against my shepherd, and against the man that is my fellow, saith the Lord of hosts: smite the shepherd, and the sheep shall be scattered; and I will turn mine hand upon the little ones. And it shall come to pass, that in all the land, saith the Lord, two parts therein shall be cut off and die; but the third shall be left therein. And I will bring the third part through the fire, and will refine them as silver is refined, and will try them as gold is tried: they shall call on my name, and I will hear them: I will say, It is my people; and they shall say, The Lord is my God."—ZECH. xiii. 7–9.

THE prophecy contained in this section appears at first sight to have no connection with that in the preceding part of the chapter; it seems rather to stand in relation with the oracle in chapter xi., where the cutting off of the shepherd is announced. This has led some to suppose that this section has been displaced and that it ought to be relegated to its proper place after the eleventh chapter. For this, however, there is no sufficient reason. A fresh start, it is true, is taken at verse seven of this chapter, and the prophecy receives a new turn, but the line of continuity is not broken with what precedes nor with what follows. The main theme of the whole prophetic utterance is the deliverance of Israel from all evil, and its ultimate complete development, after its proper type, as a people holy unto the Lord. From all outward oppression Israel should be freed, and power should be given to resist and overcome the world-powers that aim at assailing and subjugating it; the spirit of grace and supplication should be poured out upon the people, so that they should repent of their apostacy and especially of their great sin in rejecting and putting to death the Shepherd of Israel whom God had sent to them, and there should be a general turning unto the Lord, and an earnest petitioning for forgiveness and restoration. This should not be in vain; provision should be made for their cleansing, and they should be recovered from all apostacy and delivered from the influence of all false teaching. In pursuance of this, however, it was needful that there should be a severance of the ungodly from the righteous, and to effect this, judgment must come upon Jerusalem whereby the true should be separated from the false, and the latter be exterminated, while the former should be purified and refined. It is to this final purgation by trial that the section beginning with verse 7 of chapter xiii. refers; and in this section we have a summary of what is set forth more in detail in the following chapter. It is evident, therefore, that this section is in its proper place both in relation to what goes before and in relation to what comes after.

The passage commences with an address to the sword, which is personified and summoned, as if it were a living agent, to do execution: "Awake, O sword, against my Shepherd, and against a man my fellow, saith Jehovah of hosts; smite the Shepherd, and let the sheep be scattered; and I will bring back my hand over the humble ones" (ver. 7). The speaker here is Jehovah; and His call on the sword to awake intimates that it is as His instrument that it is to operate. A similar personification of the sword occurs in Jer. xlvii. 6. "Sword" is in both passages as well as elsewhere the symbol of any means of destroying life or inflicting severe penalties; cf. Ex. v. 21; 2 Sam. xii. 9; Jer. xii. 12; Rom. xiii. 4, &c. And it may be understood here of any agency the Lord may employ or overrule for the accomplishment of His purpose.* As a sword in its sheath is inoperative and, as it were, dormant, so the agency here thus indicated had up to this time remained inactive, but is now summoned to awake, to come into action against the object designated.

That object is described by the speaker as "His Shepherd;" the Shepherd, therefore, of Jehovah. In chapter xi. two shepherds are specially noted, the good Shepherd by whom the poor of the flock are fed, and the foolish shepherd by whom the flock is neglected and wasted; and to both the appellation "of Jehovah" may be applied, as both are raised up and sent forth by Him. To one or other of these the reference here must be; but to which is a question. From the piercing of the shepherd with the sword it has been concluded by some that it cannot be the good Shepherd that is intended; but this does not necessarily follow. For not against His enemies, the wicked or the foolish alone, may the sword of Jehovah be directed; even on one whom He sends forth as His approved representative to do His work, may the

---

* The anomaly in the construction here of a masculine form of the verb (עוּרִי) with a feminine substantive (חֶרֶב) is to be accounted for by the personification of the "sword;" just as in Gen. iv. 7, sin (חַטָּאת fem.) being personified as a wild beast is construed as if it were masculine.

stroke of His sword fall; as in the case of His "righteous Servant," whom He is represented as wounding and bruising and putting to grief even to the death, though "He had done no violence, neither was deceit in His mouth" (Isa. liii. 9, 10). That it is the good Shepherd that is here intended is certified by the epithet by which he is described, "a man, my fellow," for on no fair interpretation of this expression can it be supposed applicable to any but a good and worthy person. Of the various explanations which have been given of this phrase, none seems better than that of the Authorised Version, "fellow" being taken in its proper sense as indicating one in a relation of equality or companionship to another.* The word so rendered עֲמִית occurs only here and in Leviticus, where it is used several times in chap. xix. and chap. xxv., in every case as a concrete noun expressive of close personal and friendly connection, and in chap. xxv. 15 as equivalent to "brother" or a member of the same family (cf. verses 10, 15). Intimacy of relation if not equality of condition the word always implies; it could not be used of a mere servile or official relation. "No owner of a flock or lord of a flock would call a hired servant or purchased shepherd his '*amith*'" (Keil). When God, then, here calls the person against whom He summons His sword to awake, His "*amith*," His fellow, there is intimated not that He stood to God in the relation of a servant or representative merely, but that He

---

* "To be your fellow
You may deny me; but I'll be your servant
Whether you will or no."
              Tempest, act iii., sc. 1.

was in near relation to God personally, in some sense, if not on a par with the Almighty, the nearest to Him in nature and position. It is also noticeable that the word rendered "man" is not *Ish* or *Adam*, the terms commonly used with this designation, but *geber*, an emphatic word, conveying the idea of *man* in the higher sense, the designation of one in whom any of the attributes of manhood appear in pre-eminence. He, therefore, who is described as A Man, the Fellow of Jehovah, must be one pre-eminently human and yet in essence and estate closely related to God; "therefore no other than the Messiah, who is also identified with Jehovah in chap. xii. 10; or the good Shepherd, who says of Himself, 'I and My Father are one,'" John x. 30 (Keil), and whom one sent forth by Him to make known His Name calls "the Man Christ Jesus" (1 Tim. ii. 5).

The sword of Jehovah is summoned to smite the Shepherd, and as a consequence of this the sheep must be dispersed. Deprived of the Shepherd's care, exposed to manifold hostilities and trials, and in themselves helpless and ever ready to flee at the approach of danger, it cannot be but that the flock should be scattered when the Shepherd is smitten and falls. All, however, are not to be lost. God will not suffer the dispersion to be entire and final. "I will," says He, "bring back my hand upon or over the humble ones." His hand, stretched forth to smite and disperse, shall be drawn back so as to cover and protect a portion of the flock. The phrase, "to bring back the hand over (עֲל) any person," is used to express the making of that person again the object of care and action either in wrath or in mercy, either for judgment or for benefit. In the former reference it is used in Ps. lxxxi. 14 [15]: "I should have subdued their enemies, and upon their adversaries have brought back my hand." Am. i. 8: "And I will turn my hand upon Ekron." In the other reference it is found, Isa. i. 25: "And I will bring back my hand upon thee, and thoroughly purge away thy dross, and take away all thy tin." And in the general sense of recovering possession, it is used in 2 Sam. viii. 3, where David is said to have defeated Hadadezer, King of Zobah, as he was going to bring his hand back at the river, *i.e.*, to recover possession of the territory which had been taken from the kings of Zobah by Saul (1 Sam. xiv. 47).* That the phrase is used here in the good sense is certified by what follows, where it is distinctly stated that while judgment shall come upon the nation as a whole, a portion shall be rescued and brought through in safety, see vers. 8, 9, which "add the real explanation of the bringing back of the hand over the small ones" (Keil). As to the meaning of this last expression, rendered in the Authorised Version by "the little ones," there is some uncertainty. The word in the Hebrew, צֹעֲרִים, occurs only here. It is apparently the present participle in Kal of צָעַר, *to be little* or *small;* and being so it cannot be taken as synonymous with צָעִיר or צָעוֹר (Jer. xiv. 3, xlviii. 4), "the small ones," in a figurative sense, the miserable ones, those that are called the poor of the flock, in chap. xi. 7, as Keil suggests; it is rather to be taken in an *active* sense, "making [themselves] little," the humble

---

* The phrase is used in this passage without the עַל, because the object on which the hand was to be brought back is not specified.

ones, the lowly, patient, and meek. Over such the Lord would extend His protecting hand, so that though involved in the general calamity, they should not be allowed to perish, but would be sustained amid trial, and ultimately brought wholly through in safety and peace.

This scattering of the flock as a whole, and the rescuing and protecting of a portion of it, is more specifically set forth in the following verses: "And it shall come to pass in the whole land, saith Jehovah, that two parts in it shall be cut off and expire, and the third part shall remain therein. And I will bring the third part through the fire, and will smelt them as silver is smelted, and will refine them as gold is refined; it [they] shall call on my name and I will answer it [them]; I shall say, My people is it, and it shall say, Jehovah is my God" (ver. 8, 9). "The whole land" is the land of Israel, as in xii. 12, and xiv. 9, 10, not the whole earth. "Two parts," lit. a mouth, *i.e.*, a portion, of two (פִּי שְׁנַיִם), a phrase taken from Deut. xxi. 17, where it denotes the double portion inherited by the firstborn (comp. also 2 Kings ii. 9); that the phrase is used here in the sense of two-thirds is evident from there being a third part left. These two-thirds are to be destroyed by death; the "expire" is added to the "cut-off," to show that it is by death and not by mere excision from the community that they are to be punished. That these two terms indicate different modes of destruction, the cutting off being by the sword, and the expiring by pestilence or some other kind of disease (which is the opinion of Vatablus and Drusius), is a needless refinement, and besides is not supported by the usage of the verb גָוַע,

which is not limited to death by disease, but is used also of death by violence, as in Gen. vii. 21 by drowning, and Josh. xxii. 20 by stoning. The two-thirds were to perish by death, by whatever means inflicted. "The whole Jewish people appears here as one heritage left by the slain Shepherd, which is divided into three portions, of which death, claiming the right of the firstborn, seizes two, while one is assigned to life; a division analogous to that made by David with the Moabites, 2 Sam. viii. 2" (Hengstenberg). There is a striking resemblance between what is here announced and what is declared by Ezekiel concerning the judgment that was to come upon the Jewish people for their apostacy (Ezek. v. 12). There is no difference of any moment between the two representations; in both the whole is represented as divided into three portions, of which two are wholly to be destroyed, and one to be delivered through trial and suffering. The only difference is that in Ezekiel the instruments of destruction and trial are specified, while in Zechariah this is omitted, and only general terms are employed. In regard to the third part, Zechariah describes it as to be brought through the fire and subjected to a severe process of purgation and refining, but by what means this is to be effected is not declared; in Ezekiel this is said to be by their being dispersed and persecuted by enemies. The effect of this disciplinary treatment shall be beneficial; those subjected to it shall be wholly delivered from apostacy and confirmed in allegiance to Jehovah, who on His part will hear them when they call on Him, and will acknowledge them as His people.

Having thus explained the passage as it stands, we

have now to attend to its reference and application. And 1, of the *Person* here represented as *smitten by the sword of Divine justice.* This, as already intimated, is none other than the Messiah, the Christ. To Him alone can the language here used to describe the object of the smiting apply. No other being but He is at once man and the fellow of Jehovah the Lord of hosts; and He alone is the Shepherd whom God promised to set over His people Israel to feed them as a flock (Ezek. xxxiv. 23; Isa. xl. 11). Both these our Lord asserted for Himself. "I am," said He, "the Good Shepherd, and know my sheep and am known of mine" (John x. 14); and in relation to God He said, "I and my Father are one;" and when adjured by the High Priest to say whether He was the Christ, the Son of God, He responded to the charge, thereby, as the Jews rightly concluded, "making Himself equal with God" (Matt. xxvi. 63, 64, xxvii. 43; John xix. 7, v. 18). Without doubt, therefore, it is of Him that the prophet here speaks, for to Him alone can the words of the prophecy apply. None but Him did God set over Israel as their Shepherd; none but Him could Jehovah call "a man my fellow."

2. *The stroke inflicted on Him.* This, as we have seen, was the deadly stroke of Divine justice. The sword had long slept in its scabbard, but when the fitting time arrived God summoned the sword to awake and do execution on the appointed victim. As there is but one being to whom the description of the prophet can refer, so there is but one event to which the command here given can be understood as pointing—the slaying of Him who, as the Good Shepherd, laid down His life for

the sheep. His death was perpetrated by the "wicked hands" of men, but they were in this only the instruments by which God fulfilled His own purpose and counsel. The Jews had power to take Jesus and give Him to be "crucified and slain," because He was "delivered up by the determinate counsel and foreknowledge of God" (Acts ii. 23). He was a willing victim; He laid down His life of Himself (John x. 18); but He at the same time recognised the hand of God in the infliction, and held it as a fulfilment of the prediction here recorded. Speaking by anticipation of His death as near at hand, He said to His disciples, "All ye shall be offended because of Me this night, for it is written, I will smite the Shepherd, and the sheep shall be scattered" (Matt. xxvi. 31) And at an earlier season He said to them, with evident allusion to this passage, "Behold the hour cometh, yea is now come, that ye shall be scattered, every man to his own, and shall leave Me alone" (John xvi. 32). And when thus left alone, the sword which at the Divine call had sprung from its sheath, smote Him with a deadly stroke. And wherefore was He thus smitten? He had done no evil; He had neglected no duty; He was absolutely blameless, perfectly good. Why then was He thus dealt with, "smitten of God and afflicted"? Because, though Himself sinless, He bore the sins of others. He was wounded for their transgressions, He was bruised for their iniquities, the chastisement of their peace was upon Him (Isa. liii. 5). The flock had gone astray and incurred the penalty of apostacy, and He, the Shepherd, had come to give His life for theirs. He stood before God bearing their sins in His own body (1 Peter ii. 24);

and on Him the stroke of Divine justice fell. In Him, therefore, was this ancient prediction fulfilled.

3. *The consequence to the flock of this smiting of the Shepherd.* It was twofold. The sheep were to be scattered, but God was to turn back His hand over the humble and meek ones of the flock. The former of these, as we have seen, our Lord applied to the dispersion of His disciples as consequent on His crucifixion; when the sword smote the Shepherd, those who had followed Him, and been guided by Him, and had waited on His teaching were scattered abroad, and had to hide themselves and meet in secret "for fear of the Jews" (John xx. 19). The other consequence was realised when the Lord, having been raised from the dead, showed Himself to individuals and to groups of them, and especially when having, according to His promise given before His death, gone before them into Galilee (Matt. xxvi. 32), He met them there as a body to the number of about five hundred, and there showed Himself unto them alive from the dead, and received their worship as Lord of all. Then was the hand of God turned in mercy and love on these humble and trembling ones; then was the cloud that had settled over them and threatened to quench all the hopes they had cherished that their Lord was He who should restore the kingdom to Israel, dispelled; "then were the disciples glad when they saw the Lord," and from that meeting they went forth "to be His witnesses to the people," and to proclaim His Gospel to all nations, emboldened by His gracious assurance that He to whom all power in heaven and on earth had been given would be with them always, to guide, sustain, and

prosper them. Another dispersion of the flock ensued when the disciples that were in Jerusalem were scattered abroad upon the tribulations which arose about Stephen (Acts viii. 1, xi. 19); but then, also, God turned back His hand over the humble ones, for wherever they went "the hand of the Lord was with them," and "the Lord gave testimony to the word of His grace," which they preached, "and a great number believed and turned to the Lord" (Acts viii. 1, xi. 19, 21, xiv. 3). But though the prophecy had *a* fulfilment in these experiences of the disciples of our Lord after His crucifixion, it cannot be supposed that the whole meaning of the prophecy is thereby exhausted. The disciples were not the whole flock, they were only a part of it. The flock was the house of Israel, and the dispersion of the disciples was but the prelude and type of that greater and more terrible dispersion, when the community of Israel was broken up and the people were trodden under foot of the oppressor, and the few that escaped the sword were scattered to the four winds. But whilst the nation was thus broken up and scattered, there was a remnant over whom the Lord turned back His hand. Though the mass of the Jewish people, with their rulers, rejected the Shepherd which God had sent to them, and put Him to death, there were some who received Him and acknowledged His claims. They formed but a "little flock," but to Him they were very dear—these "little ones that believed in Him"—and it was not the will of their Father which is in heaven that one of these little ones should perish. It was the Father's good pleasure that to this little flock should be given the kingdom; on them had devolved the inheritance of Israel; being Christ's they were heirs according to the promise. Therefore were they marvellously preserved amid the destruction of the Jewish state. When the ancient institute fell into ruins the commonwealth of Israel survived in them. The hand of the Lord was upon them for good; and whilst to death was allotted the eldest son's portion, life had that of the younger son, and God blessed the inheritance of His saints so that it hath increased a thousandfold.

4. But though preserved and rescued this little flock would not escape all trouble and suffering. God would bring them through the fire and refine and purify them in the furnace of affliction; and the result of this discipline would be their recovery from all apostasy and their final establishment in the Divine favour and their full union to Jehovah as His people. This may refer to the trials, persecutions, and manifold afflictions to which the early Church of Christ was exposed, and to the effect which these had in confirming the faith of the Christians and establishing the Church in " deeper devotedness and closer union to God." But the representation has a wider reference and application than this. It sets forth God's method of dealing with His people for their good. It has been ever so. The Church has ever had this experience. Her language of old was, "Thou, O God, hast proved us, Thou hast tried us as silver is tried. Thou broughtest us into the net; Thou laidest affliction upon our loins. Thou hast caused men to ride over our heads; we went through fire and through water; but Thou broughtest us out into a wealthy place" (Ps. lxvi. 10–12). Our Lord told His disciples that in the world

they should have tribulation (John xvi. 33); but He bade them be of good cheer, for He had overcome the world and so would secure to them also the victory. And His servants, when they exhorted their converts to continue in the faith, reminded them that it must needs be "through much tribulation" that any can enter into the kingdom of God (Acts xiv. 22). Such discipline is needful for the purging out of all that stands in the way of the entire union of the soul to God. Only when the heart is weaned from the world will the love of the Father reign in the soul; only when self is subdued will men seek their all in God; and to this nothing conduces more than the discipline of affliction. No path leads more surely to the sublimer heights of the spiritual world than the path of trial and sorrow. "Blessed is the man that endureth trial, for when he hath been approved he shall receive the crown of life which the Lord hath promised to them that love Him" (James i. 12).

XXIII.

JERUSALEM ELEVATED.

"Behold, the day of the Lord cometh, and thy spoil shall be divided in the midst of thee. For I will gather all nations against Jerusalem to battle; and the city shall be taken, and the houses rifled, and the women ravished; and half of the city shall go forth into captivity, and the residue of the people shall not be cut off from the city. Then shall the Lord go forth, and fight against those nations, as when He fought in the day of battle. And his feet shall stand in that day upon the mount of Olives, which is before Jerusalem on the east; and the mount of Olives shall cleave in the midst thereof toward the east and toward the west, and there shall be a very great valley: and half of the mountain shall remove toward the north, and half of it towards the south. And ye shall flee to the valley of the mountains; for the valley of the mountains shall reach unto Azal: yea, ye shall flee, like as ye fled from before the earthquake in the days of Uzziah, king of Judah; and the Lord my God shall come, and all the saints with thee. And it shall come to pass in that day, that the light shall not be clear nor dark: but it shall be one day which shall be known to the Lord, nor day, nor night: but it shall come to pass, that at evening time it shall be light. And it shall be in that day, that living waters shall go out from Jerusalem; half of them toward the former sea, and half of them toward the hinder sea: in summer and in winter shall it be. And the Lord shall be King over all the earth: in that day shall there be one Lord, and his name one. All the land shall be turned as a plain from Geba to Rimmon, south of Jerusalem: and it shall be lifted up, and inhabited in her place, from Benjamin's gate unto the place of the first gate, unto the corner gate, and from the tower of Hananeel unto the king's wine-presses. And men shall dwell in it, and there shall be no more utter destruction; but Jerusalem shall be safely inhabited."—ZECH. xiv. 1-11.

THE prophecy in this chapter is closely connected with that in the close of the preceding; or rather, it is the same in an expanded form with fuller details. Here, as there, the dispersion of the flock, the deliverance of a portion of it, the bestowal of blessing on the rescued remnant, and the final establishment of the kingdom all over the earth by the reception into it of men of all nations, are set forth. There is a difference, indeed, in the point of view from which the prophet speaks; in chap. xiii. 7–9 it is Israel as a nation that is in the prophet's view, in this chapter it is more specially Jerusalem as the holy city, the metropolis and head of Israel, and the centre from which salvation and blessing were to flow forth to the world, that is the object contemplated; but this difference is of no essential moment, for as Jerusalem was the head of the nation, and the centre of its religious life, in its fate that of the nation was involved.

The prophet begins by announcing the judgment that is to come upon Jerusalem, against which the nations are to be gathered, who are to take her, despoil her, and disperse her inhabitants: "Behold, a day for Jehovah cometh, and thy spoil is divided in the midst of thee" (ver. 1). "A day for Jehovah" is a day appropriated by Jehovah, a day selected and taken by Him for the manifestation of His power, and the accomplishing of His purposes; not as in the Authorised Version, "The day of the Lord," which would point back to some great occasion in the past when God came forth to do battle for His people, and against their enemies, or forward to that august occasion which is described elsewhere as "The great day of the Lord"; the phrase is purposely indefinite (יום ליהוה, not יום יהוה,* comp. Isa. ii. 12);

* See Gesenius, *Heb. Gr.* § 115, 2; Ewald, *Intro. Heb. Gr.* § 292;

and simply indicates the occasion on which God will bring to pass what is here announced. "Thy spoil:" Jerusalem is here addressed, though not formally mentioned; her spoil is not, as the Targum of Jonathan suggests, the booty she has taken from the heathen, but the booty she contains, and which is taken from her by the invading foe. This is to be divided by the enemy in the midst of her, not carried off to some distant place of security, but divided in the midst of the city as wholly under the power of the conqueror.

At the outset the attention is arrested by a vivid announcement of the main fact; the details involved in it are given in what follows: "And I will gather all nations against Jerusalem to battle, and the city shall be taken, and the houses rifled, and the women ravished; and half of the city shall go forth into captivity, but the remnant of the people shall not be cut off from the city" (ver. 2). The "and" at the beginning of this verse is not a mere copulative, it has also an explicative force, and might be rendered "for" (*vaw explicativum*). God is said to gather the nations against Jerusalem because they are the instruments by which His purposes are accomplished, and He so orders their ways that they, in pursuit of their own ends, gather themselves to do what He has purposed shall be done. The expression "all nations" is not to be explained away as meaning "soldiers from all the different nations forming the Roman empire" (Henderson); nor is it to be taken literally as meaning

---

Müller, *Outlines of Hebrew Syntax*, § 83. Rosenmüller says: "ל hic notat auctorem"; but this does not necessarily follow: the ל may merely indicate the appropriating of the day by God for His own purpose.

all the peoples on the earth at any given time; it is a phrase of general import for the peoples outside the commonwealth of Israel.* To them the city shall be given up to be captured and plundered, and, as is usual when a ruthless soldiery take possession of a place they have besieged, the inhabitants are to be treated with the utmost barbarity, their houses rifled and the women ravished (cf. Isa. xiii. 16; Lam. v. 11 ff.; Amos vii. 7). One half of the people should be carried into exile, but a portion—not necessarily the other half, for many would perish in the sack of the city—should be preserved and remain in the city. In this respect a difference would emerge between this and the former overthrow of Jerusalem and the Jewish state by the Chaldeans; then all the people who were not killed were hurried into captivity, and even the miserable remnant at first left in the city were ultimately transported thence (2 Kings xxv. 22–26); whereas on this occasion a portion should be left which should not be cut off out of the city but should abide there. Thus left to remain in the city they might rest in peace, for though the heathen were gathered around them, and had captured the city, they had an Almighty protector who should appear for their defence: "And Jehovah will go forth and fight against those nations as in a day of His fighting, in a day of slaughter." The phrase "to go forth" is that generally used in Scripture of military expeditions (cf. Num. i. 3; 2 Sam. ii. 11; Ps. cviii. 11, &c.); and when used of

---

* Comp. Psalm cxviii. 10; Isa. ii. 2; Joel iii. 2, and our Lord's words to His disciples, "Ye shall be hated of all nations for my name's sake," Matt. xxiv. 9.

Jehovah, it designates His agency in the infliction of punishment on His enemies, and for the deliverance of His people. Thus, "Behold, Jehovah goeth out of His place to punish the inhabitants of the earth for their iniquity" (Isa. xxvi. 21); "the Lord shall go forth as a mighty man, He shall stir up jealousy as a man of war. . . . He shall prevail against His enemies" (xlii. 13); "For behold, Jehovah goeth forth out of His place, and will come down and tread upon the high places of the earth" (Mic. i. 3); "Thou wentest forth for the salvation of Thy people. . . . Thou woundest the head out of the house of the wicked" (Hab. iii. 13). So here, though these nations were the instruments in His hands of afflicting Israel, so as to drive out of it the unworthy and apostate, yet as they were the enemies of Israel only for their own evil ends, and had assailed it only in obedience to their own wicked passions, God would come forth as a man of war to fight against them, so that His people who were faithful to Him should escape. "A day of His fighting," not "the day," as if some special occasion were referred to when Jehovah fought against His enemies and for His people, as *e.g.*, His overthrow of Pharaoh and his host at the Red Sea (Jerome, Hengstenberg, &c.); the reference is rather to God's general way of acting in such cases as shown in many former instances (cf. Exod. xiv. 14, xv. 3; Josh. x. 10, xiv. 12, xxiii. 3; Judges iv. 15; 1 Sam. vii. 10; 2 Chron. xx. 15). The words "in a day of slaughter," are added "for the purpose of strengthening the expression" (Keil). The Lord would on this occasion do as He had been wont to do on former occasions, the day should be a day of battle and of slaughter, and He would go forth and fight against the enemy and for His people. In appearing for this end, the Lord would take His stand on Olivet, which at His touch should be cleft asunder: "And His feet shall stand in that day on the Mount of Olives, which is before Jerusalem eastwards, and the Mount of Olives shall be cleft in its midst, eastward and westward, a very great valley; and half of the mountain shall recede to the north and its (other) half to the south" (ver. 4). When the Lord descended on Mount Sinai "the whole Mount quaked greatly" (Exod. xix. 18); at the presence of the Lord the earth trembleth and the mountains flow down and quake (Ps. lxviii. 8, cxiv. 7; Isa. lxiv. 1; Mic. i. 4; Nah. i. 5). So here, as the feet of the Lord touched the Mount of Olives, there should be an earthquake, and the effect of this should be to open a great valley through the heart of the mountain, from west to east. Olivet is described as "before Jerusalem," not for the sake of determining its geographical position, which was too well known to require to be pointed out, but as indicating the direction in which the line of escape from the captured city was to be opened for those whom God would deliver. That was right through the centre of the mountain, the great chasm running from the side next Jerusalem eastward. Into this the people were to flee: "And ye shall flee to the valley of my mountains; and the valley of the mountains shall reach to Azal; and ye shall flee as ye fled before the earthquake in the days of Uzziah, king of Judah. And Jehovah my God shall come, and all the saints with Thee" (ver. 5). The valley formed by the cleaving asunder of the hill, is called by God "the valley of my mountains," because on each side of it was an elevation produced by the power of God, at whose touch the Mount of Olives had been rent in the midst. This valley should reach unto Azal or Atsal (אֶל־אָצַל). Some interpreters take the words *el Atzal* in an appellative sense, as meaning "to very near," or "to close at hand," and understand the expression as intimating that the valley was to extend to near to where the fugitives were, that is, to Jerusalem. This is the rendering of the Vulgate, "usque ad proximum;" and of Symmachus, πρὸς τὸ παρακείμενον. The Syriac has ܠܘܬ ܓܒܐ which in the London Polyglot is rendered by *ad angustum locum*, but which is probably rather a substitute for the Hebrew אצל. (See Payne Smith, *Thes. Syr.* Fasc. I. Col. 220.) By most ancient interpreters, Atsal is taken as a proper name, the designation of some place on the east side of Olivet, to which the valley was to reach, and where the fugitives should find an asylum, a view most recent expositors have adopted. It may probably be the Beth-ezel (בֵּית הָאֵצֶל) Beth Ha-etsal of Mic. i. 11, the Beth being omitted, as it not unfrequently is, from proper names, formed with it (as, for instance, Nimrah and Beth-Nimrah, Num. xxxii. 3, 36; Azmaveth and Beth Azmaveth, Neh. xii. 29, vii. 28; Beth-Ha-Gilgal, Neh. xii. 29, elsewhere Gilgal, &c.), and *atsal* being read for *atsel* because of the pause (comp. 1 Chron. viii. 38, 39). To this place the remnant should flee as the people "fled from before the earthquake in the days of Uzziah, king of Judah." The earthquake here referred to is not recorded in the Historical Books, but the prophet Amos refers to it (Amos i. 1) in a way which shows it was sufficiently memorable to furnish a date from which other events might be calculated. Great terror, apparently, was caused by it, so that the people fled before it. In like manner should they flee when God's hand should be stretched forth to smite the nations by whom Jerusalem should be taken and sacked, but on this occasion not so much in terror as in haste to escape to a place of safety. This coming of the Lord to smite His enemies and deliver His people should be with all His holy ones—" and all Thy saints with Thee." The prophet, as it were, sees Him approach, hails Him as his God, the protector of His people, and suddenly passing from the third person to the second, addresses Jehovah as actually present, attended by all the heavenly host, the holy angels (comp. Deut. xxxiii. 2, 3; Dan. vii. 9; Matt. xxv. 31). God, when He comes forth to act, comes attended by these ministers of His that delight to do His will and accomplish His pleasure.

As God should come not merely to smite His enemies, but more especially to deliver His people, the prophet goes on to depict the full salvation of such, as consequent on the coming of the Lord. He begins with a statement which is very obscure and which has been differently interpreted. The first part of the verse is plain enough, " and it shall come to pass in that day that there will not be light"; as to this all are agreed; it is in the closing words יקפאון יקרות that the difficulty lies. There is here a feminine nominative followed by a masculine verb, and though this may be got over by the suggestion that the feminine is here as a neuter, still it is not easy to make sense of the words. יָקַר occurs in this book (xi.

13) in the sense of *price*, and the feminine form from it may mean *precious*, and in the plural *precious ones or things*. The verb is the third person plural of the imperfect *niphal* of קפא to *fold or draw together, to thicken, to congeal*. The words would thus mean "The precious things will be congealed." Or קָרוֹת may be the plural feminine of יָקָר *bright, splendid*, and the phrase may be rendered by "The bright or shining ones shall be drawn together, shall be contracted," *i.e.*, as Gesenius explains it (Thes. II. 621), "the bright stars shall contract their lustre, that is, shall cease to shine." This gives a very good sense in connection with what goes before, but it is objected that the explanation goes beyond what the words express, for to be drawn together or contracted is not equivalent to withdraw or cease, and *yeqamoth* is nowhere used of the stars. These objections, however, may be obviated: the former by taking the verb in its primary meaning of folding together, so that the contracting is the huddling together in a confused heap of the objects designated by yeqamoth; the latter by referring to Job xxxi. 26, where the moon is said to walk brightly or in brightness יָקָר, which shows that brightness was regarded by the Hebrews as by other peoples as the special characteristic of the heavenly bodies. The whole passage then will run thus: —"There will not be light, the bright ones shall be heaped together": and the meaning will be that the stars or the heavenly bodies generally, instead of abiding in their courses shall be confusedly thrown together, the effect of which will be that they will no longer give light to the earth.

A very different interpretation has been suggested by

the K'ri on this passage, where for יִקְפְּאוּן is read יְקַפְאוּן, from which the reading וְקָרוֹת וְקִפָּאוֹן "both chills and frost" has been devised. This all the ancient versions support; the Seventy has καὶ ψύχος καὶ πάγος, the Vulgate, *sed frigus et gelu,* and the Targum and Syriac the same, "cold and ice." The Targum, indeed, has "booty" עֲדִי in place of "cold," by which Rosenmüller supposes the Targumist intended "res pretioras direptas;" but probably for עֲדִי should be read עֲרִי, like the Syriac (see Levy, "Chald. Wörterb," II., page 204).

This reading is adopted by Hitzig, De Wette, Rosenmüller, Maurer, and others; who understand the passage as predicting a day of darkness and full of horror ("horroris plenus ille dies erit." Maur.) Others, however, among whom are Hengstenberg and Keil, object, the latter of whom says that "the insertion of יהיה without a negation for the purpose of obtaining an antithesis" is "intolerably harsh."

But there does not seem to be much weight in this, for though in strict grammatical accuracy such insertion is not allowable, yet in ordinary speech and writing it is not found to be intolerable; at any rate it must have been regarded as allowable by the Targumist, the Seventy, and the Syriac Translator, else they would not have rendered here as they have done. Keil's own rendering and explanation far more deserve to be thus stigmatised. Understanding *yeqāmoth* of the stars, and reading the verb as the imperfect kal, יְקַפְאוּן he renders thus, "the glorious ones shall melt away," and says, "the words describe the passing away or vanishing of the brightness of the shining stars." But allowing that the stars are here intended by *yeqāmoth*, by what legitimate process can a verb which, as Keil himself tells us, "signifies to congeal or curdle," be brought to signify "to melt away" or "vanish"? What is congealed may, it is true, be afterwards melted; but the congealing and the melting are antagonistic processes, and could never come to be designated by the same word. Ewald, Bunsen, and Umbreit adopt this reading which Keil so indignantly rejects, but instead of regarding the passage as minatory, they regard it as being rather of a comforting and cheering aspect, comparing it with Isaiah lx. 19, 20, and Rev. xxi. 23. Ewald renders by, "there shall be no sunshine with cold and ice," and Bunsen, "there will not be light: storminess and freezing;" and the latter explains the meaning to be that "the heretofore interchange of summer and winter, of light and darkness, shall cease, and ever henceforward there shall be sunshine." But, as Henderson remarks, "whatever connection there may be between the absence of light and the production of cold in winter, the contrast is not so natural as that between light and darkness." Had the prophet intended to convey the idea of "pure and perennial sunshine" he would have said, "there will be light without darkness," or something equivalent to this. As for Bunsen's explanation, one can only say of it, as Maurer says of that of Gesenius, "elegans quidem sensus modo certior esset!" Much the same must be said of the explanation adopted by Henderson from Dr. Lee (Heb. Lex., p. 533), who "reads אוֹר יְקָרוֹת in construction," and renders by "there shall not be the light of the precious orbs, but condensed darkness"—a plausible conjecture if it only could be certified.

But though at first there should be gloom and calamity, this should not be lasting. This is intimated in what follows: "And it shall be one day, it shall be known to Jehovah, not day and not night; and it shall come to pass at evening time that there shall be light" (ver. 7). The phrase "one day" is often used in the sense of "a short time" (cf. Ezra x. 13; Isa. ix. 1, lxvi. 8; Zech. iii. 9, &c.); and so it is understood here by some (Cocceius, tempus non longum; Hengstenberg, "a relatively short time"), who suppose that "the allusion is to the transient character of the visitations of God," as in Psalm xxx. 5, "Weeping may endure for a night, but joy cometh in the morning;" and Isaiah xxvi. 20, "Hide thyself as it were for a little moment until the indignation be overpast." But though this in itself gives a very good sense, the words that follow, "It shall be known to the Lord," would seem to indicate that it is the *peculiarity* of the season rather than its *brevity* that is here expressed; the day shall be one of its kind, known to Jehovah, as it really is, and by implication to none else; אֶחָד has here very much the sense of *unique* or *special*, as in Ezek. vii. 5, "a special evil," one entirely *sui generis*, Cant. vi. 9, and verse 9 of this chapter. As respects outward appearance, it will be "not day and not night." This may mean either, It shall not be day and night, that is, there shall be no such distinction between day and night as that it could be said, This is day and this is night, for the heavenly luminaries being extinguished, there would be no means of determining this; or, It shall be neither day nor night, but a turbid mixture of light and darkness, a mysterious twilight, like that produced by an eclipse of the sun. In support of the latter it has been urged that "there is a gradation through three distinct stages: first, utter darkness; then a dim twilight like that of an eclipse; and at the close, when you might expect darkness soon to cover the earth, lo, the effulgence of a full and glorious day!"* But the former is what the words of the prophet more naturally suggest. And this strange day, unlike all other days, should no less strangely close: "At evening time there shall be light;" the natural order of things shall be reversed; in the evening, when darkness is expected to settle down on the earth, a bright light should break forth. This light is not to be regarded as the return of the natural light of day, for the heavenly bodies are supposed to be hidden or extinguished; it is a new, supernatural light that shall arise, a Divine lustre that shall break forth on the darkened world. An illustration may be obtained from Rev. xxi. 23 ff., though the object there referred to may not be the same as that presented here: it is the glory of the Lord that shall illuminate the earth: comp. also Isa. xxiv. 23, lx. 19, xl. 5). With this illumination shall come a season of prosperity and joy: "And it shall be on that day that living waters shall go forth from Jerusalem, the half of them towards the eastern sea and the half of them towards the western sea: in summer and winter it shall be" (ver. 8). "Living waters," that is, water fresh, pure, and salubrious, springing from a perennial source (cf. Gen. xxvi. 19; Cant. iv. 15; Jer. ii. 13). These shall flow forth from Jerusalem, the centre of the kingdom of God

---

* Cowles' "Minor Prophets," page 374, cited by Chambers, "Schaaf-Lange Commentary," *in loc.*

(cf. Ezek. xlvii. 1 ff.; Joel iii. 18, where the waters are said to issue from the Temple), and shall spread over the whole land, carrying fertility and abundance with them. The eastern sea (the sea in front קַדְמֹנִי) is the Asphaltite Lake or Dead Sea, and the western sea (the sea behind אַחֲרוֹן) is the Mediterranean, so named, because to one looking from Jerusalem, the centre to the east, "the primary point of the horizon with the Orientals," the Dead Sea is before him and the Mediterranean behind him (cf. Joel ii. 20; Ezek. xlvii. 18, 20). These streams should be perennial; in summer and winter they should flow, neither bound by frost in winter nor dried up by heat in summer. That the representation is wholly figurative is evident from the fact that natural waters could not flow in all directions at once from the same point. Elsewhere, as here, the flowing forth of waters over the land is figurative of the diffusion of blessing, temporal and spiritual; cf. Joel iii. 18; Ezek. xlvii. 1–12. Over the land thus inundated with blessing Jehovah should reign, and His name should alone be revered and invoked: "And Jehovah will be King over all the land; in that day will Jehovah be one and His name one" (ver. 9). כָּל הָאָרֶץ is here not "the whole earth" (A. V.), but "all the land," the land of which the Dead Sea and the Mediterranean are extreme boundaries, the land of Israel, the sphere of the ancient kingdom of God on earth. At the same time, as Canaan was the type of that spiritual kingdom which is in the latter day to extend over the whole earth, it is in substance, and virtually, the whole earth that is here intended. Of this kingdom, "the field is the world," and over this (when "the kingdom of the world" has become "the kingdom of our Lord and of His Christ") Jehovah shall be King, "the blessed and only Potentate, King of kings, and Lord of lords." The expression "Jehovah will be one and His name one," intimates that Jehovah shall thus be acknowledged universally as the one and only God, that men everywhere shall be "turned to God from idols to serve the living and true God," and that "the Name which is above every name" shall be the only name on which men shall call all over the earth (comp. Ps. lxxii. 8–11; Dan. ii. 44; Zech. ix. 10).

Consequent on the exaltation of Jehovah as King shall be the exaltation of Jerusalem, the city of the great King, over all the land; "And the whole land shall turn to [become as] the Plain from Geba to Rimmon, south of Jerusalem, and she shall be high, and shall dwell in her place, from the gate of Benjamin to the place of the first gate, to the corner gate, and from the tower of Hananeel to the wine presses of the king" (ver. 10). Geba was situated on a rocky ridge overlooking the eastern slopes of the mountains of Benjamin, about six miles to the north of Jerusalem (*Hod.* Jeba); Rimmon was a city on the southern border of the territory originally assigned to Judah (Josh. xv. 21, 32), here described as to the south of Jerusalem, to distinguish it from the Rimmon in Galilee, to the north of Nazareth and the Rock Rimmon (Judges xx. 45), probably represented now by the ruins of Um-er-Rummanim, four hours north of Beersheba. These places marked the northern and southern extremities of the territory of Judah; and the phrase "from Geba to Rimmon," equivalent to "from Geba to Beersheba" (2 Kings xxiii. 8), describes the whole land of

Judah. This is for the most part a hilly region; but this whole district should become like the Arabah (Deut. i. 7; Josh xii. 1, 3, 8, &c.), the Great Plain (τὸ Μέγα πεδίον καλεῖται, Jos. *de Bell. Jud.* iv. 8, 2) extending from the Sea of Tiberias to the Elanitic Gulf. Thus a way would be made for the waters to flow from Jerusalem, and the city itself should become relatively elevated, so as to tower over the whole land,—" a figurative representation of the spiritual elevation and glory which it is to receive" (Keil). It should also dwell in its own place, that is, shall occupy to the full extent its proper site, shall be restored to its former dimensions from the ruin caused by its capture and sack (ver. 1). The boundaries of the city, as here given, cannot in every particular be determined. The gate of Benjamin is undoubtedly the northern gate opening on the road to the land of Benjamin, called elsewhere "the gate of Ephraim" (2 King xiv. 13; Neh. viii. 16), the same road leading both to Benjamin and Ephraim. The tower of Hananeel was near to the sheep-gate on the eastern side of the city (Neh. iii. 1, xii. 37, 39). Between it and the Benjamin gate was probably "the place of the first gate," *i.e.*, the place occupied by the first gate, as the city was before it was everted by the Chaldeans. What is here called the "first gate" is probably the same as "the gate of the old town," הַיְשָׁנָה שַׁעַר (gate of the old one (fem.), Jerusalem being personified, like cities generally, as a woman) mentioned Neh. iii. 6, xii. 39, here called "the first" because in a part of the city first built. This gate was probably at the north-eastern end of the wall. "The gate of the corner" was on the other side of the gate of

Benjamin or Ephraim, to the west, about 400 cubits distant from that gate (2 Kings xiv. 13); in Jer. xxxi. 38, it is mentioned as opposite to the tower of Hananeel, to indicate the whole extent of the city. A fresh departure is taken from the tower of Hananeel, and a line is drawn thence to "the king's presses." These were in all probability in the king's gardens, which were on the south side of the city (Neh. iii. 15). The limits of the city are thus given to the four points of the compass. In the city thus restored and exalted peace and blessedness should reign: "And they shall dwell in her, and there shall be no more curse, and Jerusalem shall dwell in security" (ver. 11). The dwelling here is in contrast to the going out from the city as captives or fugitives, in ver. 2 and ver. 5. The expression "there shall no more be a curse," has reference to the *cherem* or *ban* which came upon those who were idolaters, or who rebelled against Jehovah, or violated certain laws of the Theocracy, and which entailed on the transgressor condign punishment, either by death or by confiscation of goods and excision from the community (Exod. xxii. 20; Deut. vii. 26, xiii. 12 ff.; Ezra x. 8; Isa. xliii. 28; Mal. iv. 6). As the infliction of such a curse implied the existence of sin on the part of those on whom it was sent, the removal of the curse implied the remission of guilt to the transgressor; and, in accordance with this, the declaration, "there shall be no more curse," is equivalent to a declaration of the abolition of sin, and the cessation finally of all ungodliness and transgression. What is here intimated, then, is that the city shall be inhabited by a people wholly the Lord's, a holy nation, devoted to God, at peace with Him, "righteous before Him, and walking in all the commandments and ordinances of the Lord, blameless." The city and its inhabitants will, consequently, be in perfect security, there being no occasion any more for chastisement to come upon them at the hand of the enemy (comp. Isa. lxv. 17 ff.; Joel iii. 17-21; Jer. xxxi. 38-40; Rev. xxi. 2-5, xxii. 3 ff.).

At this point we may conveniently pause to inquire into the meaning and intent of the oracle, the signification of the language of which we have been engaged in investigating. As it is an expansion with fuller details of the prophecy in the close of the preceding chapter, we must start from the assumption that what is referred to here is not any one great historical event, or any series of events, but the kingdom of God in its experience and development and ultimate triumph, in the world. The highly figurative description of the prophet, couched in language which does not admit of a literal interpretation, of itself necessitates our resorting to a spiritual application of his utterance. The appearance of Jehovah on Mount Olivet, the sudden cleaving of that mountain by an earthquake, so as to cause a valley to stretch through its centre, the extinguishing of the heavenly luminaries, causing a darkness that might be felt to overspread the land, the breaking forth of light at evening when, according to natural law, darkness should begin to assume the sway, the sending forth of streams from one point in diametrically opposite directions, the making of the whole hilly region round Jerusalem into a plain like the Arabah, so as that Jerusalem should come to be elevated over the whole land—all that is so conspicuously figurative that a literal interpretation of it has never been seriously proposed by any one except some of the Rabbins. Figurative also is the representation of a gathering of all nations against Jerusalem; this at no time has been realised, nor could it be so at any time. But if all this be figurative, it cannot be of Jerusalem as the actual metropolis of Judea that the prophet here speaks; it must be to Jerusalem as to the centre of the kingdom of heaven upon earth, and as representing that kingdom that the oracle relates. Hence in the overthrow and ruin of Jerusalem here described we are to find the abolition of the ancient economy, the decaying and vanishing away of the former under which the kingdom had been established of old, an event which was brought about by the assault of the hostile heathen powers of the world. The kingdom itself, however, was not thereby averted; amid the general ruin a remnant was preserved, and that not by flight *from* the city but *in* it, there permanently to abide. Around this, the nucleus of the renovated kingdom, the protecting care of the Omnipotent should be vouchsafed; on the enemy His judgments should fall, and lest His people should be involved in these, a way of escape should be made for them, and they should flee and be in safety. Seasons of darkness and calamity might come, and amid the ominous gloom the face of heaven might be obscured, and it might seem as if God's favour was withdrawn; but this should be only for a season; the dark day would in due time decline, and at the evening there should be light. Ways should be made by which the kingdom, as it expanded, might extend over the earth—a path should be cut through the most obdurate obstacles, obstructions should be removed, and streams of blessing should flow in all directions over the earth. Then should Jehovah be recognised as King over all the earth, and be worshipped as the one and only God. Then should Jerusalem, "the new," "the heavenly Jerusalem," "Jerusalem the free," which is the mother of all the people of Christ (Rev. iii. 12, xxi. 2; Heb. xii. 22; Gal. iv. 26; comp. Phil. iii. 20), "the Church of the living God" (1 Tim. iii. 15), be exalted, and be filled with inhabitants to the full extent of her proper boundaries. Then shall the saints inherit the earth; then shall the true people of God, being all righteous, be free from all calamity, injury or assault; perfect security shall be enjoyed and the calm of a great peace shall settle down on the world, so long troubled and vexed by the storms of evil. The ban which has rested on the race because of sin since the first transgression, shall then be for ever taken off; there will be no need to make men acknowledge God's supremacy by the judgments which He executes; a willing obedience shall be rendered to Him by all; His servants shall serve Him, they shall see His face, and His name shall be on their foreheads.

XXIV.

THE PERFECT AND SPIRITUAL KINGDOM.

"And this shall be the plague wherewith the Lord will smite all the people that have fought against Jerusalem: their flesh shall consume away while they stand upon their feet, and their eyes shall consume away in their holes, and their tongue shall consume away in their mouth. And it shall come to pass in that day, that a great tumult from the Lord shall be among them; and they shall lay hold every one on the hand of his neighbour, and his hand shall rise up against the hand of his neighbour. And Judah also shall fight at Jerusalem: and the wealth of all the heathen round about shall be gathered together, gold, and silver, and apparel, in great abundance. And so shall be the plague of the horse, of the mule, of the camel, and of the ass, and of all the beasts that shall be in these tents, as this plague. And it shall come to pass, that every one that is left of all the nations which came against Jerusalem shall even go up from year to year to worship the King, the Lord of hosts, and to keep the feast of tabernacles. And it shall be, that whoso will not come up of all the families of the earth unto Jerusalem to worship the King, the Lord of hosts, even upon them shall be no rain. And if the family of Egypt go not up, and come not, that have no rain; there shall be the plague, wherewith the Lord will smite the heathen that come not up to keep the feast of tabernacles. This shall be the punishment of Egypt, and the punishment of all nations that come not up to keep the feast of tabernacles. In that day shall there be upon the bells of the horses, HOLINESS UNTO THE LORD; and the pots in the Lord's house shall be like the bowls before the altar. Yea, every pot in Jerusalem and in Judah shall be holiness unto the Lord of hosts; and all they that sacrifice shall come and take of them, and seethe therein: and in that day there shall be no more the Canaanite in the house of the Lord of hosts."—ZECH. xiv. 12-21.

THE oracle in this section is best regarded not as another and distinct from that which precedes, nor as a mere

THE PERFECT AND SPIRITUAL KINGDOM.

continuation of it, but rather as a résumé or repetition of it in which the same things are depicted as in the former, but more explicitly and in language less figurative and symbolical. As in the former the prophet here begins by a reference to the overthrow of the peoples that had fought against Jerusalem (verses 12–15), and then proceeds to describe the conversion of the residue of the peoples, and the diffusion of a universal reign of holiness and godliness all over the earth (verses 16–21); just as in the preceding section he had described the levelling of the whole land so as to become a plain, over which the living and life-giving waters of salvation are to flow to the ends of the earth, and the reign of peace and godliness and blessedness under Jehovah, as King and only Lord over all the earth, shall be inaugurated.

In the preceding oracle it is declared that the Lord shall go forth and fight against the nations that had captured and plundered Jerusalem (verse 3). How this is to be done is now described. "And (or Now) this shall be the smiting wherewith Jehovah shall smite all the peoples which have warred against Jerusalem. He causes to waste the flesh of each whilst standing on its feet, and the eyes of each shall be wasted away in their sockets, and the tongue of each shall be wasted in their mouth." *The smiting* (magêphah); the word is used generally of an infliction sent by God, such as a pestilence or epidemic, disease or slaughter, which He has purposed or ordained; comp. Ex. ix. 15; Num. xiv. 37; 1 Sam. vi. 4; and the use of the cognate verb in Ex. xii. 23; Judges xx. 35; Is. xix. 22. That *magêphah*, however, "always denotes a plague or punishment sent by God" (Keil) cannot be maintained in the face of such usages of the noun and verb as in 1 Sam. iv. 17; 2 Sam. xvii. 9, xviii. 7; Ex. xxi. 22, 35; Prov. iii. 23. *The flesh of each*, etc., lit., his flesh, his eyes, his tongue; "sc. unius cujusque" (Ros.); the singular suffixes are to be taken distributively. In the close of the clause the singular passes into the plural. *Causeth to waste away*: הָמֵק, inf. abs. hiph., *causing to waste*, used for the finite verb. Jehovah makes the flesh of the enemy to waste or rot whilst he stands on his feet, *i.e.*, whilst he is still alive. The wasting of the eyes in their sockets and of the tongue in the mouth is specially mentioned, not only to give greater emphasis to the denunciation, but because it was by these organs that the enemy had most conspicuously offended; their eyes were evil against the city of God and searching out Jerusalem for plunder, and their tongue crying out for its destruction, saying, "Raze it, raze it even to the foundations thereof" (Ps. cxxxvii. 7; cf. Mic. iv. 11). Besides this judgment from God, destruction should come upon them from among themselves: "And it shall come to pass in that day that there shall be a mighty confusion from Jehovah among them, and each shall grip the hand of his neighbour, and his hand [the hand of each] shall rise up against his neighbour; and also Judah shall fight against Jerusalem, and the wealth of all the nations round about shall be gathered together, gold and silver and apparel in much abundance" (verses 13, 14). *Confusion from* (lit., *of*, *i.e.*, caused by, gen. of cause) *Jehovah*. The Lord should cause a panic to fall upon the host of the enemy, by which they should be thrown into confusion, and should turn their weapons against each other so as to complete their destruction; just as He had done on former occasions to the enemies of Israel (cf. Judges vii. 22; 1 Sam. xiv. 20; 2 Chron. xx. 23; comp. Is. xxii. 5, *yom mehumah*, and Deut. vii. 23). *Mighty*, רַבָּה, is *vast, widespread*, rather than *great;* a confusion spreading through the entire host. *Grip*, הֶחֱזִיק, to lay hold of, to fasten on, with יָד, either to take the hand to assist (Gen. xix. 16, xxi. 18; Is. xlii. 6), or to grasp it with a hostile intent as here. Each should seize the hand of his neighbour to hold him, that he might smite him; and so a hand-to-hand fight between neighbours should ensue (cf. xi. 6). The scene of this internecine conflict should be Jerusalem, which the enemy had besieged and taken; but the city having been sacked, and its inhabitants either slain or utterly cowed and put to flight, no advantage could be taken by them of the confusion and disaster into which their assailants had been thrown. From the nation at large, however, a force should come which, falling upon the disordered and struggling host, should complete their destruction. Judah also shall mingle in the fray. Instead of "at Jerusalem," some (Rosenmüller, Maurer, etc.), with the Targumist, Jerome, Jarchi and other Jewish interpreters, read " against Jerusalem," and understand the meaning to be that the people of Judah, compelled by force (*coacti*), had joined the heathen in their attack upon Jerusalem. In support of this it is urged that the preposition בְּ, following a verb of fighting, and prefixed to the names of persons or places, is to be taken adversatively, as in Judges ix. 45; 1 Sam. xxiii. 1. But this is not conclusive, for though generally the preposition in such a collocation denotes the object of attack, it is also used to point to the place of the fighting; cf. Ex. xvii. 8; 1 Kings xx. 25; 2 Chron. xxxv. 22. The rendering "at" or "in Jerusalem" is therefore legitimate, and the meaning thus obtained is much more apt than the other. There is no indication in the passage of any hostility between Jerusalem and Judah; and the supposition of an enforced service of Judah by the heathen against the metropolis of their own land is wholly gratuitous as well as improbable. Besides, such an announcement as that Judah should fight against Jerusalem would be altogether out of place and incongruous here, in the midst of a passage describing the overthrow and rout of the assailants of Jerusalem; whereas the coming of Judah to fight at Jerusalem against its assailants, comes in naturally as an adjunct to the previously announced means by which the invading host are to be destroyed. This assault by Judah should complete the rout of the heathen; the wealth which they had accumulated should be gathered together to be carried away by the victors, and all the rich booty, gold and silver and apparel, which they had taken from Jerusalem, should become the spoil of the victors. Even the beasts of burden and the cattle which they had with them in the tents should be destroyed; the same plague as had come on their owners should fall upon them. "And as this plague, so shall be the plague of the horse, of the mule, of the camel, and of the ass, and of all the cattle that are in these tents [in this encampment, *in castris illis*]" (verse 15). To the כְּ at the beginning of the verse responds the כְּ in the last clause; more usually the order of these particles is the reverse. When nations or individuals came under the Divine curse, not only they but their possessions and dependents along with them were exposed to destruction; cf. Joshua vii. 24. This was the doom threatened to Israel through Moses in case of rebellion and apostacy, Deut. xxviii. 18 ff.

From this infliction only a remnant of those who had come up against Jerusalem and had plundered it, should escape; but this remnant should be spared only to become subject to the kingdom of which Jerusalem is the metropolis and centre: "And it shall come to pass the whole that is left of all the nations which came against Jerusalem shall go up from year to year to worship the King, Jehovah of hosts, and to observe the Feast of Tabernacles" (verse 16). The heathen came up to Jerusalem to destroy it; but now after the judgment by which they were themselves overwhelmed and ruined, the remnant that should be spared should be converted to the Lord, acknowledge Him as King, and come up to Jerusalem as the city of the Great King to offer worship and observe His ordinances. That this is not to be taken literally, as it is by the Jews, is evident as well from the general tenor of the whole prophecy as from the nature of the case; for as on the one hand a gathering every year from all the nations of the earth at Jerusalem to observe a religious festival is a simple impossibility, so on the other such a gathering would be incongruous with the character and purpose of that spiritual reign which the prophet is here announcing. In accordance with what goes before and what follows in this prophetic utterance, the coming of all nations to worship at Jerusalem can only be understood of the conversion of the heathen to God under the reign of the Messiah, an event which is here presented under forms borrowed from the ordinances and usages of the ancient dispensation; "the representation is founded upon the manner in which the fear of God and connection with His kingdom manifested themselves under the Old Covenant, and the prophet employs this as a type of the higher form in which they would be manifested in the Messianic times" (Hengstenb.); cf. Isa. lxvi. 23, ii. 2, 3. The phrase מִדֵּי שָׁנָה בְשָׁנָה is rightly rendered by "from year to year," as in 1 Sam. vii. 16; 2 Chron. xxiv. 5; Isa. lxvi. 23. Why the Feast of Tabernacles is specified by the prophet is to be accounted for not because it was the most important of the three great festivals of the Jews, for in this respect it was inferior to the Passover, which had the highest place in the esteem of the nation, nor because it was held in the autumn, the time most convenient for travelling (Theodoret, Grotius, Rosenmüller), nor because it was the Feast of the Ingathering of the Harvest (Köhler), nor because such a festival may be observed without any compromise of the principles of the New Dispensation (Henderson); but because, from its original intention and its internal spiritual significance, it was the fittest to form an element in the prophet's representation here. The Feast of Tabernacles (חַג הַסֻּכּוֹת festival of booths) was not only a feast of the ingathering, when the people appeared before the Lord with "fruits of goodly trees" (said to be the citron, but perhaps also the vine), branches of palm and other trees, to rejoice and give thanks for the bounteous produce of the year, but also a festival of remembrance, when the people, by dwelling for a season in booths, commemorated the journeyings of the Israelites through the wilderness when they dwelt in booths (Ex. xxiii. 16; Lev. xxiii. 40–43). It was a season of great festivity, and was celebrated by the Jews with special solemnity and jubilation. See also Plutarch, Symposiai, Book IV., qu. 6. One of Plutarch's interlocutors describing this festival of the Hebrews, says that from the time and manner of its celebration it was evidently a festival to Dionusos, whose cultus he represents the Jews as following. Tacitus has been charged with making the same misrepresentation (Horne's Introduction, Vol. III., p. 316, 8th ed.); but this is a mistake. Tacitus refers to this as an opinion ("quidam arbitrati sunt"), but declares it to be untenable—"nequaquam congruentibus institutis" (Hist. V. 5). In the opinion of the haughty Roman, the usage of the Jews was too "absurd," "gloomy" and "sordid," to be compared with the mirthful rites of Bacchus. (ἑορτὴ σφόδρα παρὰ τοῖς Ἑβραίοις ἁγιώτατη καὶ μεγίστη.) Joseph. Ant. Jud. viii. 4, 1. Fittingly, therefore, is it introduced by the prophet here as symbolic of that season of joy and worship in the kingdom of heaven, when the heathen, gathered from wandering in the wilderness, shall enter with songs and everlasting joy into the kingdom of God, when the fulness of the Gentiles shall be brought in, and so all Israel shall be saved.

In keeping with this symbolical representation is the description of the punishment that should come on those of the heathen who should refuse or neglect to join in this procession to the Holy City to observe the Feast: "And it shall be that whoso will not come up of the families of the earth to Jerusalem to worship the King, the Lord of hosts, on them shall be no rain" (verse 17). As without rain the land which God had given to Israel for an inheritance would have ceased to be the goodly land, the land flowing with milk and honey He had promised, He assured them by Moses that His care for the land should be manifested by His giving them the rain of the land in its season, so long as they continued to hearken diligently to His commandments to do them; and, on the other hand, should they become rebellious and disobedient, He would mark His displeasure by withholding rain from the land, so that it should become arid and barren (Deut. xi. 13–17). Rain thus became to the Hebrews the type of blessing, of temporal blessing first and then also of spiritual blessing, or both included (cf. Isa. xlv. 8, xxx. 23; Hos. vi. 28; Joel ii. 23, iii. 18; Amos ix. 13). There being no rain, therefore, on those who came not up to the Feast, implies the withholding from them of the Divine blessing, their being left to the emptiness and vanity of a world that is at enmity with God, their dwelling "in parched places in the wilderness, in a salt land" (Jer. xvii. 6). "The meaning of the threat is that those families which do not come to worship the Lord will be punished by Him with the withdrawal of the blessings of His grace" (Keil). Such are regarded as enemies of the kingdom of God. This is implied in the special allusion to the family of Egypt as not coming up to the Feast: "And if the family of Egypt go not up, and come not, there shall be on them no [rain]; there shall be the plague wherewith Jehovah shall plague the nations [the heathen] that go not up to observe the Feast of Tabernacles. This shall be the guilt [the penalty] of

Egypt, and the guilt [the penalty] of all the nations that go not up to observe the Feast of Tabernacles" (verses 18, 19). The words, וְלֹא עֲלֵיהֶם *and not on them*, in verse 18, present a difficulty. What shall not be on them? The sentence is incomplete, and something must be supplied to complete it. In the Authorised Version a supplement is taken from the preceding clause, "rain is not to them" = "they have no rain." This is the most natural supplement; but the form in which the clause is thus presented is unfortunate, for it is made to assert what is not the fact, seeing the Egyptians are not wholly without rain, and what if it were a fact, would be irrelevant here in a description where it is not the natural history of Egypt that is described, but the punishment that should come on the family of Egypt, along with others of the heathen who came not to the Feast. As Egypt, however, is not so dependent for its fertility on rain as other lands, but has an abundant source of irrigation in the annual overflow of the Nile, it has been suggested that it is the withdrawal of this that is here threatened, as what would be equivalent in effect to the Egyptians with the withholding of rain to the inhabitants of other lands. The Targumist accordingly thus paraphrases the clause: לֹא להון יסק נילוס *not to them shall rise the Nile*. But had the prophet intended to convey any such meaning he would have intimated it in some way, and not have left in his text words which do not even suggest this as a conjecture. Besides, there would thus be intimated that on the Egyptians would come a calamity different from that threatened to other nations, which is incompatible with what is stated in verse 19, that the penalty of Egypt and the penalty of all nations should be the same. The LXX ignore the negative and connect this clause with what follows, thus: καὶ ἐπὶ τούτους ἔσται ἡ πτῶσις ἣν πατάξει κύριος πάντα τὰ ἔθνη κ.τ.λ. *And on them shall be the infliction with which the Lord shall smite all the nations*, &c.

But the neglect of the negative vitiates this rendering and forbids its acceptance. To escape this objection Hitzig proposes to read the clause interrogatively: And if . . . shall there not be on them the plague wherewith, etc.; and this Bunsen adopts, and Lange commends it as not only doing justice to the prophet's language but also setting forth his thought. It has been questioned, however, whether such a construction of the clause be grammatically admissible; as it is considered doubtful if the apodosis in the form of a question to a conditional clause can begin with וְלֹא. But for such doubt there seems no sufficient reason, as the same construction may be found elsewhere; comp. 1 Sam. xx. 9, "If I knew . . . should I not (ולא) tell it thee?" Jer. xxiii. 24, "If a man hide himself . . . shall I not (ולא) see him?" Amos iii. 6, "If a trumpet be blown in the city shall not (ולא) the people be afraid?" &c. On the whole, however, it seems best to adopt the simple expedient of taking וְלֹא עֲלֵיהֶם as the apodosis to the conditional clause introduced by אִם, and supplying יִהְיֶה הַגֶּשֶׁם from verse 17 to complete the sentence. There is thus no allusion to the climatic peculiarity of Egypt (which would be strangely out of place here), but only a declaration that if the family of Egypt came not up to the Feast, from them should be withheld the blessing which should be bestowed on all that came up to worship at the Feast. This has been adopted by Hengstenberg, Keil, Henderson, and others, and seems to be that intended by the Vulgate, non super eos erit [*sc.* imber.] sed erit ruina. Egypt, it may be presumed, is specially referred to because it was the type of hostility to the people of God, and thus is indicated that refusal to come up to the Feast was prompted by enmity to Jehovah, the King over all the earth, and was not the result of mere ignorance or inability. In verse 19 the whole is wound up by general affirmation: "This," *i.e.*, there being no rain, will be the guilt (חַטָּאת), the judicial penalty (cf. Lam. iv. 6 and חֲטָא iii. 39), of Egypt and of all the nations that persist in opposition to Jehovah and His kingdom. Within that kingdom there shall be nothing that is profane, abominable, or idolatrous (Rev. xxi. 27, "anything that is common or that maketh an abomination and a lie"). But not only shall there be the absence of all that is unholy and vile, there shall also be the presence of entire and absolute holiness and consecration to God: "In that day there shall be on the bells of the horses Holiness to Jehovah, and the pots in the house of Jehovah shall be as the sacrificial bowls before the altar" (verse 20). Among many nations of antiquity it was customary to hang bells on horses and mules partly for ornament, partly for use, as is still the practice in many places in modern times; and it is probable this usage prevailed also among the Jews in Palestine. As the tinkling of these bells announces the presence of the animal on which they are suspended, they may be held as representing the animal itself; and thus the inscription upon them of Holiness to Jehovah would imply that they, though only belonging to the lower part of creation and in no wise connected specially with religious worship, should be consecrated to the Lord. There is manifestly an allusion to the golden plate on the tiara of the High Priest on which were engraven the words קֹדֶשׁ לַיהוָה, Holy or Holiness to Jehovah: and as this was not a profession put forth by the High Priest, but was an ascription put upon him to indicate his entire consecration to the Lord, so the putting of this on the bells of the horses signifies that they, though mere outward objects, should be as entirely consecrated to God as were the most holy objects in the service of the sanctuary. Involved in this as a necessary conclusion is the abolition of the ceremonial distinction between the common and the holy; for if even beasts of burden were to be as much holy to Jehovah as was the High Priest there was an end of that distinction for ever, not by sinking the holy in the profane, but by stamping on everything, even the most common, the character of holiness by consecration to God. Involved also in this is the abolition of gradations of sanctity, as is explicitly indicated in the following clause, where it is said that the vessels the least esteemed for holiness, the pots in which the meat of the sacrifices was boiled, should be as holy as the sacred basins into which the blood of the animals was poured that it might be sprinkled upon the altar. And as this consummation was uniform so it should be universal: "And every pot in Jerusalem and in Judah shall be holy unto Jehovah of hosts, and all they that sacrifice shall come and take of them and boil therein; and in that day there shall be no more the Canaanite in the house of Jehovah of hosts" (verse 21). Not only the pots in the Temple but all the pots, those in common use in Jerusalem and Judah, shall be consecrated to Jehovah and be used as well as those in the Temple for sacrificial purposes. "In this priestly-levitical drapery the thought is expressed that in the perfected kingdom of God not only will everything without exception be holy, but all will be equally holy" (Keil). No element of evil or ungodliness shall remain within the pale of that perfected kingdom; its "people shall be all righteous" (Isa. lx. 21); "the Canaanite shall no more be in the house of the Lord of hosts." The Canaanites were a people defiled, accursed and utterly estranged from the commonwealth of Israel (Lev. xviii. 24 ff.; Deut. vii. 2, ix. 4, xviii. 12). Hence in the mind of the Jews a Canaanite was the type of the ungodly and profane, and the name might be applied to anyone whether Jew or Gentile who was of this character; just as Daniel is represented as addressing to the wicked elder whom he had come to judge, the epithet, "Thou seed of Canaan and not of Judah" (Hist. of Susannah, verse 56); or, as Isaiah calls the princes and people of Judah, "rulers of Sodom" and "people of Gomorrah" (i. 10). When the prophet, then, says here, "The Canaanite shall no more be in the house of Jehovah of hosts," the meaning is that though in the congregation of Israel there had been often those who were not true Israelites in heart, persons ungodly and profane, in the perfected kingdom it should not be so. Into that hallowed Temple none should come but the holy and the pure.

The prophet thus follows to its glorious consummation

the development of that heavenly kingdom which was to rise upon the ruins of the ancient kingdom of Israel, and was to be the reality of which that was the type and shadow. The picture he presents is vested in the drapery of the ancient institute, but it is not of Israel after the flesh that the prophet speaks. The abolition of the ancient system, with its "carnal ordinances," is referred to, but it is as these should be superseded by passing into that great spiritual system of universal consecration to God of which it was the type. Nor is it the Church as a visible institute that is the object of the prophet's delineations; the fates and fortunes of that institute which history may relate it is not the object of prophecy to delineate. The kingdom whose development amidst mundane conditions and circumstances the prophets of the old economy describe, is that kingdom of God which cometh not with observation (Luke xvii. 20), which is not in word but in power (1 Cor. iv. 20); that kingdom which was set up when God raised His Son from the dead and set Him as His King on His holy hill of Zion. Of the progress of this kingdom through varied scenes of trial and of triumph the prophet had a vision which he has here unfolded. With the final triumph and the glorious consummation, when all hostility shall have been quelled and the whole world shall have been turned to the Lord, the prophet's vision closes. Through the ages, ever since the Christ took His seat on the throne, "crowned with glory and with honour," His prediction has been and is being fulfilled. In degree as the kingdom extends and its influence is felt, the curse is lifted from the race, and Holiness to the Lord becomes inscribed on those who have been in arms against Him, enemies by a mind in evil works. The end is not yet; we see not yet all things put under Him. But we see the kingdom advancing, and in due time the mystery of God shall be finished, as He hath declared to His servants the prophets (Rev. x. 7)—that mystery which is also "the mystery of the Christ," that the Gentiles ($\tau\grave{a}$ $\ddot{\epsilon}\theta\nu\eta$, those outside the Israel of God) are fellow-heirs [with Israel] and of the same body, and partakers of the promise in Christ by the Gospel (Eph. iii. 3–6). This mystery, which was kept secret since the world began, but is manifested now in this latter time, it was given to Zechariah, as to other prophets of the former dispensation, to make known.

THE END.

NISBET'S THEOLOGICAL LIBRARY.

I.

Crown 8vo.   Price 6s.

IMMORTALITY:

A Series of Papers by the

Rev. Principal CAIRNS, D.D.,

Rev. Canon KNOX-LITTLE, M.A.,

Right Rev. THE BISHOP OF AMYCLA (Coadjutor of H.E. Cardinal MANNING),

Rev. Professor J. RADFORD THOMSON, M.A.,

Rev. EDWARD WHITE,

Rev. J. E. PAGE HOPPS,

Rev. CROSBY BARLOW, M.A.,

And Others.

Reprinted from the Symposium in the Homiletic Magazine.

II.

Crown 8vo.   6s.

ZECHARIAH:

HIS VISIONS AND WARNINGS.

BY THE LATE

REV. W. LINDSAY ALEXANDER, D.D.

Y

NISBET'S THEOLOGICAL LIBRARY—Continued.

III.

Crown 8vo.   6s.

ATONEMENT:

A Clerical Symposium on the Atonement.

By the Revs. Dr. LITTLEDALE, A. MACKENNAL, J. PAGE HOPPS, Dr. OLVER, Principal RAINY, D.D., EDWARD WHITE, Professor ISRAEL ABRAHAMS, Dr. PATON GLOAG, Ven. Archdeacon FARRAR, Right Rev. BISHOP OF AMYCLA, and Others.

CRITICAL OPINIONS.

The Literary Churchman.

"We recommend our readers to purchase the work. Although the papers are naturally argumentative and not devotional, the record of the effort of different minds to grasp the doctrine of the Atonement cannot but be helpful."

The Irish Ecclesiastical Gazette.

"The volume contains many thoughts of value."

The Literary World.

"A valuable addition to the theological literature of the day."

The Baptist.

"To the trained theologian it will have all the interest of a well-ordered battle between well-trained disputants."

Liverpool Mercury.

"The volume is one of permanent value, and will save both time and research in wading through theological dictionaries to find what lies here ready to hand."

Newcastle Journal.

"We question if any volume has yet been published on the Atonement which sets forth the views of Christendom in so many varied lights, and at the same time with so much mutual toleration and modesty. This is a book which ought to find a place in every theological library."

NISBET'S THEOLOGICAL LIBRARY—Continued.

IV.

Crown 8vo.   6s.

INSPIRATION:

A Clerical Symposium on In what Sense and Within what Limits is the Bible the Word of God?

By the Ven. Archdeacon FARRAR, the Rev. Principal CAIRNS, the Rev. Prebendary STANLEY LEATHES, the Rev. Prebendary Row, the Rev. Professor J. RADFORD THOMSON, the Right Rev. the BISHOP OF AMYCLA, and Others.

CRITICAL OPINIONS.

The Church Times.

"The volume is an interesting one, written throughout in a temperate and scholarly spirit, and likely to prove useful to the higher stamp of theological students."

The Scotsman.

"These clever papers, written for the most part by men of mark and standing, although they may have an unsettling tendency, are well calculated to attract attention and to repay perusal."

The Freeman.

"Every side of the question is, if not fully, at any rate candidly and reverently discussed; and as an epitome of the various conceptions which are now current on this momentous theme, there can be no better or more useful work than this."

The Literary Churchman.

"If any book were designed to show that the Bible was never intended to stand alone, but that a supernatural revelation must of necessity be committed to a supernatural custodian, it could not have better fulfilled its object than this 'Clerical' Symposium."

The Edinburgh Courant.

"A most valuable contribution to inspirational literature. A great variety of views, all falling within the lines of recognised orthodoxy, are brought together, and made to act and react on each other. Their individual weight is thus more clearly ascertained, and a stronger impression is given of the force of argument in favour of inspiration."

Aberdeen Free Press.

"This valuable and suggestive book ought to have a place in every minister's library."

RECENT WORKS

IN

BIBLICAL AND THEOLOGICAL LITERATURE

PUBLISHED BY

JAMES NISBET & CO.

THE TEACHING OF THE TWELVE APOSTLES: A Page of First Century Christian Life, with Translation, Notes, and Dissertations. By Canon SPENCE, M.A., Vicar of St. Pancras. Crown 8vo, 6s.

"Canon Spence's notes are generally excellent. The excursus in this volume are an able though far from exhaustive treatment of the several points of interest raised by this treatise."—*Academy.*

THE EMPIRE OF THE HITTITES. By WM. WRIGHT, D.D. With Decipherment of Hittite Inscriptions by Professor SAYCE, LL.D.; A Hittite Map by Col. Sir CHARLES WILSON, F.R.S., and Captain CONDER, R.E.; and a complete set of Hittite Inscriptions by W. H. RYLANDS, F.S.A. Royal 8vo, 17s. 6d.

"Any one who wishes to know more about this remarkable people must read this book, in which Dr. Wright has brought together in a popular form all that has been yet extracted from the various sources that have recently been laid open. Its value is attested by no less an authority than Mr. Gladstone."—*Guardian.*

METAPHORS IN THE GOSPELS: A Series of Short Studies. By the Rev. DONALD FRASER, D.D. Crown 8vo, 6s.

"It will open the eyes of ministers to a fact of which they often seem unaware, that in the Gospels a metaphor is never introduced for the mere purpose of decorating a sentence or gratifying a poetic fancy."—*Daily Chronicle.*

SYNOPTICAL LECTURES ON THE BOOKS OF HOLY SCRIPTURE. By the Rev. DONALD FRASER, D.D. New Edition.

"Singularly interesting, instructive, and comprehensive."—*Record.*
"There is a great deal of common sense and clear thought in these volumes."—*Nonconformist.*

OVER THE HOLY LAND. By the Rev. A. J. WYLIE, LL.D., Author of "History of Protestantism." Crown 8vo, 7s. 6d.

"Dr. Wylie's observations on the true sites of the holy places at Jerusalem will be read with interest, as well as his disquisitions on the present physical desolation of the country and the possibility and method of restoring it to its ancient fertility. Some of his descriptions of scenery are very striking and effective."—*Record.*

THROUGH BIBLE LANDS: A Narrative of a Recent Tour in Egypt and the Holy Land. By PHILIP SCHAFF, D.D. With Illustrations. Crown 8vo, 6s.

"Full of scholarly estimates of knowledge, and written with perfect simplicity and flowing ease."—*British Quarterly Review.*

DAYS AND NIGHTS IN THE EAST; OR, ILLUSTRATIONS OF BIBLE SCENES. By HORATIUS BONAR, D.D. With Illustrations. Crown 8vo, 3s. 6d.

THE KINGDOM OF ALL ISRAEL: Its History, Literature, and Worship. By JAMES SIME, M.A., F.R.S.E. Crown 8vo, 15s.

"The book is admirable in its arrangement, lucid in its style, and rich with the results of careful and wide reading."—*Dundee Advertiser.*

TREASURES OF THE TALMUD: Being a Series of Classified Subjects Compiled from the Babylonian Talmud, and Translated by PAUL J. HERSHON, with Notes and Indexes, and an Introductory Preface by Canon SPENCE, M.A., Vicar of St. Pancras. Demy 8vo, 12s. 6d.

"No more interesting book for students of Oriental and Biblical literature has for a long time been published than this volume."—*Bookseller.*

THE BOOK OF DANIEL; OR, THE SECOND VOLUME OF PROPHECY. Translated and expounded, with a Preliminary Sketch of Antecedent Prophecy. By the Rev. JAMES G. MURPHY, D.D., Professor of Hebrew, &c. Small crown 8vo, 3s.

"With a perfect mastery of the literature of his subject, Dr. Murphy gives his readers results rather than references, and brings within most moderate compass all that the ordinary Bible student needs to know. Through the visions of the prophet the reader proceeds with confidence, for he feels that all through he has the advantage of a most capable and trusty guide."—*Presbyterian Churchman.*

THE LAST PROPHECY: Being an Abridgment of the late Rev. E. B. ELLIOTT's "Horæ Apocalypticæ." To which is subjoined his last paper on "Prophecy Fulfilled and Fulfilling." By H. E. E. Third Edition, as Revised by the late Rev. E. B. ELLIOTT. Crown 8vo, 5s.

"There are few better books of its class accessible to the general reader."—*Aberdeen Free Press.*

"Very valuable for its large amount of condensed information concerning the chief events in Church history."—*Christian Age.*

FOR THE WORK OF THE MINISTRY: A Manual of Homiletical and Pastoral Theology. By W. G. BLAIKIE, D.D., LL.D., Professor of Apologetics and of Ecclesiastical and Pastoral Theology, New College, Edinburgh. Fourth Edition. Crown 8vo, 5s.

"A volume which displays a considerable amount of wide and varied reading, much thought and ability, great good feeling, and an earnest and charitable desire to further the attainment of the highest ends of all right human thought and action."—*Guardian.*

THE PUBLIC MINISTRY AND PASTORAL METHODS OF OUR LORD. By Prof. W. G. BLAIKIE, D.D., LL.D. Cr. 8vo, 6s.

"Should be very acceptable and profitable, not only to those whose life-work is the ministry of the Gospel, but also to those who in other ways take their share of active service for the spiritual good of men, and we heartily commend it to them."—*Messenger*.

ABRAHAM, THE FRIEND OF GOD: A Study from Old Testament History. By J. OSWALD DYKES, D.D. Third Thousand. Post 8vo, 6s.

"It is beyond doubt one of the most fascinating as well as most valuable contributions to the religious literature of this country that has appeared for some years."—*Record*.

THE MANIFESTO OF THE KING. Comprising "The Beatitudes of the Kingdom," "The Laws of the Kingdom," and "The Relation of the Kingdom to the World." By J. OSWALD DYKES, D.D. Second Edition. Crown 8vo, 6s.

"A model of spiritual discernment, vigorous grip, and succinct practical application, in which the sentiment of religion is very beautifully blended with its precepts."—*British Quarterly Review*.

THE SELF-REVEALING JEHOVAH OF THE OLD TESTAMENT THE CHRIST OF THE NEW TESTAMENT. By S. M. BARCLAY. Demy 8vo, 7s. 6d.

"Never, perhaps, has the argument for this doctrine been more clearly or exhaustively stated than in the present work."—*Scotsman*.

THE PERSON OF CHRIST: The Perfection of His Humanity Viewed as a Proof of His Divinity. By PHILIP SCHAFF, D.D. Small crown 8vo, 3s. 6d.

"While the book is intended, and in every way suitable, for general reading, scholarly care and accuracy are everywhere manifested."—*Christian*.

CHRIST AND THE CHURCH: Nine Lectures on the Apostolic Commission. By the Rev. ADOLPH SAPHIR, B.A. Crown 8vo, 6s.

"Eloquent, beautiful, and profoundly evangelical."—*Literary World*.

THE LORD'S PRAYER: A Series of Lectures. By the Rev. ADOLPH SAPHIR, B.A. Crown 8vo, 5s.

"A work so wide in its range of thought and so concentrated in its doctrinal teachings, so rich and well packed, yet so simple and interesting, and so clear, pure, and intelligible in expression, does not often make its appearance."—*Christian Work*.

CHRIST CRUCIFIED: Lectures on 1 Corinthians ii. By the Rev. ADOLPH SAPHIR, B.A. Crown 8vo, 3s. 6d.

"A valuable commentary."—Mr. C. H. SPURGEON in the *Sword and Trowel*.

THE BIBLE TRUE TO ITSELF: A Treatise on the Historical Truth of the Old Testament. By the Rev. A. MOODY STUART, D.D. New Edition. Crown 8vo, 5s.

"It is highly worthy of the attention of all Biblical students, and cannot be too warmly commended as an aid to Christian knowledge and to Christian faith."—*Messenger and Missionary Record*.

MOMENTS ON THE MOUNT: A Series of Devotional Meditations. By the Rev. GEORGE MATHESON, D.D., Author of "The Natural Elements of Revealed Theology," &c. Crown 8vo, 3s. 6d.

"This little volume is not one to be read through at a sitting and then laid aside. Rather each meditation is to be pondered over and enjoyed singly and separately, and to be dwelt upon till it becomes a permanent possession."—*Scotsman.*

MODERN ATHEISM; OR, THE HEAVENLY FATHER. With an Appendix on the More Recent Development of Atheism. By M. ERNEST NAVILLE. Translated by the Rev. HENRY DOWNTON. Crown 8vo, 6s.

"The author has few rivals on the Continent in the graces of polished eloquence, and his arguments are stated with that peculiar clearness and elegance of illustration which gives a charm and freshness to the best kind of French literature."—*Record.*

ROCK *versus* SAND; OR, THE FOUNDATIONS OF THE CHRISTIAN FAITH. By J. M. GIBSON, D.D. Small crown 8vo, 1s. 6d.

"A weighty, original treatise. The author puts the argument with much directness and force. The views of Clifford, Spencer, Mill, Huxley, are noticed and met."—*London Quarterley Review.*
"Dr. Gibson is an acute observer and a cogent reasoner. His little book is strong and timely."—*British Quarterley Review.*

A TRANSLATION OF THE OLD TESTAMENT FROM THE ORIGINAL HEBREW. By H. SPURRELL. Demy 8vo, 10s. 6d.

"It is well worthy of being in the hands of all teachers of Divine truth."—*Christian World.*

THE NATURAL ELEMENTS OF REVEALED THEOLOGY. By the Rev. GEORGE MATHESON, D.D. Crown 8vo, 6s.

"It would be hard to find any small volume in which the immense need for the Christian revelation, and the Divine, all-satisfying character of that revelation, are more lucidly and attractively set forth."—*Expositor.*

CHARACTERISTICS OF CHRISTIANITY. By the Rev. Professor STANLEY LEATHES, D.D. Crown 8vo, 6s.

"Professor Leathes always writes with sound scholarship, great good sense, and intellectual vigour. The evidential value of these characteristics is here well arrayed."—*British Quarterly Review.*

THE RELATIONS OF CHRISTIANITY TO CIVIL SOCIETY. By SAMUEL SMITH HARRIS, D.D., LL.D., Bishop of Michigan. Crown 8vo, 4s. 6d.

A WISE DISCRIMINATION THE CHURCH'S NEED. By J. W. DUDLEY, D.D., Assistant Bishop of the Diocese of Kentucky. Crown 8vo, 4s. 6d.

"A thoughtful, eloquent book; one which will prove suggestive to many, and may contribute to calm the minds of some who read it."—*John Bull.*

Published Monthly. Price One Shilling.

THE HOMILETIC MAGAZINE.

THE FAVOURITE PERIODICAL OF CLERGYMEN, MINISTERS, AND LAY PREACHERS FOR THEOLOGICAL ARTICLES, PRACTICAL HOMILETICS, AND SUGGESTIVE EXPOSITIONS.

Among other Contributors to this Serial are

The Right Rev. Lord A. C. Hervey, D.D.; The Right Rev. H. Cotterell, D.D.; The Very Rev. J. S. Perowne, D.D.; The Very Rev. E. H. Plumptre, D.D.; The Ven. Archdeacon F. W. Farrar, D.D.; The Rev. Canon Knox-Little, M.A.; The Very Rev. Principal Tulloch, D.D.; Rev. Prof. S. Leathes, D.D.; Rev. Prof. A. B. Bruce; Rev. Prof. Blaikie, D.D.; Rev. Canon Rawlinson, M.A.; Rev. Principal Rainy, D.D.; Rev. Prof. H. Reynolds, D.D.; Rev. Principal Cave; Rev. Prof. W. B. Pope, D.D.; Rev. Dr. Littledale; Prof. G. G. Stokes, F.R.S., &c.

Published Quarterly, in January, April, July, and October.
Price 3s. 6d.

The British and Foreign Evangelical Review.

EDITED BY

H. SINCLAIR PATERSON, M.A.

LONDON:
JAMES NISBET & CO., 21 BERNERS STREET.